LEGENDARY WHITETAILS II

LEGENDARY WHITETAILS II

Wildlife Images

Mequon, Wisconsin

LEGENDARY WHITETAILS II
Stories And Photos Of 40 More Of The Greatest Bucks Of All Time
Copyright © 2001 by Wildlife Images

Compiled by: Larry L. Huffman

Contributing Writers:

J.D. Andrews, Mike Beatty, Craig Bobula, Ken Cartwright, Les Davenport, Duncan Dobie,
Jack Ehresman, Alan Foster, Dick Idol, Bruce Jameson, Dale Larson, Larry Lawson, Todd Loewen,
Orlan Love, Todd Murray, Ron Osborne, Brenda Potts, Ernest D. Richardson, Ken Shane,
Jim Shockey, Richard P. Smith, Richard Stahl, Sam Townsend, Brenda Valentine,
Dr. Rob Wegner, Gordon Whittington, Bobby Willis, Ron Willmore, Bill Winke

Contributing Photographers/Photography Providers:

Charles Alsheimer, Bass Pro Shops, Keith Benoist, Jamie Boardman, Kim Boes, Craig Bobula,
Ron Brown, George Chase, Russ Clarken, Sam Collora, Danny M. Critser, Les Davenport, Duncan Dobie,
Tom Evans, Alan Foster, Fred Goodwin, Billy Hanson, Elisha Hugen, Larry L. Huffman, Dick Idol,
Bruce Jameson, Tom Johnson, Dale Larson, Legendary Whitetails Collection, Orlan Love, Kirsten Lyons,
Rod McClanahan, Cindy Moleski, Locie Murphy, North American Whitetail, Brenda Potts, Pat Reeve,
Jamie Remmers, Mike Rowe, Cindy Sexton, Ken Shane, Ron Sinfelt, Richard P. Smith, Lyle Spitznogle,
Bryce Towsley, Brenda Valentine, Gordon Whittington, Jamie Willis, Ron Willmore, Bill Winke

Published by Larry L. Huffman of Wildlife Images,
1115 West Liebau Road in Mequon, WI 53092

Printed in the United States of America
Second Edition

Edited by: Gordon Whittington
Designed and Produced by: Mark S. Kaiser

Library of Congress Catalog Card Number: 2001092954
ISBN 0-9711762-0-5

Dedication

The hunters featured between these covers are an elite group, one whose accomplishments are revered by everyone who dreams of harvesting a legendary whitetail. These men and women are our heroes, and it is to them that this book is dedicated.

ACKNOWLEDGMENTS

BY LARRY L. HUFFMAN

When I was compiling the original *Legendary Whitetails*, I commented on what a privilege it was to work with some of the finest people in the business to make that book a reality. Now I realize how fortunate I am to have that privilege a second time.

This book, like the first, would not have been possible without the contribution of many individuals. It is impossible to name everyone who played a role in producing *Legendary Whitetails II*, but I will attempt to acknowledge as many as possible on the front lines, in the trenches and behind the scenes.

Let me first extend a very special "thank you" to Jimmy Stewart and his staff at *North American Whitetail* magazine. It was through their assistance and cooperation that we adapted many feature articles from past issues of that publication. Gordon Whittington, editor of *North American Whitetail* and co-editor of the original *Legendary Whitetails*, unselfishly found time to serve as editor of this second volume. I consider Gordon my friend, and his professionalism and knowledge of trophy whitetails are second to none. How can one measure his contribution?

Special thanks also go to all of the writers who contributed chapters to *Legendary Whitetails II*. Of these, Mike Beatty, Ken Cartwright, Bruce Jameson, Dale Larson, Ron Osborne, Ken Shane, Richard Stahl, Sam Townsend and Bobby Willis wrote their own stories.

In addition, the following also authored chapters that have been adapted from *North American Whitetail*: J. D. Andrews, Craig Bobula, Les Davenport, Duncan Dobie, Jack Ehresman, Alan Foster, Dick Idol, Larry Lawson, Todd Loewen,

Todd Murray, Brenda Potts, Ernest D. Richardson, Jim Shockey, Richard P. Smith, Brenda Valentine, Ron Willmore and Bill Winke. Their writing expertise and knowledge are much appreciated.

Legendary Whitetails II features four stories not previously published in *North American Whitetail,* and I want to extend thanks to these writers: Orlan Love, for the Lyle Spitznogle chapter; Brenda Potts, for the Jamie Remmers and Stan Potts chapters; and Dr. Rob Wegner, for the Fred Goodwin chapter. I also wish to acknowledge the research and help of my friend Phil Osborn on the great story of the Goodwin buck.

Of course, this book would not even have been possible without the hunters who allowed us to detail their historic accomplishments. Most of them are dedicated and experienced hunters, though some others had very little hunting experience at the time they made whitetail history. The one common denominator in all of their stories was they were in the right place at the right time.

I also wish to acknowledge the tremendous contributions made by Johnny Morris' Bass Pro Shops and their staff. *Legendary Whitetails II* features the stories of 16 great trophy bucks from their tremendous collection: the giants taken by Ken Cartwright, Brian Damery, Kenny Fowler, Hill Gould, Bruce Jameson, Duane Linscott, Jerry Martin, Ronald Martin, Kevin Naugle, Ron Osborne, Jamie Remmers, Peter Rutkowski, Shawn Sears, Lyle Spitznogle, Richard Stahl and Sam Townsend. Bass Pro Shops worked closely with us in compiling these stories, providing us with photography and research on each trophy, and I extend my sincere appreciation to Jerry Martin for heading up this effort. To Rick Collins, Terry Snowden and Becky Gann of the museum staff and to staff photographers Chris Irwin, Brian Gibson and Mike Shepherd, thanks!

Helpful assistance also was provided by my good friend Brad Gsell, who graciously allowed us to feature two great trophies from his own personal collection: the Neil Morin buck and the Joe Waters buck.

Thanks to my good friend Craig Calderone and his Michigan Whitetail Hall of Fame Museum for making the Michigan state-record typical, the Troy Stephens buck, available to us.

A very special "thank you" also goes to Jack Reneau of the Boone and Crockett Club and Kevin Hisey of the Pope and Young Club for providing me with scoring data. Along the same lines, I appreciate the assistance of my friends Dave Boland and Bill Lilienthal, who helped me obtain scoring details on several deer in this book.

I also would like to acknowledge all of the hard work and effort by those closest to me. First and foremost, thanks to Mark Kaiser for his expertise and dedicated effort in the design and production of this book. It is great to have someone this talented on your own staff. Thanks as well to the other Wildlife Images staff members who assisted with *Legendary Whitetails II:* Tom Johnson, Sheryl Wolf and Mary Ellen Mortensen.

Finally, where would I be without my family? My sons, Greg, Troy, Todd and Doug, I thank for their assistance and moral support. And then, there is my wife, Joyce, who must put up with my love of whitetails every day.

TABLE OF CONTENTS

"Becoming a legend is a two-step process.
First, you must be extraordinary.
Second, fate must let you prove it."

from the Introduction by Gordon Whittington

FOREWORD

BY LARRY L. HUFFMAN

Five years now have passed since *Legendary Whitetails* was first published. Yes, it was back in 1996 when I approached Dick Idol and David Morris about putting together a book featuring 40 of the greatest whitetails of all time. Shortly afterwards, we added editor Gordon Whittington to our team and published what many in the hunting community have described as "a book of dreams."

For some whitetail enthusiasts, that might have been enough. But I still dream about trophy bucks every day, and I realized that there were many more great bucks that needed to be brought to the attention of the hunting world. I knew that a follow-up book was necessary. The result is *Legendary Whitetails II*,

a collection of 40 more stories of world-class deer.

All of the bucks featured in this second volume were harvested by hunters, most of them during the past two decades. In fact, several actually were tagged while this book was being researched. It is truly amazing how many world-class bucks are being taken today. As I often have said in my seminars, "The good old days of deer hunting are now."

Overall, there now is more opportunity to harvest a trophy buck than ever before. Today's whitetail hunter has many advantages over his counterpart from yesteryear. He has far more biological data at his disposal and so many more sources of hunting knowledge with which to educate himself. He has much better equipment as well. He can fool a deer's sense of sight with today's camouflage. In fact, with modern scent-control clothing, he can even fool its nose.

Let's take a moment and look at some of the improvements in hunting equipment, for they certainly have played a role in helping whitetail hunters become more successful than ever. The improvements in our archery equipment alone are mind boggling. Today's bows are faster and flatter shooting, especially when carbon arrows are used. In addition, broadheads flying almost identical to field points and penetrating much better than earlier heads are being introduced every year. Modern rangefinders also have taken much of the guesswork out of where to aim, leading to more accurate shooting and thus, improved odds of recovering game.

In the past, a shotgun or muzzleloader hunter generally had to get within 75 yards or so of a deer to harvest it cleanly. That no longer is the case. Today, we have shotguns and muzzleloaders capable of taking deer at ranges of 150 to 200 yards. In fact, with the right gun and the right load, two-inch groups now are not uncommon at distances of 200 yards or even farther.

The recent trend toward better deer management also has played a huge role in helping trophy prospects. Hunters are spending much more time afield all year long, installing food plots and engaging in other forms of habitat management. They also are spending more time scouting because of these management practices. And many of today's hunters also have specific trophy goals, making them willing to hold out for older bucks instead of shooting younger animals. They are simply working harder than ever to reach their goals — and as the old saying goes, "The harder you work, the luckier you get."

"It is truly amazing how many world-class bucks are being taken today. As I often have said in my seminars, 'The good old days of deer hunting are now.'"

So here it is, *Legendary Whitetails II: 40 more bucks to dream about.* I know I have had my share of dreams of harvesting a legendary buck, and you can bet that many of the hunters featured in this book had similar dreams about their bucks before they were successful.

Through hard work, countless hours of scouting and ultimately ending up in the right place at the right time, their dreams finally came true. Perhaps yours can too!

INTRODUCTION

BY GORDON WHITTINGTON

Becoming a legend is a two-step process. First, you must be extraordinary. Second, fate must let you prove it.

The fact that mankind has so few legendary figures shows how rarely both parts have coincided throughout human history. Sometimes special persons have passed through this world unknown and unappreciated, simply for lack of an opportunity to display their talents. In other instances the chance was there, but no one seized it.

The process by which a whitetail buck can become a legend is similar. First, it takes the right animal, one of such tremendous antler size that he ranks among the biggest ever known. But growing that rack just might be the easy half of the equation. Bucks of legendary size simply aren't eager to be made famous, for that usually requires a pit stop at a taxidermy studio en route.

If a giant whitetail has his way — and he usually does — he'll live out his full life span, then die of natural causes in some quiet spot where only nature's scavengers ever will find his bones. Even his glorious crown of antlers eventually will be absorbed by the same forest that nurtured him throughout his life. And so will pass through this world yet another potential legend left unknown and untold.

Fortunately for those of us who appreciate magnum deer, there are occasional exceptions to this rule. Every so often, a hunter will down a buck so big that all trophy aficionados across North America must sit up and take notice. And over time, as word of the deer spreads and the details of his story becomes known, out of death a whitetail legend is born.

Even after roughly a century of regulated hunting, during which literally millions of fine bucks have traveled from the woods to den walls, whitetail enthusiasts still regard only a few dozen of these animals as true legends. We know these deer by name, or at least the names bestowed on them by virtue of whose tags they once wore. And in death they're now honored in ways they never were in life. The deer themselves might be gone, but the bony headgear they've left behind will remind us of their greatness for decades or even centuries to come.

Back in 1996, the first edition of *Legendary Whitetails* broke new ground in paying tribute to these great deer. For the first time ever, 40 of history's top trophies were assembled under one cover and presented in a way that brought lasting respect to the animals and to the hunters who had taken them.

Readers were treated to the saga of Ohio's incredible "Hole in the Horn" buck, whose story took more than 50 years and a bizarre twist of fate to unravel. They also got the story of the famed James Jordan buck, the former Boone and Crockett world-record typical shot in Wisconsin way back in 1914 — but not recognized as the world's top trophy until the 1960s. And those stories were just the beginning.

There also were full chapters on four other former or current world records: rifleman John Breen's 1918 giant from Minnesota, Del Austin's 1962 bow non-typical from Nebraska, Mel Johnson's 1965 bow typical from Illinois and Lloyd Goad's 1962 bow typical from Iowa. Never before had so many of the world's top trophy deer been brought back to life in a single publication.

As a result, immediately after its release, *Legendary Whitetails* was hailed as

The legend of all legends: Ohio's famous "Hole in the Horn."
Photo courtesy of the Legendary Whitetails Collection.

nothing less than the finest big-buck book ever to roll off the press. It was soon something of a legend in its own right.

This volume is cut of much the same cloth. With the expert help of the world's top whitetail writers and photographers, we've combed the back roads for the stories and photos of 40 more great bucks, and we've gathered them under one cover as a special tribute that picks up right where the first book leaves off.

If you're among the thousands of readers who have enjoyed *Legendary Whitetails*, you'll see a few subtle differences in these two volumes. For instance, whereas the first focused heavily on world-class deer from yesteryear, the second has a more contemporary flavor. Yes, *Legendary Whitetails II* does contain some deer from the old days, including a state record taken way back in 1910; however, for the most part, the bucks featured here were taken by men and women who still walk the woods each fall.

What's that? Trophy bucks shot by women? Indeed. The number of female whitetail hunters in North America continues to grow, and it's currently the highest since anyone started keeping records of such trends. But that really shouldn't come as much of a surprise. Unlike some other types of big-game hunting, in which sheer physical strength might offer a decided advantage in climbing mountains or handling the requisite big-bore rifles, whitetail hunting rewards participants who can think strategically, be patient and then keep it all together at the moment of truth. That's an apt description of many women who hunt… and perhaps even the occasional man!

Of course, there always have been some women in the deer woods, and they've been shooting big deer since way back when. A classic case in point is the Flora Campbell buck from Maine. Back in 1953, while Flora and her husband were running their trapline, she downed a 228 7/8-point Boone and Crockett non-typical that at the time was the world's highest-scoring whitetail ever taken by a woman.

The Campbell buck held the women's world record for more than four decades; then, on one of the most odds-defying days in hunting history, it was shattered not once but twice. On the afternoon of Dec. 7, 1997, Jamie Remmers of Kansas and Barb Brewer of Illinois each downed

Flora Campbell's buck held the women's world record for over 40 years. Photo by Dick Idol, courtesy of North American Whitetail.

massive non-typicals scoring in excess of 250 points! In fact, their bucks turned out to be the world's two biggest whitetails of the year! The Remmers and Brewer bucks are among those profiled in the volume you're holding, as are Jill Adcock's giant 10-pointer from Illinois and Elisha Hugen's world-class 8-pointer from Iowa.

In addition to featuring several top bucks taken by female hunters, another departure from the first volume is the number of self-authored stories in *Legendary Whitetails II*. Because almost all of the bucks in the first book were taken long ago or found dead, none of the chapters in it were written by the hunter himself. This time around, we were working largely with bucks taken since 1980, and often we were able to have the hunters tell the stories in their own words. Getting the details of a hunt straight from the central figure is always interesting, especially when the animal taken is of record size.

Some of the mighty deer profiled in *Legendary Whitetails II* were shot by hunters in single-minded pursuit of those animals. These stories make for particularly engaging reading, because they contain all of the emotions that are part of any successful trophy quest: anticipation, self-doubt, suspense and ultimately, great satisfaction. Some of these accounts are classic hunting tales that over time have become almost as legendary as the deer themselves.

But just as interesting, in a way, are the stories of fortunate hunters and unfortunate bucks whose paths crossed only as a result of fate. Of course, good luck is a vital component of

The massive James Jordan buck from Wisconsin.
Photo courtesy of the Legendary Whitetails Collection.

chooses, and our success or failure as hunters largely depends on which trail he decides to travel on a given day. We often talk of the need to be selective if we're to take trophy deer, and rightly so; however, it could be argued that the buck ultimately has a say in deciding who among us will get an opportunity to become part of whitetail history and who won't. If that's not irony, I don't know what is.

Sit back

any successful hunt, for no matter how well we plan or how cleverly we pursue our quarry, certain variables are simply out of our control. But some of the stories in this book show just how much a hunt's outcome can hinge on an event that, at the time, seems of very little consequence.

The wildest of wild cards in this great game of chance is the buck himself. At any time he can go wherever he

and enjoy these 40 tales of triumph, of men and women whose lives changed forever with the squeeze of a trigger or the release of a bowstring.

Share their joy as they achieve something most other deer hunters have done only in dreams. And finally, wonder how it would have felt to be in these fortunate hunters' boots the day their greatest whitetail fantasies came true. It's as close as most of us ever will get.

◇

Chapter One

THE JILL ADCOCK BUCK

188 3/8 TYPICAL, ILLINOIS, 1993

One of the Largest Typicals Ever Taken by a Lady Hunter

BY LES DAVENPORT

I t's no secret that whitetail hunting has long been a male-dominated activity. However, the number of female hunters is rising, and many sportsmen are thrilled with this trend. You can count Therry Adcock of Peoria, Illinois, among them.

Therry and his wife, Jill, had special cause to be anxious as the 1993 firearms season approached. After five years of searching for hunting property to buy, they finally sealed a deal on 40 acres of timber in Peoria County. The bank closing was shortly after the end of the 1992 deer season. Hunting their own ground the following November would be a dream come true.

Therry had begun his deer-hunting career in 1979, and over the years had hunted mostly with Jill's brother, Jack Loughridge. When Jack moved in 1988, Therry mentioned to Jill that he would be hard pressed to find a hunting buddy as good as Jack.

"I'd like to hunt with you," Jill replied without hesitation. Although his wife had never been a deer hunter, Therry suspected she would enjoy it, so he gave her a

Jill Adcock, Illinois, 1993

	Right Antler	Left Antler	Difference
Main Beam Length	27 7/8	27 6/8	1/8
1st Point Length	6 2/8	6 1/8	1/8
2nd Point Length	13 2/8	12 4/8	6/8
3rd Point Length	13 0/8	12 5/8	3/8
4th Point Length	5 2/8	10 1/8	4 7/8
5th Point Length	—	—	—
1st Circumference	5 0/8	5 1/8	1/8
2nd Circumference	4 6/8	4 7/8	1/8
3rd Circumference	4 6/8	5 1/8	3/8
4th Circumference	4 4/8	5 0/8	4/8
Total	**84 5/8**	**89 2/8**	**7 3/8**

Main Characteristics: Great height, with five tines over 10". Damage to right G-4 tine reduced score.

MISCELLANEOUS STATS	
No. Of Points–Right	5
No. Of Points–Left	5
Total No. Of Points	10
Length Of Abnormals	0
Greatest Spread	23 7/8
Tip To Tip Spread	16 3/8
Inside Spread	21 7/8

FINAL TALLY	
Inside Spread	21 7/8
Right Antler	84 5/8
Left Antler	89 2/8
Gross Score	195 6/8
Difference (–)	7 3/8
Subtotal	188 3/8
Abnormals (–)	0
NET TYPICAL SCORE	**188 3/8**

thumbs-up reply and began training her immediately.

The Adcocks love venison and categorize themselves primarily as "meat hunters." Therry usually fills at least one tag, but going into the fall of 1993, Jill had yet to cut a notch on her gun stock. As Therry would say, at that point Jill was not yet "one with her weapon." Although previously an Army air-traffic controller who had handled guns well in basic training, she seemed to lose control of her 20 gauge whenever a deer was in the cross hairs.

Therry worked more intently with Jill, hoping to eliminate glitches that previously had cost her deer. He drilled her to reload more quickly during trap-shooting outings, and she became almost robotic at exploding three clays and reloading in time to hammer a fourth. Her slug accuracy also improved with regular practice. Therry was confident she soon would take her first whitetail.

By November, the Adcocks and their two children, 12-year-old Leon and 8-year-old Rilla, knew every nook and cranny of the acreage they'd bought. They learned from a neighbor that back in 1965, Mel Johnson's 204 4/8-point Pope and Young world-record typical (featured in *Legendary Whitetails*) had been arrowed just down the road from what was now their private deer haven. The friendly informant also told of two hunters who had fought over a stand site in the nucleus of the tract. Supposedly, it was a major funneling area for some giant bucks.

Bluebird weather prevailed on Nov. 19, opening day of shotgun season, and disappointingly, neither of the Adcocks saw a deer. Jill announced that she was changing stand locations for morning No. 2, while Therry elected to stay put.

In the pre-dawn of Saturday, Jill boarded a 12-foot ladder stand in the center of the property. Therry had placed the stand there in bow season, and it looked good. Several trails intersected nearby, and an excellent crop of acorns enhanced the location's appeal to deer.

The air was frigid, and things were uneventful for the first hour of the morning hunt. Then oak leaves crunched underneath heavy hooves, and Jill spotted a large deer paralleling her position. She shouldered her gun, took aim and squeezed the trigger. A single shot rang through the woods.

The buck froze, showing no sign of injury. Startled by his lack of reaction, Jill fired twice more, but he still didn't respond! The hunter reloaded immediately and fired three more times, and only after the sixth did the deer turn and bound away!

Thirty minutes past before Jill exited the stand and looked for the buck. As it turned out, he was mortally wounded and lying not far from the ambush site. She dispensed him with one more shot and tagged her prize.

The first shot had hit near the base of the buck's main beam, apparently stunning him but not dislodging the antler. The sixth shot had hit him in the neck and eventually was what downed the trophy whitetail. Although Jill's aim still remained a bit suspect, quick reloading saved the day.

Two hours passed before husband and wife met at their agreed-upon rendezvous point. "I got one!" Jill reported with a smile. "It was a big one! I didn't know which of the 10 points to put the head tag on. Some of the points were this long," she said, displaying a hand spread of about 14 inches as she spoke.

Surely the tines aren't as long as Jill described, Therry thought as he and Jill walked to where the deer lay. But words failed him when he saw the monster!

Jill gave her husband a verbal depiction of the morning's hunt, ending with, "Well, what do you think, Honey?"

"Damn... Jill," was all that Therry could muster.

The giant grosses 195 6/8 B&C points and nets 188 3/8, and almost all of the deductions are for one pair of mismatched tines. The G-4 tine on the right antler is malformed, and that alone reduces the net score significantly. The deer, which field-dressed 193 pounds, was aged at just 4 1/2 years.

While more female hunters are joining the hunting ranks every year, this great deer remains among the world's top typicals ever taken by a woman.

✦

Chapter Two

THE
MIKE BEATTY BUCK

304 6/8 Non-Typical, Ohio, 2000

The Highest-Scoring Whitetail Ever Harvested by a Hunter

By Mike Beatty

When I moved to western Ohio from Pennsylvania years ago, my brother-in-law, Jerry Michael, told me I was moving to an area where the bucks get really big. On Nov. 8, 2000, I learned just how right he was.

At 4 p.m. that day, I pulled in to park my truck near the edge of a corn field on the Greene County farm I had permission to hunt. The temperature was in the mid-50s, with a fog and a light breeze. As I drove down the lane to park, I looked to the left and saw two does bedded in grass alongside the field. I rolled down the truck window to snap some photos of the deer, but they were out of good camera range.

After parking and gathering my gear, I walked over a grassy knob and entered the field, moving quietly through the wet corn stalks. When I reached a narrow finger of woods on the far side of the corn, I set out some scent bombs near my tree stand, which was 18 feet up in a pin oak roughly 10 yards from the field's edge. Within a few minutes I'd climbed into the stand and prepared myself for action.

Photo by Ron Sinfelt, courtesy of North American Whitetail.

Main Characteristics: Phenomenal mass and the most total inches of abnormal points of any top buck by bow.

MIKE BEATTY, OHIO, 2000

	Right Antler	Left Antler	Difference
Main Beam Length	26 2/8	26 1/8	1/8
1st Point Length	8 3/8	8 6/8	3/8
2nd Point Length	8 5/8	10 5/8	2 0/8
3rd Point Length	8 2/8	9 5/8	1 3/8
4th Point Length	6 3/8	5 4/8	7/8
5th Point Length	—	—	—
1st Circumference	6 6/8	6 3/8	3/8
2nd Circumference	4 7/8	5 3/8	4/8
3rd Circumference	8 3/8	7 3/8	1 0/8
4th Circumference	6 3/8	6 2/8	1/8
Total	84 2/8	86 0/8	6 6/8

MISCELLANEOUS STATS

No. Of Points–Right	18
No. Of Points–Left	21
Total No. Of Points	39
Length Of Abnormals	115 5/8
Greatest Spread	31 0/8
Tip To Tip Spread	25 0/8
Inside Spread	25 5/8

FINAL TALLY

Inside Spread	25 5/8
Right Antler	84 2/8
Left Antler	86 0/8
Gross Score	195 7/8
Difference (–)	6 6/8
Subtotal	189 1/8
Abnormals (+)	115 5/8
NET NON-TYPICAL SCORE	304 6/8

I saw no deer for a while. Then, at around 5 p.m., I hit my Primos doe-bleat call. Perhaps five minutes passed before I saw a deer sneaking in from behind me at a range of roughly 40 yards.

The animal was to the southwest of my stand and was moving upwind toward me. As I watched, I saw it was a big buck; in fact, it was the high, wide 8-pointer my 10-year-old son, Andrew, and I had been watching throughout the summer.

As the buck stopped to work a scrape perhaps 30 yards from me, I hit the doe-bleat call one more time. Suddenly, here he came, walking to within 15 yards of my position before stopping behind a thorny locust tree.

While he was standing there, his body hidden in the branches, I was shaking so badly I felt my knees knocking. I was at full draw, but with no shooting lanes cut, I couldn't get a clear shot. All I could do was hope the buck walked into an opening.

He didn't. Instead, he turned and walked away, back down that brushy draw in which he'd approached. As he did, I disappointedly let my bow down. *I just watched the buck of a lifetime walk away,* I said to myself as the 8-pointer faded away in the thick cover.

Once he was out of sight, I tried my grunt call a couple of times, then very lightly rattled a set of antlers. After that I watched and waited for his return, but saw nothing.

Reasoning that the doe bleat might work again, I finally gave three more calls on it, waiting a bit between each one. Sure enough, after several minutes I again spotted a buck roughly 30 yards away, sneaking up that thick draw toward me. Although the wind had started to pick up on the back of my neck, pushing my scent in the deer's direction, he apparently couldn't smell me.

Assuming this was the big 8-pointer, I stood up, grabbed my bow and prepared for a shot. But as the buck got closer, I could tell he wasn't the same deer. This one had an even bigger and more massive rack — much bigger and much more massive! And he was heading toward one of the scent bombs I'd hung. At this point, all I could tell about the buck was that he was huge. As he ducked his head to go under a low-hanging branch on the thorn tree, I seized my chance to draw.

Focus… just focus, I said to myself as I stood there at full draw, trying to maintain what was left of my composure.

As I watched through my peep sight, the buck kept moving toward me. Finally

> *"As the arrow struck, the buck whirled and took off, resembling a bull elk as he bolted through the trees. It sounded as though his massive antlers hit every branch in the woods as he ran."*

he was within 12 yards, quartering in and facing straight toward me.

I began hunting deer with a gun in my native Pennsylvania at the age of 12, and three years later I took up bowhunting. Going into the 2000 season I'd been hunting with archery gear for 16 years, and in that span I'd arrowed perhaps 10 whitetails. But my biggest had been an 8-pointer that would score around 120 points — not exactly the size deer that would fully prepare a person for a chance at a world-class non-typical. Still, here I was, looking through my peep sight at this great buck.

The buck apparently then caught a whiff of one of the scent bombs, because after ducking under that limb, he began to do a lip curl. As his head came up, I saw the chance I'd been hoping for.

Given the position of the deer's body, I reasoned that if I hit him in the right spot on the neck, my arrow should angle back into the chest cavity, taking out a lung in the process. And so, with the buck's head tilted upward in that classic lip-curl position, I settled my sight pin on what I figured was the right point and tripped my release.

Smack! As the arrow struck, the buck whirled and took off, resembling a bull elk as he bolted through the trees. It sounded as though his massive antlers hit every branch in the woods as he ran. After watching the monster for perhaps 100 yards, I lost sight of him in the cover.

By then my adrenaline was flowing nonstop, and I was frantic. I took a few deep breaths and began to shuffle around on the 18 x 24-inch platform of my stand. Finally, I decided I should lower my bow to the ground and climb out of the tree — before I *fell* out of it!

Once safely on the ground, I sat down for perhaps five minutes to gather my thoughts, then went to look for my arrow. Only 10 paces from my tree I found a single white feather of my fletching, but the arrow was nowhere in sight.

I looked a bit more and discovered a bit of dark-red blood, so I knew the buck was hit. At that point, I went back to my bow and other gear and sat back down. By then it was 5:45, and with the cloud cover, darkness was rapidly approaching.

After waiting an excruciating 30 minutes, I grabbed my flashlight, bow and knife and went out in search of the buck. Once I'd followed his blood trail a short distance, it became easier to follow; in fact, there suddenly was so much blood it looked as though someone had tipped over a can of red paint and run through the woods with it. Every so often I'd find a large patch of blood, and at one point thick, foamy pink blood, which indicated to me that my arrow had indeed reached the lungs.

The buck had headed down the draw southwest of my stand, zig-zagging through thick brush en route. Never having had an arrowed deer travel more than 60 yards after the shot, I soon began to shine my light ahead of me in the woods, as I figured the buck would be lying dead just up the trail. But the blood kept going and going.

Finally, when I was a bit over 250 yards from my stand, I heard a deer blow. I turned off my flashlight and listened. I could hear a deer milling around in the woods. But was it *my* deer?

After turning my light back on, I followed the blood only another 10 yards or so before coming to the edge of a fenced cattle pasture containing some timber and open areas. Now I had a choice: Should I keep going or wait for daylight to continue? It was the toughest decision I've ever had to make as a deer hunter.

When I reached the pasture fence, instead of crossing, I placed one of my arrows against it, turned around and walked back to my truck. Despite the wet weather and uncertain trailing conditions, I'd elected to wait until morning to take up the trail again. If the buck was still alive, I didn't want to risk pushing him farther.

As I was driving home that evening the drizzle stopped, which made me feel better about my decision to leave the trail. But needless to say, I couldn't sleep at all that night, because I was so worried about the risk that rain would wash away the blood. Sure enough, at around 1:30 a.m. it began to rain — hard.

As I listened to the downpour my stomach twisted up in knots, and I felt physically ill. I'd arrowed the buck of a lifetime, and he'd left behind a good blood trail. Now I could only hope there would be enough sign left for me to recover him in daylight.

Andrew and I got dressed early and headed out to look for the buck. We got to my hunting area just as dawn was breaking. Rather than retrace the trail from the stand, we walked across the cattle pasture to pick up the buck's trail where I'd left it the night before.

At least, that was our plan. It changed entirely before we got there. As we came over a high spot in the pasture, Andrew tugged on my jacket. "Dad,

Mike Beatty's huge buck has one of the widest spreads of any non-typical taken by bow. Photo by Ron Sinfelt, courtesy of North American Whitetail.

there he is!" he said, pointing ahead. It was my buck — which had died only 30 yards from where I'd quit looking for him the night before.

The closer we got to the deer, the more massive the antlers appeared. There was no ground shrinkage — instead, there was ground *growth!* I just couldn't believe the size of the wide, palmated rack. Later that day I checked in at the Division of Wildlife office in Xenia, where District Wildlife Supervisor Todd Haines and his staff examined the deer and estimated his age at 4 1/2 years.

On Jan. 7, 2001, Boone and Crockett measurer Ron Perrine gave the 39-point rack an official entry score of 304 6/8

non-typical. At that score, he's not only the tentative world record for archery but also for any hunter-taken whitetail — bow or gun!

It's certainly an honor to have shot such a tremendous deer. But whether or not a B&C panel eventually confirms him as the first 300-inch whitetail ever taken by a hunter, my fondest memories of the 2000 season won't be of this buck. Instead, I'll most remember being able to share the deer season with my son. Having Andrew there when my deer was found was a special moment for me. And when my boy shot his first buck later that season, what had already been a magical year got just that much better.

Chapter Three

THE KIM BOES BUCK

222 7/8 NON-TYPICAL, ILLINOIS, 1989

Illinois' Oddest Deer Story

BY ALAN FOSTER

You wouldn't think a telephone call canceling a previously planned deer hunt would result in the encounter of a lifetime with a trophy whitetail. Yet, that's exactly what happened to an Illinois bowhunter during the 1989 season.

Kim Boes, then a 35-year-old maintenance man from Douglas County, had been bowhunting successfully for seven years. At least once or twice each year he'd get together with close friend Stan Duzan for a hunt, taking turns traveling to each other's hunting areas. During the 1989 season, they'd set aside Nov. 26 for a day afield, and it was Kim's turn to play host.

Kim had stands prepared and ready for Stan's arrival. However, the evening before the big day, that plan fell through. Stan couldn't make it, due to illness.

The call immediately changed Kim's plans for the next morning. He had an area he was hunting for the first time, and it had all of the potential to be a real hotspot. However, Kim only had permission to hunt the farm by himself, so when Stan called up and canceled, he decided to try this new place.

Photo by Larry L. Huffman.

KIM BOES, ILLINOIS, 1989

Main Characteristics: World-class beam and tine length. Left G-2 tine is among the longest on record.

	Right Antler	Left Antler	Difference
Main Beam Length	27 5/8	28 1/8	4/8
1st Point Length	3 1/8	3 4/8	3/8
2nd Point Length	14 6/8	17 3/8	2 5/8
3rd Point Length	14 0/8	14 4/8	4/8
4th Point Length	11 1/8	9 5/8	1 4/8
5th Point Length	—	—	—
1st Circumference	5 0/8	5 0/8	0/8
2nd Circumference	4 6/8	4 6/8	0/8
3rd Circumference	5 0/8	4 6/8	2/8
4th Circumference	5 0/8	4 5/8	3/8
Total	**90 3/8**	**92 2/8**	**6 1/8**

MISCELLANEOUS STATS	
No. Of Points–Right	9
No. Of Points–Left	7
Total No. Of Points	16
Length Of Abnormals	27 5/8
Greatest Spread	23 2/8
Tip To Tip Spread	1 4/8
Inside Spread	18 6/8

FINAL TALLY	
Inside Spread	18 6/8
Right Antler	90 3/8
Left Antler	92 2/8
Gross Score	201 3/8
Difference (–)	6 1/8
Subtotal	195 2/8
Abnormals (+)	27 5/8
NET NON-TYPICAL SCORE	**222 7/8**

Located in nearby Coles County, the new area consisted of 150 acres of brush with a similar amount of tillable land. The farmland once had been in hardwood timber, but several years before it had been almost completely logged off. A small but deep creek flowed through the center of the area, and one end of the property (near the landowner's home) had been fenced off and pastured. The rest had grown back into one of the nastiest thickets imaginable.

The first time Kim had walked around this area, it had seemed impossible to bowhunt. Besides the thicket being almost impenetrable, there were very few trees large enough to support a stand. However, Kim kept scouting and studying the terrain, and finally he'd found a clue to hunting the land successfully.

An old fence line ran east-west across the extreme north end of the thicket. About 100 yards from the thicket's northwest corner a draw jutted out from the fence line and thicket into a bean field. The draw was wide and had gently sloping sides, creating a "bowl" overgrown with clumps of black locust, multiflora rose and tall grass. Farther north, on the other side of the bean field, was a harvested corn field which hadn't yet been turned under. The deer were feeding in the corn at night and then coming back across the fields to meander down through the draw to the thicket, where they bedded during daylight hours.

The key was the old fence line separating the draw from the thicket. A few sizeable trees along the fence had been neglected by the loggers, and one 50-yard stretch of fence had collapsed from neglect. Several well-used trails showed deer were filtering down the draw and crossing there.

Kim had placed his portable stand high in one of the mature trees overlooking the crossing. It looked like an ideal setup, and the bowhunter had high hopes for the spot. So when Stan canceled their hunt for the next day, Kim knew exactly where he was going to sit, provided the wind would cooperate.

A calm, overcast morning greeted Kim as he anxiously checked the wind direction. It was in his favor, so he drove quickly to his parking place on the west side of the farm. Cautiously walking down the fencerow until he reached the west side of the draw, he then eased down a deer trail paralleling the fence. Kim didn't like walking on a deer trail, but he was wearing high-topped rubber

"It was immediately apparent when the coyotes found the dead deer. 'I've never heard anything like it,' Kim recalls. 'The sounds coming from that thicket turned my blood cold.'"

boots, and the trail was the only quiet way into the thicket.

Reaching his stand tree, Kim carefully climbed 20 feet up to his portable, then settled back to await dawn. Apparently he had made it into position without spooking any deer.

At 7 a.m. three does and then two more appeared, walking down the trails toward Kim's stand. The first three passed on one side of his tree, and the next two passed on the other. The does were very close but didn't notice the hunter above as they began browsing around the stand.

Suddenly, movement in the draw captured Kim's attention. Excitement washed over him as he saw antler tines flickering above the high grass. The dense brush hid the approaching buck until he was fairly close to the stand, where the undergrowth opened up a bit. Reaching the small clearing, the buck finally stepped into the open, giving the hunter his first good look.

"I almost came apart when that buck stepped into the open," Kim says. "It's a good thing I was sitting down. I knew the buck was huge, and that was bad enough. But when I saw that mass of wire wrapped up in his antlers I just couldn't believe it."

Sure enough, the tremendous buck had gone through what must have been an epic battle with an electric fence. He had almost 100 feet of electric fence wire wrapped around his ears and antlers, making him an imposing sight as he stood motionless, watching the does.

After a seemingly endless period the buck slowly made his way past Kim's stand and into position for a shot. The archer now had regained his composure and waited for the right moment to shoot, praying all the while that the does would not spoil his opportunity.

Fifteen yards from his stand, the buck stopped and offered a broadside opportunity. Drawing his 70-pound Martin Lynx compound ever so carefully, Kim centered the sight pin on the buck's lungs and released a perfect arrow. The buck gave one tremendous leap when the arrow struck; then, to Kim's amazement, he stopped and looked back at the suddenly alert does!

Quickly but quietly getting another arrow nocked, Kim once again drew, aimed and released. At the exact moment he touched off his second arrow, one of the does blew an alarm and the buck lunged ahead, causing the arrow to hit a bit farther back than intended. Deer exploded everywhere as the buck disappeared into the depths of the thicket.

About 20 minutes later, as Kim sat on stand waiting for the deer to die, he again noticed movement coming off a slight ridge to the east. As he watched, a large pack of coyotes appeared 50 yards from him, ghosting down through the brush into the thicket. Kim quickly counted at least a dozen coyotes, and he thought there were still more in the brush. The pack was returning from the fields after a night of hunting and was going to bed in the thicket.

> *"Although there are many outstanding features on this buck's rack, probably most noteworthy is the left G-2 tine. It's a whopping 17 3/8 inches long, with a 10 2/8 inch fork to boot. That would even be impressive on a mule deer!"*

As fate would have it, their route crossed the trail of the wounded buck, and when the first two coyotes hit the blood trail, bedlam ensued. Sounding like a frenzied pack of beagles, the whole pack raced down the trail as the stunned bowhunter watched in horror.

It was immediately apparent when the coyotes found the dead deer. "I've never heard anything like it," Kim recalls. "The sounds coming from that thicket turned my blood cold. They were screaming, snarling and yowling as they fought over the carcass, and I didn't know what to do. I'm not normally scared of coyotes, but there were a lot of them, and they were obviously in a frenzy back in that jungle. It just didn't seem like a good place for a lone bowhunter with two arrows in his quiver!"

Kim finally decided discretion was the better part of valor; he bailed out of his stand and headed home for help. Once back in Hindsboro, the shaken hunter managed to find his brother and convince him to come back and help run off the coyotes. They returned to the area a little over an hour later, intentionally making a lot of noise as they did.

The woods were quiet when the brothers located the ample blood trail and began following it cautiously into the depths of the thicket. After about 150 yards they came upon a small knoll overlooking the creek. As the profuse buck sign indicated, it was obviously one of the big deer's favored bedding areas, and it was here that the giant had fallen.

Great tine length makes the Kim Boes buck one of the most impressive whitetail bow trophies ever. Photo courtesy of Kim Boes.

Sick at heart, Kim looked at what was left of his once-beautiful trophy. In a very short time the hungry pack had literally destroyed the carcass. All the bowhunter could salvage was the head and antlers. The antlers and all that wire tangled around them, that is!

Marveling over the sight, the men couldn't imagine how the buck had managed to wrap himself up so thoroughly. The deer had wrapped the wire so tightly around his head that the wire literally was cutting into the ears.

The brothers stopped at the farmer's home to show him the deer and tell the story. The man took one look at the wire around the buck's head and knew at once where the deer had become entangled. The landowner then took them to a section of his property that he had just fenced in for pasture. Signs of the buck's furious battle with the fence were readily apparent, and a long stretch of wire had been torn loose!

Evidently, the deer had first become entangled some distance from the corner post. By tossing his head around and around, he'd evidently wrapped the fence wire around his antlers and ears until he worked his way to the corner, where he'd managed to break the wire and thus free himself.

Although there are many outstanding features on this buck's rack, probably most noteworthy is the left G-2 tine. It's a whopping 17 3/8 inches long, with a 10 2/8-inch fork to boot. That would even be impressive on a mule deer!

Nov. 26, 1989, definitely was a day Kim Boes won't forget. After all, how often does a phone call canceling a hunt result in an encounter with a giant buck, an electric fence and a hungry pack of coyotes, all in the same morning?

Chapter Four

THE BARB BREWER BUCK

---

253 3/8 NON-TYPICAL, ILLINOIS, 1997

A Veteran Hunter's Hard Work Pays Huge Dividends

BY BRENDA POTTS

There are plenty of stories about first-time hunters who make the shot after blundering into the path of a record-book buck. This isn't one of them. Barb Brewer is a veteran hunter who'd seen her monster buck before and was doing her best to tag him.

Prior to the 1997 shotgun season, Barb and her husband, Jim, applied for either-sex permits in Hamilton County, Illinois, which is not far from where the Brewers live. They'd been invited to hunt with Barb's brother, Brad.

"My brother owns 100 acres that is almost all timber except for an open ridge in the center," she says. "It's not very hilly around here, so that is one of the tallest ridges in the area. The back side of the property is mainly timber and some pasture, but there are some crops in the area, too. The deer don't usually come into the timber until after those crops are harvested, though."

There was reason to think big bucks were in the area. "Brad and Jim had hunted the year before on this property and had seen two huge bucks," Barb explains. "One of the bucks got into some heavy brush and had to back out, swinging his head,

Photo by Mike Rowe.

BARB BREWER, ILLINOIS, 1997

	Right Antler	Left Antler	Difference
Main Beam Length	27 2/8	27 6/8	4/8
1st Point Length	6 4/8	6 2/8	2/8
2nd Point Length	11 3/8	12 1/8	6/8
3rd Point Length	10 1/8	10 3/8	2/8
4th Point Length	8 2/8	6 2/8	2 0/8
5th Point Length	—	—	—
1st Circumference	5 7/8	6 0/8	1/8
2nd Circumference	4 4/8	4 6/8	2/8
3rd Circumference	4 5/8	4 1/8	4/8
4th Circumference	4 5/8	4 4/8	1/8
Total	**83 1/8**	**82 1/8**	**4 6/8**

Main Characteristics: Above-average width, even for a world-class rack. Exceptionally symmetrical for a non-typical.

MISCELLANEOUS STATS	
No. Of Points–Right	11
No. Of Points–Left	13
Total No. Of Points	24
Length Of Abnormals	69 3/8
Greatest Spread	29 0/8
Tip To Tip Spread	17 5/8
Inside Spread	23 4/8

FINAL TALLY	
Inside Spread	23 4/8
Right Antler	83 1/8
Left Antler	82 1/8
Gross Score	188 6/8
Difference (–)	4 6/8
Subtotal	184 0/8
Abnormals (+)	69 3/8
NET NON-TYPICAL SCORE	253 3/8

trying to get its antlers loose from the brush. "I hadn't hunted that area before, but I did go there with Jim one time," she adds. "We were on the ridge, and I was facing him as he was explaining how nice it would be to have a house right there. Then, all of a sudden, he just quit talking, and I knew something was up. About 40 yards behind me, a big old buck with his hair all bristled up stepped out. He had a big typical rack on him, and he just stood there and watched us

before he blew and took off. Jim said he was a Boone and Crockett-class buck."

About three weeks before the 1997 gun season, Barb and Jim scouted for stand locations. Barb tried to get into one of Jim's stands, but it was too high and difficult to climb into. Her husband told her to pick any place she wanted, and he'd help her get a stand into place.

"We went east of Jim's stand and found a trail coming in off the ridge," she recalls.

"We put up a wooden stand into a big tree with trails on each side of it. I could see out onto the ridge — not real well, but it looked like a good spot with a lot of sign."

On the opener of Illinois' three-day first season, Barb headed for the 100 acres. "I took the truck around to my stand on the northeast side of the timber. It was drizzling rain that day, and I thought it might really start pouring. But luckily, it didn't. It just kept misting off and on without getting too bad."

At about 8:30 a.m., a big doe came in. "She was just running around, making a circle in the woods near the stand I had trouble getting into," Barb recalls. "Then, she suddenly ran out of the woods and immediately came back in — running all around, crazy. I thought maybe she had winded me and couldn't figure out where I was. Then she disappeared. About 45 minutes later, I heard a buck grunt."

Barb knew it was time to go meet the other hunters, so she decided to ease through the timber near where she'd heard the grunt. As she made her way through an area choked with small saplings, she saw a doe out on the ridge.

"The doe swung her head around to the east, and I saw a huge buck," Barb says. "He was headed down the second gully, and I thought I would be able to get a shot if I just stepped out a little bit. He came right to the edge of the gully and spotted me. He stopped, dead in his tracks, and went into a sneak position with his head down real low." Barb then lifted her gun slowly, and the buck raised his head slightly. With only the deer's head and neck visible, she shot.

Barb and Jim later trailed the buck for some distance, but with no blood or hair to suggest otherwise, they finally concluded that he hadn't been hit. The widest part of Barb's size 7 1/2 boot wouldn't cover the buck's track!

Jim had to work that afternoon, but Barb was able to get off her scheduled shift from her job at an ambulance service. So she and her brother Brad returned to the woods. Unfortunately, the big buck didn't show that day, but Brad got a nice doe.

Most hunters wouldn't dream of sharing their stand after such a close encounter with a trophy buck, but Barb was happy to let others give it a try. Brad's wife, Marsha, hunted from the stand the next day, seeing 57 turkeys but no deer. Later, Marsha's brother hunted there and saw a different big buck, but couldn't get a shot.

For the rest of the first slug season, Barb opted to try a tent-style camouflage ground blind her dad had been using. Three does walked right up to her in the blind, but no bucks. All too soon, the three-day season had ended.

Prior to the second season, Barb asked Jim to set up a tripod stand closer to the ridge. After the stand went up, Barb found out she wouldn't be able to hunt much during the second season — it's only four days long, and Barb was scheduled to work the first two.

Jim sat in the stand for two days and nearly froze. No big bucks showed. Then Brad tried the stand on the third day... he didn't see anything good either. Finally, on Sunday afternoon — the year's last few hours of shotgun hunting — Barb went out to her spot at around 1 o'clock.

She hadn't been there long before she started blowing on her grunt call. And not long after that, a deer approached.

"Off to my left, I saw the top of a buck's rack," she remembers. "But I couldn't get a clear shot. He was there for about 10 minutes, and I was just sick. After a few minutes, he turned his head and I could see the drop tines. Then I really got nervous. I just kept thinking, I've got to get myself together and not blow this."

"When I raised my gun a bit, I bumped the grunt call around my neck," Barb says. "I thought, Well, I've ruined it now. He threw his head up and tried to wind me, but he couldn't."

After a few more tense minutes, the buck started rubbing his antlers. He finally took a few steps forward, giving Barb a clear shot.

"I shot him at about 30 or 40 yards, and he took off running like I had never hit him," she recalls. "As he was running off, I shot at him again. Then the buck went over a ridge, and I just shot up in the air, thinking, I can't believe this!"

As Barb replayed the events in her mind, she remembered seeing steam coming from the buck's sides as he turned at the bottom of the ridge. "Then I was pretty sure I had gotten him, and then I *really* started shaking!" she says.

"My Dad taught me never to get down right away, because you might push the deer and never get it," Barb notes. "So I sat there for about 20 minutes. It was the longest wait of my life. As I climbed down, the stand was really shaking from my legs quivering so badly. I went out to where I thought I had first hit him and couldn't find anything. Then, after another 10 yards, I found a drop of

"...The widest part of Barb's size 7 1/2 boot wouldn't cover the buck's track!"

blood. Then it started to spray the grass red and was an easy trail to follow.

"As I peeked over the hill, I could see him lying there with that rack sticking up. I waited to make sure he was dead before I went over to him. When I saw he was dead for sure, I let out the biggest 'war whoop' you've ever heard in your life!

"Brad had a buck on him right down the ridge below me at that time," she says. "I didn't know it, but I scared it away from him going to get him. He came out of the woods and said, 'I had a whole herd of them around me, and you scared them off. What are you doing?'"

Of course, Brad soon learned why Barb had come to get him. She was afraid to leave her buck — there were fresh ATV tracks in the area, and she'd found where some trespasser had dragged out a deer.

Barb and Brad tried to cover the buck's antlers with a jacket, though even that couldn't completely hide the rack. Then they walked over to Jim's stand and told him they had a "little doe" they needed to get out.

In an effort to convince Jim of the urgency of the situation, Barb said she was concerned that coyotes might get her doe. She laughs as she recalls her husband's reaction. "He said, 'I can't believe you come in here on the last day, an hour before dark, to tell me you need help getting a doe. Can't it wait until dark?'"

Barb and Brad were having trouble keeping straight faces as they carried out their mischievous prank. "We walked out to get the four-wheeler, and I rode back with him (Jim) on it, and he was complaining the whole way back in," Barb says. "But then, when Brad pulled the coat off of it and he saw the buck, he really started cussing me!" she says with a laugh.

Of course, Jim really wasn't the least bit angry about Barb getting the monster — in fact, he was as excited as anyone. They loaded the deer and headed for the nearby town of Carmi, to share the story with family and friends.

Brad locked the buck in his storage shed for the night, and Barb's dad guarded the deer the next day as onlookers streamed past to get a glimpse of the gigantic non-typical with four drop tines. At the coffee shop the next morning, Barb was overwhelmed with questions and congratulations. Everyone wanted to know more about the amazing deer that would go on to be ranked as the state's No. 4 non-typical.

A proud Barb Brewer with her trophy buck, which has a huge 5x5 typical frame and 69 3/8 inches of abnormals. Photo courtesy of Brenda Potts.

As the days passed, stories of the monster began to spread across the nation. And with that talk came the usual nonsense surrounding any trophy whitetail taken these days.

One tale even claimed Barb had shot the buck in the mouth during the first season, causing him to lose so much weight that her finishing shot was little more than a "mercy killing." It seems that often the size of the lies told about a trophy is in direct proportion to the size of his antlers!

Some hunters who bag exceptional deer develop the attitude that the world owes them a new pickup truck. Perhaps this is what's best about Barb's story. She's an ethical, knowledgeable hunter and just a bit uncomfortable with all the attention this huge whitetail focused on her. All she wants to do is keep hunting big bucks!

Chapter Five

THE KEITH BROSSARD BUCK

197 6/8 TYPICAL, WISCONSIN, 1999

A Stunning Whitetail from Southern Wisconsin

BY CRAIG BOBULA

Going into the 1999 firearms season, southeastern Wisconsin's Kenosha County was considered one of the state's least likely places to shoot a monster deer. In fact, it had never produced a Boone and Crockett whitetail. But what happened that November changed the way Wisconsin hunters view this county south of Milwaukee.

The day before gun season opened, Keith Brossard headed out to hang his stand in a tree he'd hunted from for the past six years. Known to Keith and his brothers as "the slot," the area was a typical funnel of woods linking two larger pieces of cover.

Keith hung his stand on one end of the bottleneck, where deer typically exited it on their way into bigger woods. The funnel was only 150 yards wide, and the woods were fairly open. Because Keith typically hung his stand a dizzying 38 feet off the ground, almost any deer passing through the funnel was visible and within shotgun range. Going into that season, Keith had shot many nice deer from that tree, including a 147 4/8-inch 12-pointer in 1995 and a 144 3/8-inch 9-pointer in 1997. These

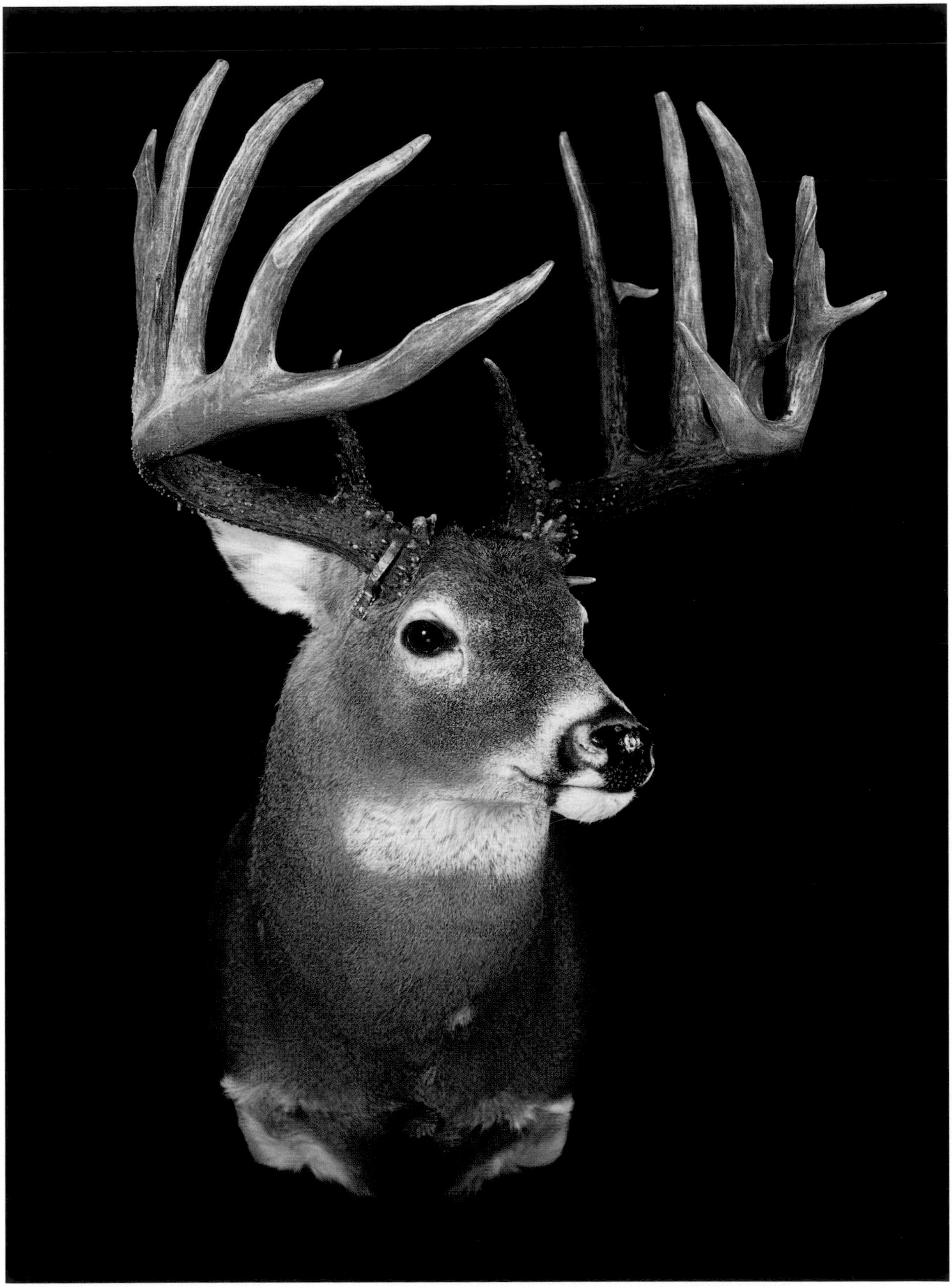

Photo by Tom Johnson.

Main Characteristics: Tremendous mass and character to go with great tine length and beam length.

KEITH BROSSARD, WISCONSIN, 1999

	Right Antler	Left Antler	Difference
Main Beam Length	30 0/8	26 7/8	3 1/8
1st Point Length	6 0/8	5 4/8	4/8
2nd Point Length	11 2/8	12 0/8	6/8
3rd Point Length	11 2/8	11 7/8	5/8
4th Point Length	10 1/8	12 0/8	1 7/8
5th Point Length	9 2/8	7 7/8	1 3/8
1st Circumference	5 7/8	6 0/8	1/8
2nd Circumference	5 2/8	5 3/8	1/8
3rd Circumference	5 2/8	5 4/8	2/8
4th Circumference	5 0/8	5 2/8	2/8
Total	**99 2/8**	**98 2/8**	**9 0/8**

MISCELLANEOUS STATS	
No. Of Points–Right	7
No. Of Points–Left	10
Total No. Of Points	17
Length Of Abnormals	9 5/8
Greatest Spread	21 3/8
Tip To Tip Spread	5 2/8
Inside Spread	18 7/8

FINAL TALLY	
Inside Spread	18 7/8
Right Antler	99 2/8
Left Antler	98 2/8
Gross Score	216 3/8
Difference (–)	9 0/8
Subtotal	207 3/8
Abnormals (–)	9 5/8
NET TYPICAL SCORE	197 6/8

trophies, along with several other bucks and does Keith had shot from the stand, all had ended up traveling within 20 yards of that tree.

Despite such successes, Keith actually considered going elsewhere for the 1999 opener. His alternative was a spot his brother Dave had bowhunted earlier that fall. Located 600 yards from Keith's usual stand in "the slot," Dave's stand hung in a large piece of cover on the far end of the funnel.

The stand was next to a large tract of hardwoods where several trails merged on the edge of good bedding cover.

Dave had seen a big buck within bow range there in early season, and Keith knew it was an outstanding spot. The problem was that the tree stood only 30 yards from a property line and a frequently hunted stand on the other side of the line. So, Keith finally decided not to risk going there and having his hunt ruined by another hunter.

Opening day dawned cloudy with light winds and temperatures in the low 40s. Hunting alone, Keith got to his stand at 5:50, a half-hour before shooting light, and settled in to hunt all day if necessary.

For several hours, it seemed such a long vigil might be in order; Keith had seen no deer and hadn't even heard many shots. Then, at 10:30, he caught a flash of brown roughly 100 yards behind his stand. As Keith turned to get a better look, he realized the deer was a buck — in fact, the biggest he'd ever seen!

The huge deer kept making his way closer, walking slowly and stopping often. Such casual behavior seemed unusual for a trophy buck on opening morning of gun season, but Keith wasn't about to complain. Remaining seated, he moved his 12-gauge shotgun into position for a shot. By now, the buck was 75 yards away… and still coming.

As the monster approached, Keith grew more nervous. But he was in no hurry to shoot. Based on the buck's direction of travel and calm demeanor, he'd eventually pass within close range. And within two or three minutes, he was indeed close — a mere 18 yards from Keith's tree!

Suddenly, the deer sensed something was wrong. "I was breathing really hard, and with almost no wind and the cool temperatures, I know he heard me," Keith says.

The buck stopped behind limbs and vines, well within range but too hidden for a good shot. If he took two or three steps he'd be in the clear… but for three nerve-wracking minutes he just stood there, surveying

Brossard's massive trophy was Kenosha County's first B&C buck. Photo by Craig Bobula.

the scene with great caution. He kept bobbing his head and peeking over and through the brush.

By now, Keith had been holding his open sights on the buck for five or six minutes, and the shotgun's barrel was swaying back and forth. Several times, the hunter had to lift his face off the stock and take deep breaths just to relax himself. Meanwhile, the buck kept looking in his general direction, though never directly at him way up in that tree.

Finally, the buck took two steps forward, and as soon as he did, Keith shot. The deer arched his back slightly, and before he had much chance to do anything else, Keith shot again. It was over.

Keith had known the buck was big, but when he reached the animal, he couldn't believe the sheer amount of antler. All of that bone translated into a tremendous score — in fact, the second-highest typical score ever recorded for a Wisconsin whitetail!

When a panel of Wisconsin Buck & Bear Club measurers put a tape to the massive rack, they came up with a gross typical score of 216 3/8 points and a net of 197 6/8. Only a whopping 18 5/8 inches of deductions for asymmetry and abnormal points had kept the Brossard buck from shattering James Jordan's state record of 206 1/8. The Jordan buck, which once held the B&C world record (see *Legendary Whitetails*), had been shot in 1914, so Keith's deer was Wisconsin's top typical in 85 years!

It's safe to say that Kenosha County's big-buck reputation is better these days.

Chapter Six

THE BILL BROWN BUCK

251 6/8 NON-TYPICAL, ILLINOIS, 1999

A Shift in the Wind and Behold — a Shift in the Luck

BY RON WILLMORE

At first glance, Bill Brown of Pekin, Illinois, might not fit your usual image of a hard-core whitetail bowhunter. When the season's closed, he spends a lot of time at the office (he's an attorney) and at the golf course (during any kind of reasonable weather). But then, when you learn that Bill's other primary off-season activity is planting food plots on his hunting land, you start to realize just how serious he is about hunting trophy deer.

During the fall of 1999, that pursuit paid off in a huge way — as in a non-typical buck that nets a stunning 251 6/8 Pope and Young points! That score shattered the long-standing Illinois bow record of 245 5/8 points, set by Robert Chestnut in 1981.

Bill's unique buck has it all: a wide basic 6x5 typical frame, tremendous mass and drop tines up to 13 5/8 inches long (two of them forked). There's no doubt that this trophy ranks among the world's greatest bucks by bow.

The story of this buck actually began six years before the hunt, when Bill and his partner, Leroy Compton, bought 200 acres in Fulton County. Their idea at that time

*Main Characteristics:
Spectacular drop
tines, spread and
beam length. One of
the largest frames of
any archery buck ever.*

BILL BROWN, ILLINOIS, 1999

	Right Antler	Left Antler	Difference
Main Beam Length	30 4/8	31 6/8	1 2/8
1st Point Length	9 0/8	9 0/8	0/8
2nd Point Length	9 6/8	11 1/8	1 3/8
3rd Point Length	7 3/8	9 2/8	1 7/8
4th Point Length	2 0/8	3 1/8	1 1/8
5th Point Length	—	5 0/8	5 0/8
1st Circumference	5 5/8	5 3/8	2/8
2nd Circumference	4 7/8	4 5/8	2/8
3rd Circumference	5 2/8	5 2/8	0/8
4th Circumference	3 7/8	5 1/8	1 2/8
Total	78 2/8	89 5/8	12 3/8

MISCELLANEOUS STATS	
No. Of Points–Right	12
No. Of Points–Left	13
Total No. Of Points	25
Length Of Abnormals	71 0/8
Greatest Spread	30 5/8
Tip To Tip Spread	20 0/8
Inside Spread	25 2/8

FINAL TALLY	
Inside Spread	25 2/8
Right Antler	78 2/8
Left Antler	89 5/8
Gross Score	193 1/8
Difference (–)	12 3/8
Subtotal	180 6/8
Abnormals (+)	71 0/8
NET NON-TYPICAL SCORE	251 6/8

was not only to have a place of their own to bowhunt, but also to do everything they could to properly manage the deer herd. They shoot enough does for herd control and don't take immature bucks. They work with biologists to improve the habitat, increasing the amount of available forage for those times when local agricultural crops aren't available. And as important as anything else, these guys don't feel that they must kill bucks every year to have a successful season.

On the hunting side of the equation, one of the most important tricks Bill and Leroy rely on is locating major bedding areas and then keeping them secure by not hunting in them or otherwise disturbing deer there.

Like thousands of other bowhunters, Bill began his 1999 season with high hopes. He'd seen some good bucks during the summer, especially on the ladino clover plots. He also had in his mind an image of a tremendous non-typical he'd seen in 1997. Although Bill hadn't taken a buck with his bow in two years, he'd decided that the only buck he'd consider shooting would be mature and at least a high-end P&Y trophy, if not of Boone and Crockett caliber.

In Illinois, unusually warm, dry weather held on well into the fall of 1999, causing most rut activity to be nocturnal. Bill considered giving up and going home for a few days, to wait for conditions to improve. But then, after returning to his cabin, he made a decision that ultimately started the wheels of fate turning in the right direction. Bill decided to stay and hunt Monday morning. His reasoning was simple: No hunter has ever taken a buck unless he was in the woods!

Well before dawn on Monday, Bill went through his ritual of picturing in his mind which stand to hunt under the prevailing wind conditions. After weighing the wind and other factors, the bowhunter headed for the woods.

But then, fate intervened again. Between Bill's departure from the cabin and his arrival at his chosen morning stand, the wind direction shifted 90 degrees. When Bill realized that the wind now was blowing from the east, he knew conditions finally were perfect for his favorite stand. So, rather than stick with his original plan, he got back into his truck and headed that way.

Bill's new destination was a tree that had rarely been hunted all fall, because of the unusually persistent southerly winds. It lay in the middle of a river bluff between two major bedding areas for does, making it a likely travel corridor for any big buck out looking for love. Several big bucks had been seen there over the years, and the bowhunter hoped one would cruise through this morning.

Bill climbed the 22 feet up to the stand and settled in. Nothing showed up right after daybreak, but at 8 a.m. a doe and two fawns appeared. They came toward the stand, then bedded in a thicket about 40 yards away.

The three deer had been bedded for about 45 minutes when suddenly they jumped up and began staring north. Two or three minutes later, they ran out of the thicket to the south. Although Bill didn't know what had spooked them, when they were out of sight he stood up and got ready for a possible shot.

It wasn't long before Bill heard the approach of what sounded like a big deer, off in the direction in which the doe and fawns had been looking. He scanned the woods in an effort to pinpoint the sounds, which were growing ever louder.

Suddenly, the bowhunter saw a huge left antler 50 to 60 yards away. When the right antler came into view, Bill's first thought was that the buck "looked like he had a cage around his head."

The huge deer continued on, moving down a sapling-choked trail that passed some 30 yards from the tree stand. As he did, it occurred to Bill that his rack wouldn't fit through the saplings!

"The buck kept backing up and turning his head sideways, so he could get his antlers through the brush (much as an elk does to get his rack through timber)," the bowhunter recalls.

Bill typically clears his shooting lanes out to only 25 yards, because he doesn't feel comfortable shooting any farther. This buck now was at 30 yards, putting him just into the brush and just out of reach. So, with no reason to think a reasonable shot was imminent, the archer began thinking of how to lure him in.

Several grunts had no visible effect; the giant buck continued on, perhaps out of Bill's life forever. But then, when the deer stopped approximately 100 yards away, Bill remembered he had a Primos "Hands Free" adjustable call in his pocket, its O-ring set to imitate a doe bleat. He quickly grabbed the call and gave three bleats.

The huge buck's head shot up, and he immediately turned and started back toward the stand — this time on a trail that would lead him into a shooting lane.

At 80 yards and with the deer closing the distance, it was time to grab the bow. As the monster drew ever nearer, Bill told himself, *Here we go… it's for real now. Concentrate.*

Throughout his final approach, the buck was straight downwind of the stand. Still, he kept coming until he was within 15 yards of Bill's tree and just two steps from the shooting lane. Then, he stopped in his tracks!

Imagine watching this monster stand just 15 yards from your stand, sticking his nose into the air and rotating his giant antlers. Suddenly, the colossal deer decided to change directions. He turned and cut diagonally in behind Bill.

Bill was in position for a shot off to his right — difficult for a righthanded archer. Now, with the buck taking a new route, he had to turn all the way around to prepare for a shot.

After completing that maneuver, and with the monster buck now entering the second shooting lane, Bill brought his 58-pound PSE bow to full draw. As the deer

"The huge deer continued on, moving down a sapling-choked trail that passed some 30 yards from the tree stand. As he did, it occurred to Bill that his rack wouldn't fit through the saplings!"

came into the clear, quartering away at 20 yards, the bowhunter took careful aim at the vitals and released his arrow.

In an instant, the shaft buried itself to the fletching within two inches of the point of aim. The buck whirled and ran off into a nearby bottomland bean field.

The flood of adrenaline finally caught up with Bill as he tried to keep the buck in sight with his binoculars. He was shaking so badly that he finally lowered the glasses, just as the deer began to stumble. When he looked through the binoculars again, the buck was nowhere in sight!

Recognizing the danger of trying to climb down from his tree while still excited, Bill took a few minutes to regain his composure — and perhaps to convince himself that the episode really had just happened. Then, he carefully climbed down from the stand and returned to his truck. After attempting to find help to no avail, Bill drove back to the field where he'd last seen the buck.

The archer walked only 15 feet before spotting the immense deer lying in the ditch next to the field. Although he'd been shot through both lungs with a 100-grain Thunderhead that had then wedged in an offside rib, the buck had traveled almost 400 yards before dying.

With the warm weather, Bill headed for the meat locker. Interestingly, when Bill arrived, another hunter was there with a 200-class non-typical taken the evening before. Imagine: another Boone and Crockett bow kill — same county, shot 10 miles away and 16 hours earlier!

Great width, mass and spectacular drop tines make Bill Brown's trophy a world-class non-typical. Photo by Ron Willmore.

After getting his buck skinned out, Bill took the antlers and cape to taxidermist Locie Murphy of Bushnell. One glance told Locie the rack was world class, and he quickly called me to come over for a look.

Following the 60-day drying period, fellow P&Y measurer Tim Walmsley and I scored the Brown buck at 264 1/8 gross points, 251 6/8 net. The rack is exceptional in every way: beam length, spread, mass, points and uniqueness.

This historic deer is an example of what can happen when you combine proper management with the right mental approach to trophy hunting. It takes an extremely dedicated hunter to pass up smaller deer to the point of going several years without killing a buck, but Bill was willing to do just that. In fact, only six days after taking the non-typical, he sat in the same tree and let two P&Y-class bucks walk by — broadside at 15 yards!

Managing your hunting area might never give you a shot at a state-record deer, but it definitely will improve your chances. Bill Brown has all the proof anyone should need.

Chapter Seven

THE JEFF BRUNK BUCK

199 4/8 TYPICAL, MISSOURI, 1969

A Three-Year Quest for a Buck Known as the Phantom

BY DUNCAN DOBIE

Nineteen-year-old Jeff Brunk had every reason to call the deer he was pursuing a "phantom" buck. It was late in Missouri's 1969 gun season, and Jeff felt he was no closer to catching up with the tall-tined giant than he had been when he'd first resolved to go after him three years before.

During all of that time, Jeff only had glimpsed the incredible buck on two occasions, but each sighting had been more than enough to keep him on the trail. The first sighting had taken place two years earlier, as Jeff and some friends were returning home after a day of quail hunting. Two does had run out of a wooded draw across an opening, with a giant buck following.

"He was tremendous," Jeff remembers. "And his rack was pure white, with huge tines. He was by far the largest buck any of us had ever seen."

Northern Missouri's gun season hadn't yet opened, so Jeff and his friends rushed home, grabbed their bows and hurried back to the scene. The buck had gone into a stand of woods surrounded by several open fields. A well-executed drive failed to produce another sighting of the buck, however.

Photo by Danny M. Critzer.

Main Characteristics: Incredible rack height, due to length of G-2 and G-3 tines and upward angle of beams.

JEFF BRUNK, MISSOURI, 1969

	Right Antler	Left Antler	Difference
Main Beam Length	27 2/8	26 2/8	1 0/8
1st Point Length	10 4/8	8 7/8	1 5/8
2nd Point Length	17 0/8	16 6/8	2/8
3rd Point Length	13 5/8	14 6/8	1 1/8
4th Point Length	6 7/8	7 3/8	4/8
5th Point Length	1 2/8	—	1 2/8
6th Point Length	1 6/8	—	1 6/8
1st Circumference	5 4/8	5 1/8	3/8
2nd Circumference	4 4/8	4 2/8	2/8
3rd Circumference	4 4/8	5 2/8	6/8
4th Circumference	4 4/8	4 2/8	2/8
Total	**97 2/8**	**92 7/8**	**9 1/8**

MISCELLANEOUS STATS	
No. Of Points–Right	8
No. Of Points–Left	5
Total No. Of Points	13
Length Of Abnormals	1 4/8
Greatest Spread	22 4/8
Tip To Tip Spread	10 3/8
Inside Spread	20 0/8

FINAL TALLY	
Inside Spread	20 0/8
Right Antler	97 2/8
Left Antler	92 7/8
Gross Score	**210 1/8**
Difference (–)	9 1/8
Subtotal	**201 0/8**
Abnormals (–)	1 4/8
NET TYPICAL SCORE	**199 4/8**

During the gun season, Jeff hunted for the big buck every time he went out, but no one saw him again that year. "We started calling him the 'Phantom' shortly after that," Jeff recalls. "His horns were so white and ghostly that the name seemed to fit. It also was fitting because we all knew he was in the area, but no one had ever seen him. He must've stayed pretty much to himself in the thickest cover he could find. I believe he had to be almost entirely nocturnal. If he had

moved around at all during the day, someone probably would have seen him."

Jeff lived with his family in Clark County, in the extreme northeastern corner of the state. His dad had purchased a hog farm near the small town of Kahoka in 1960, when Jeff was nine years old. The Brunks raised registered Hampshires and grew about 300 acres of corn and other crops. The terrain was ideal for whitetails, having mineral-rich soil, flat-to-rolling topography and numerous patches of isolated woods and dense cedar thickets.

The second sighting of the Phantom occurred during the 1968 gun season, after Jeff had hunted the entire archery season without success. On the second or third day of gun hunting, he was slipping along the side of a deep draw when he jumped four does. "As I was watching the does run off, the Phantom suddenly jumped up and took out after them," the hunter recalls. "I was shooting a Browning automatic shotgun with slugs. I shot at him twice, but I knew it was hopeless. He was too far out. I was sick."

Frustrated over this incident, he stormed home and raised Cain with his dad. "I told him I wanted a deer rifle, and that by the next deer season I was going to buy one. Money was tight in those days, but the following spring, when I graduated from high school, Dad bought me a Browning .30/06 as a graduation present."

Jeff's missed opportunity at the Phantom during the 1968 season certainly had been disappointing, but the season wasn't a total loss. If nothing else, the hunter now knew far more about the buck's home range.

"For one thing, I found that he ranged a much wider area than I originally had thought," Jeff says. "The two places where I had seen him were several miles apart. I also located several of his scrapes and rubs, and I learned to recognize his tracks. Most importantly, though, I realized that he was almost exclusively nocturnal."

At the ripe old age of 19, Jeff was already something of a sensation among the local deer-hunting fraternity. He'd killed several nice bucks, one of which

fell during his first year of gun hunting in 1965.

On the third day of gun season that year, he jumped a large buck while still-hunting and dropped the deer with a slug from the family's old 20-gauge single-shot Springfield. The deer turned out to be a 215-pound 12-pointer: the largest buck anyone had seen in the area in years!

"You ought to be really happy, son," Jeff's dad told him after the hunt. "That's probably the largest buck you'll ever see." What Mr. Brunk didn't know was that in a few short years, his son would kill a buck far bigger!

By the time the 1969 gun season opened, Jeff pretty well knew the Phantom's home range, and he spent day after day still-hunting the cedar thickets where he believed the giant stayed during daylight hours. But when the final day of gun season arrived, there hadn't been so much as a glimpse of the deer.

It was about 9 a.m. and as usual, Jeff was still-hunting. "I was walking up a hillside that was covered with cedar, moving extremely slow and not making a sound," he remembers. "It was in an area where the Phantom had several large scrapes, and I knew he was in there somewhere. I had started walking up this draw right after daylight, and it had taken me several hours to go a short distance.

"Suddenly, I looked up, and there he was. He was slowly walking through the woods. The first thing I saw was that huge set of white antlers, then the rest of his body."

Jeff dropped to one knee, raised his rifle and waited. When the deer stepped into a small opening about 50 yards away, the rifle spoke. However, the huge buck turned and ran off, giving no indication of a hit.

Jeff immediately began looking for a blood trail, but his search turned up nothing. "He had headed toward an area where there were several thick draws, one right after the other, and the cover was so heavy I figured he'd be in one of those draws. Sure enough, he was in the first draw. When he heard me, he came rushing out, but it was too thick for me to shoot."

The Phantom ran over a rise and into the next draw, then again stopped. "He had to be badly hurt, because he kept stopping, but I still hadn't found any blood and didn't know whether he was hit or not," Jeff remembers.

When the hunter moved down into the second draw, the buck evacuated the area once again. This time, Jeff got off two quick shots. "I don't know if I hit him or not, but I did find blood," he says. "It could have been from the first bullet. There wasn't much, only a few drops, but at least I knew he was hit."

The Phantom went out across a field and into some big timber. When Jeff reached it, nearly all traces of blood had disappeared, and he was forced to crawl on his hands and knees to look for sign. "I tracked him for a long time. I lost the trail several times. Once, I completely lost it on one side of a creek bottom. I began circling and found a drop of blood 300 yards away.

"I started following the blood trail again," Jeff says, "and as I reached the top of a ridge, I jumped him. He started

running straight away from me, and I was able to get off three rapid shots. The third shot hit his femoral artery, and that really slowed him down. He finally stopped, but I couldn't see him."

As Jeff worked his way to a better vantage point, the Phantom saw movement and began running again. The hunter aimed and fired, this time hitting the deer in the back leg.

"That last shot slowed him down to a walk," Jeff recalls. "He was dragging his back leg, and I was beginning to feel terrible. I wanted to get it over with so he wouldn't suffer, but he just kept on going."

Finally, at a distance of about 100 yards, the Phantom stopped and turned broadside. Jeff took careful aim through the trees and fired for the eighth time of the day, and the big buck dropped in his tracks. Greatly relieved that the ordeal was finally over, Jeff began walking toward the buck — which then, to his utter amazement, jumped up and tried to stagger off! At a distance of less than 20 yards, Jeff fired a final round, and the incredible deer went down for the last time. By then, over three hours had passed since the hunter's first shot.

"I had only carried 10 bullets with me that morning, and when it was all over, I had one bullet left," Jeff says. "When I field dressed the Phantom, I found that my first shot had nicked a lung. Out of nine shots, I hit him seven times. Most of the wounds were superficial, but three of the shots had hit him right in the boiler room. The thing that amazed me was the fact that he should have died from the

"To match wits with a really big one, then do everything right when the time comes — that's what deer hunting is all about."

first shot, but he wouldn't give up."

Jeff knew he'd killed a record buck. He hurriedly field dressed his prize and then covered him up with brush. Although Jeff was deep in the woods on private property, he wasn't about to take any chances with a stray hunter sneaking up and stealing his hard-earned trophy. It was two miles back to Jeff's house as the crow flies, and he covered the entire distance at a dead run. He quickly rounded up his dad, several uncles and a cousin, and the party set off to retrieve the huge trophy.

High, white tines give Jeff Brunk's buck a mystical appearance. Photo by Duncan Dobie, courtesy of North American Whitetail.

"I felt both sad and happy," Jeff says. "When you kill an animal like that, you always have some regrets. Over the years, the Phantom had outsmarted a lot of hunters, including me."

At the deer cooler in nearby Revere, the buck caused quite a stir. He was hung on a meat pole with seven or eight other bucks, and he dwarfed them all. His head was lying on the floor, while those of the other bucks were all at least six inches off the ground!

But the Phantom's rack drew even more attention. After the 60-day drying period, official Boone and Crockett measurer Dean Murphy scored Jeff's

buck at 197 2/8 net, making him a state record. Later, a B&C judges panel elevated the final score to 199 4/8, which was No. 4 in the world.

The Phantom reigned as the Missouri champion for only two years. In 1971, Larry Gibson shot a Randolph County 12-pointer that netted 205 0/8 typical, making him not only the Missouri record but also No. 2 in the world. As of this writing, the Phantom still ranks second to that buck on the Missouri list.

Jeff didn't kill his record whitetail by accident. From the time he first saw those huge white antlers, he methodically set out to get the deer. And while he had many disappointments along the way, he never gave up. Since that memorable hunt Jeff has killed numerous bucks, some of them outstanding trophies. Many have been taken while still-hunting with the same .30/06 that downed the Phantom better than three decades ago.

"I have always hunted in a variety of ways," Jeff says, "but I enjoy still-hunting best of all. To me, one on one is the ultimate challenge in hunting a big buck. To match wits with a really big one, then do everything right when the time comes — that's what deer hunting is all about."

Chapter Eight

THE KEN CARTWRIGHT BUCK

250 6/8 NON-TYPICAL, KANSAS, 1994

Playing a Hunch
Pays off Big

BY KEN CARTWRIGHT

Although taking a giant buck is every whitetail bowhunter's dream, only for a few does this fantasy ever come true. So, what are the odds that two buddies in Kansas each would arrow Top 10 Pope and Young non-typicals — and that they'd do so only two seasons apart?

In December 1992, while bowhunting in Anderson County, my friend Richard Stahl took a 246 3/8-inch buck that went on to be recognized as the No. 4 non-typical in P&Y history. (See Chapter 36). This extraordinary kill encouraged me that it was possible to arrow a buck of that class. Of course, I knew it would take luck, along with skill and patience, to do so. Even in Kansas, which has produced several of the world's top bucks by bow, giant non-typicals aren't exactly common!

Let's fast-forward to Dec. 19, 1994, almost exactly two years after Richard shot his trophy. Long before daylight that morning, as I was getting ready to head for the woods, the phone rang. It turned out to be another one of my hunting buddies, calling to let me know he'd seen three does and two bucks the previous evening in an area I

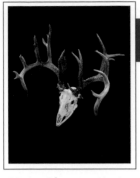

KEN CARTWRIGHT, KANSAS, 1994

	Right Antler	Left Antler	Difference
Main Beam Length	29 4/8	26 7/8	2 5/8
1st Point Length	10 2/8	10 4/8	2/8
2nd Point Length	13 5/8	12 6/8	7/8
3rd Point Length	11 3/8	11 1/8	2/8
4th Point Length	8 2/8	8 2/8	0/8
5th Point Length	4 5/8	4 6/8	1/8
1st Circumference	5 3/8	5 4/8	1/8
2nd Circumference	5 0/8	4 6/8	2/8
3rd Circumference	4 7/8	4 6/8	1/8
4th Circumference	4 2/8	4 3/8	1/8
Total	97 1/8	93 5/8	4 6/8

Main Characteristics: Outstanding typical frame, among the largest basic 5x5 racks ever. Unique downward-projecting beam tips.

MISCELLANEOUS STATS

No. Of Points–Right	12
No. Of Points–Left	12
Total No. Of Points	24
Length Of Abnormals	40 6/8
Greatest Spread	26 6/8
Tip To Tip Spread	22 4/8
Inside Spread	24 0/8

FINAL TALLY

Inside Spread	24 0/8
Right Antler	97 1/8
Left Antler	93 5/8
Gross Score	214 6/8
Difference (–)	4 6/8
Subtotal	210 0/8
Abnormals (+)	40 6/8
NET NON-TYPICAL SCORE	250 6/8

often hunt. He gave me a strong impression that one of the bucks was a monster.

Within a few minutes of leaving home that foggy morning, I entered the area where my friend had spotted the deer. I decided they probably were using the area at night, then following a certain trail as they left in the morning. I elected to climb into a familiar tree near that trail and wait for dawn.

Not long after I'd climbed into place, I heard footsteps approaching. As it was get-

ting light enough to see a bit, I spotted a set of deer legs, and my heart began to pound. It turned out to be a pair of does, and I couldn't help but wonder if that monster buck was behind them. He wasn't.

Perhaps another hour passed before the swirling fog finally began to lift. By now it was light enough for me to see fair detail in my surroundings. But I also was starting to feel hunger pangs. I'd brought no food with me, so I'd have to leave the woods if I wanted breakfast. I decided to stay another 30 minutes; then, if I hadn't seen anything of note, I'd go grab a bite.

The minutes dragged by with no more deer sighted. I was just about to climb out of the tree when I felt an urge to look to my left. As I did, I noticed a very tall set of antlers turning slowly in the brush. A big buck was scanning his surroundings!

Eventually, he proceeded down the trail the does had followed, and I felt good about my chances of getting a shot. When he reached an opening within comfortable shooting range, he did everything you could ask for: He stopped broadside and looked directly away from me. I drew, placed my sight pin behind his shoulder and released.

The shot felt great, and I was confident of a solid hit as the buck scooted out of sight. I waited only 10 minutes before the tension forced me down to look for blood. Once on the ground, I studied the area for several minutes, trying to figure out where the buck had headed. Then, I caught a flicker of a deer's tail in the cover; he was still just 50 yards from me, but he didn't know I was there. As he walked away, I could see he was as huge as I'd thought!

With the wind in my favor, I sneaked along behind the buck for perhaps a quarter-mile, all the time wondering at which moment he might drop. Eventually he moved out across an open pasture, where he entered a weed patch and bed-

> *"I was just about to climb out of the tree when I felt an urge to look to my left. As I did, I noticed a very tall set of antlers turning slowly in the brush. A big buck was scanning his surroundings!"*

ded. Even though I knew he was there, he still was hard to see in the vegetation.

By now I was certain the buck was badly hurt, and I really figured he'd die in his bed. It was time to go home for some help in recovering him. As my dad and I returned to the area, I figured the deer might already be dead, but I still had my bow ready as I stalked toward the weed patch.

It's a good thing I did. As I was easing up to the bedding spot, I got to within perhaps 20 yards of the buck's position before realizing his ears were up and scanning for danger! I drew my bow and took a few soft steps, trying to find a hole through which to shoot. Suddenly, the deer stood and offered a broadside shot for the second time that day. My arrow hit him well, and he went only about 10 yards before collapsing.

Actually, I hadn't looked closely at the deer's rack until my dad and I walked up to him. Now there was ample time to do so, and we were overwhelmed. The two massive drop tines, split brow tines and awesome tine length were more than impressive.

As I sat down to catch some air, I thanked God for the privilege of being allowed to take this beautiful animal.

In 1997, my buck's score was verified by P&Y officials at 250 6/8 net points, which at that time made him the No. 3 non-typical in P&Y. I guess my buddy Richard hadn't shot the last eastern Kansas giant after all!

<figure>
❖
</figure>

Chapter Nine

THE RUSS CLARKEN BUCK

236 7/8 NON-TYPICAL, IOWA, 1994

Iowa's Awesome Non-Typical by Bow

BY BILL WINKE

Shredded trees the size of a man's leg left little doubt that Russ Clarken was on the trail of a buck the size of which most hunters only dream about. "It was Nov. 6 when I finally saw the buck," Russ says of that day back in 1994.

"I was looking into the woods along the road as I drove to my stand and saw a decent buck standing on the top of a creek bank. I slowed down to take a look when a monstrous set of antlers rose above the weeds next to him. This other buck was incredible! I watched him at 70 or 80 yards for a couple of minutes, but since he was on property I couldn't hunt, I decided to go back to town to get a video camera. If I couldn't shoot the buck, I at least wanted to get him on video."

"Driving quickly to the archery shop, I grabbed my friend Clark Brittain and his video camera," Russ continues. "We drove back out, and the buck was still standing there. We got about five minutes of footage before the doe he was guarding finally got spooky and ran off."

*Main Characteristics:
Among the widest
inside spreads of any
bow buck. World-
class mass.*

RUSS CLARKEN, IOWA, 1994

	Right Antler	Left Antler	Difference
Main Beam Length	28 0/8	27 0/8	1 0/8
1st Point Length	8 7/8	8 2/8	5/8
2nd Point Length	6 2/8	6 6/8	4/8
3rd Point Length	8 5/8	8 5/8	—
4th Point Length	7 1/8	7 4/8	3/8
5th Point Length	—	—	—
1st Circumference	5 3/8	5 4/8	1/8
2nd Circumference	5 1/8	5 1/8	—
3rd Circumference	6 0/8	6 4/8	4/8
4th Circumference	5 6/8	5 0/8	6/8
Total	**81 1/8**	**80 2/8**	**3 7/8**

MISCELLANEOUS STATS	
No. Of Points–Right	11
No. Of Points–Left	10
Total No. Of Points	21
Length Of Abnormals	54 0/8
Greatest Spread	28 0/8
Tip To Tip Spread	21 1/8
Inside Spread	25 3/8

FINAL TALLY	
Inside Spread	25 3/8
Right Antler	81 1/8
Left Antler	80 2/8
Gross Score	186 6/8
Difference (–)	3 7/8
Subtotal	182 7/8
Abnormals (+)	54 0/8
NET NON-TYPICAL SCORE	**236 7/8**

The property Russ was planning to hunt that evening bordered the one where the buck had just been seen. In fact, it was the same location where he'd found the huge rubs. Although the buck didn't show up that day, Russ was determined to get him. Arriving back in town after the hunt, he immediately got together with his friends to watch the video footage.

"We couldn't tell exactly how big the buck was," Russ notes. "It was a little too far away and kind of blurry. But we could tell he was enormous. Now, after watching the video, my friends also knew where he lived. During the next week there were at least three or four guys seriously hunting him."

"Right after I watched that video, I called my partner and told him I wouldn't be coming to work for a while," Russ says with a smile. Self-employed as a dry-waller, he was able to take time off work, and he began hunting the buck immediately. Every day, before going to his afternoon stand, he shot dozens of arrows, every one mentally destined for the big buck.

Because Russ had seen the bruiser and knew from the huge rubs that the buck was hanging out in the area, he was able to stay after him. But hunting hard isn't enough to put a monster whitetail on your wall; you also must hunt carefully. And Russ certainly went to great lengths to put the odds into his favor.

"I didn't spook a single deer that season," the bowhunter claims. "After seeing that buck, I became fanatical about my scent and went to great lengths to make sure that I was clean and that my clothing was clean before each hunt. I also sprayed scent eliminator on my clothing. I knew I couldn't let the buck know that I was hounding him."

The terrain within Russ' 40-acre hunting area consisted of a wooded ridge connecting a brushy creek bottom to a large woods above. Thick bedding cover ran along the ridge on its east slope, while the west side was open timber. Russ had placed two homemade portable stands in the area to give him options for various wind conditions. Of the two, his favorite was situated 12 yards from a well-used trail leading into and out of the ridgeline bedding thicket. A huge rub near the stand was evidence that the giant had used the trail at least once in the past weeks, and Russ was planning on staying there until it happened again.

One week of hard hunting later, on Nov. 12, the bowhunter finally got his chance. "I went to the stand a little before 4," he recalls. "The wind was from the southeast, which blew my scent away from the thick cover and into an area of open woods, allowing me to hunt the stand near the big rub. I had been there for about an hour when I looked down the ridge toward the creek bottom and saw a doe about 80 yards away, coming toward me. Right behind her was the huge buck I had seen a week earlier!

"I was shocked when I saw the buck, but I quickly regained composure and stood up so that I would be ready for a shot, regardless of which side of the tree he passed on," Russ says. "They kept coming. When the doe was still 20 yards away, I realized she would pass behind me and that the buck would be right under my stand. I didn't want that, but there was nothing I could do.

"After the doe went by, she started to blow. My stands are 18 to 20 feet high, and she was upwind of me, so I knew she couldn't have scented me. Though I didn't know what was going on, I figured it was all over. Immediately the buck went on alert. He was now 20 yards away and broadside, but limbs covered his vitals, and I had no shot. He turned toward the cover and was trying to plow into it, but his wide rack was catching in the brush.

"I knew I had to try something or he would be gone, so I grabbed my call and grunted," Russ remembers. "He turned and looked my way, then took two more steps in the other direction. I grunted again, and again he stopped and looked.

> *"He was now 20 yards away and broadside, but limbs covered his vitals, and I had no shot. He turned toward the cover and was trying to plow into it, but his wide rack was catching in the brush."*

We did this a couple more times before he finally raised his head above the thicket and grunted back at me."

That's when the bowhunter heard something shuffling through the leaves down the slope from where he and the buck were exchanging conversation. The hunt of a lifetime was deteriorating right before Russ' eyes. "It sounded like a person walking toward me," he recalls. "I figured someone was scouting the area after hearing about the big buck. Being close to a city, the area gets a lot of hunting pressure. Finally, out of the corner of my eye I saw that it was an old gobbler instead of a person. (There was actually an entire flock of turkeys.) This must have made the buck curious, because he turned around and came out of the thicket and began angling toward the turkeys. When he got closer to them, he took a good look and then snorted loudly. Now I knew why the doe had mysteriously blown earlier," Russ says.

Seemingly relieved that no danger was present, the big buck continued walking through the open timber down the sidehill, away from Russ' stand. Again, it appeared as if the buck was destined to walk out of range without offering a shot. "Looking ahead, I saw one opening that he would have to pass through at about 25 yards," the archer notes. "Quickly drawing my bow, I got in position, and when he stepped into the opening I released. I couldn't see the arrow in flight, but I thought I heard it

"…when he stepped into the opening I released. I couldn't see the arrow in flight, but I thought I heard it hit the leaves. I had been surprisingly calm through the whole thing, so I couldn't believe I had missed. How could I have missed the most important shot of my life?"

hit the leaves. I had been surprisingly calm through the whole thing, so I couldn't believe I had missed. How could I have missed the most important shot of my life?"

It took only seconds, however, before all doubt was erased. The buck ran only 40 yards before getting a serious case of the "wobblies" and going down!

Emotionally exhausted, Russ dropped onto the stand seat and just sat there for 15 minutes. "My first reaction was, 'Oh my gosh, I got him!'" the hunter says. "After climbing down and looking at the buck, I went back into town to get a camera and some help getting him out."

Returning with his brothers-in-law, Bill Roach and Mike McGuigan, Russ began field-dressing the 21-point buck and soon learned exactly where his arrow had hit: straight through the center of the heart!

Clark Brittain, who'd gone with Russ to shoot the video of the live buck earlier in the season, did the taxidermy work.

At the time of the kill, this monster was the top-scoring Pope and Young non-typical in Iowa. The state record has been broken twice since then, but Russ' tremendous deer still ranks among the top few dozen whitetails taken by bow anywhere in North America. And with an inside spread of 25 3/8 inches, the Clarken buck is one of the widest-racked archery bucks ever, typical or non-typical.

Russ Clarken arrowed this dream 236 7/8 Pope & Young buck as the Iowa monster trailed a doe in the late afternoon. Photo courtesy of Russ Clarken.

As well as the Clarken buck scored, he could have ended up much higher still. Apparently, two good-sized points had broken off shortly after the buck shed his velvet. One was a large drop tine that could have contributed as much as 10 additional inches of abnormal growth. Thus, it's possible that the buck could have netted better than 250 non-typical if in fact he was shot earlier in bow season.

Of course, you aren't likely to hear any complaints out of Russ. He likes his deer just fine as is!

Chapter Ten

THE SAM COLLORA BUCK

193 3/8 TYPICAL, IOWA, 1996

An Unexpected Bonus for an Afternoon Off Work

BY BILL WINKE

Southeast Iowa is rolling farm country, a transition zone between the big corn fields of the state's center and the wooded bluffs of the Mississippi River valley to the east. Medium-sized rivers, such as the Skunk, Cedar and Des Moines, cut wide swaths through the terrain, with cover-choked draws reaching into the surrounding corn and soybean fields like long fingers. Peppered among the fields beyond these ravines are wood lots of various sizes, linked by brushy fencelines and shallow waterways.

It's in this ideal whitetail world that Sam Collora has pursued his passion of bowhunting big bucks for more than 25 years. And it's where on Oct. 11, 1996, he shot one of the world's biggest typicals ever taken by bow.

"The hunting season sneaked up on me," Sam recalls. "I work full-time, and on the side I operate a deer-scent business (Mrs. Doe Pee's Buck Lures) with my wife, Judi. That keeps me very busy. I still hadn't been out yet when one of my buddies, Curt, came by in the middle of the afternoon on Oct. 11. He stopped by to get

SAM COLLORA, IOWA, 1996

Main Characteristics: Classic "rib cage" look, formed by long, heavy tines. Two "typical" tines ruled non-typical.

	Right Antler	Left Antler	Difference
Main Beam Length	28 4/8	27 3/8	1 1/8
1st Point Length	8 7/8	7 2/8	1 5/8
2nd Point Length	12 6/8	13 3/8	5/8
3rd Point Length	12 0/8	12 5/8	5/8
4th Point Length	8 3/8	9 3/8	1 0/8
5th Point Length	4 5/8	6 1/8	1 4/8
1st Circumference	4 3/8	4 5/8	2/8
2nd Circumference	4 4/8	4 5/8	1/8
3rd Circumference	5 7/8	5 5/8	2/8
4th Circumference	5 7/8	5 5/8	2/8
Total	**95 6/8**	**96 5/8**	**7 3/8**

MISCELLANEOUS STATS

No. Of Points–Right	8
No. Of Points–Left	6
Total No. Of Points	14
Length Of Abnormals	12 5/8
Greatest Spread	23 4/8
Tip To Tip Spread	16 2/8
Inside Spread	21 0/8

FINAL TALLY

Inside Spread	21 0/8
Right Antler	95 6/8
Left Antler	96 5/8
Gross Score	213 3/8
Difference (–)	7 3/8
Subtotal	206 0/8
Abnormals (–)	12 5/8
NET TYPICAL SCORE	193 3/8

clothing he had left hanging where the air circulating through my deer-scent collection room exhausts. Several of us keep our stuff in the exhaust room so that we'll smell like deer when we hunt.

"I sat and watched him gather up his gear, and I said to myself, 'All work and no play makes Sam a dull boy.' Right then, I knew I had to get out and do what I love. I was getting burned out and needed a break. I asked Judi if there was anything else that absolutely had to be done, and when she said, 'Nope,' I was on my way to the woods.

"It was a beautiful fall day," Sam notes. "The morning had been chilly, but it warmed up to around 65 during the day, as a light but steady breeze was blowing from the south. The stand I was heading to was located in a travel route between a feeding and bedding area. I had put the stand up the previous year, about 12 to 14 feet high in a big oak tree. A trail ran right under it.

"You wouldn't believe how particular I am about my scent while hunting," Sam says. "I put my Scent-Lok suit, my outer clothes and my rubber boots in a Rubbermaid container as soon as I take them out of the exhaust room, and they stay in the box until I get to the edge of the woods. I slip them on and tie a drag rag to my ankle. I put a few drops of our Doe in Estrus scent on the drag rag. I always put only a small amount of scent on to start out and add more as I walk toward my stand, so a buck will track me in the direction I've walked.

"I went out of my way to cut across two or three good travel routes in a loop that took me on about an eighth-mile to a quarter-mile loop out of my way," the bowhunter remembers. "When I got to the stand, I went on past the tree, so that a trailing buck wouldn't stop right at the tree. About 20 yards from the stand, I untied the drag rag and hung it about three feet up in a tree. The sun was still high when I got into my stand, maybe 45 minutes to an hour before sunset.

"I've always made it a habit to look over my equipment as soon as I get comfortable in my stand," Sam says. "That's when I noticed that the rubber tube that aligns my peep sight was torn about 95 percent of the way through. I was positive that the tube wouldn't have made another draw. I broke it the rest of the way. I had to get that tube back on the small peg of the peep sight, so I got a little saliva to lubricate it. I knew I had to see to shoot, even though I hated the idea of letting even that much scent out.

"I'd spooked a doe while making the final approach to the stand," Sam continues. "She didn't smell me, but she heard me, and she finally bounded off after a 10-minute stare-down. I sat on my stand for about 45 minutes, pretty sure that I wasn't going to see another thing for the rest of the evening, but I didn't care. It was a great evening to be out, with the warm sun and light breeze and all the squirrels running around. Plus, I really needed the chance to just relax and get away from work for a while.

"I was soaking up the evening when all of a sudden I noticed this huge buck straight downwind from me. He was about 75 to 100 yards away, in a direction I didn't expect a deer to come from. When I saw him, the first thought that entered my mind was 'this is the biggest buck I've ever had a shot at' — only I hadn't gotten the shot yet.

"I just ate the whole thing up," Sam says. "Surprisingly, I wasn't shocked when I first saw him. I remained fairly calm. The situation just felt good. I thought — let's get it done. The buck came in with his nose in the air, smelling the drag rag the whole way. He was still straight downwind, coming right at me!

"About 30 yards away, the buck turned to his left and looked across a fence. That was when I first started getting a little rattled," the archer admits. "I thought maybe he was getting ready to leave, so I drew on him. But there was no clear shot. That's where he stopped.

"Eventually I had to let the string down, and when I did, my left knee started shaking," Sam says. "I was losing it. I said to myself, 'You'd better settle down, Sam, or you're going to screw this clear up. Pay attention and relax. He's going to give you a shot in a second.' I got back under control again, only my heart was slapping so hard inside my chest that I was afraid he'd hear it.

"With all the time I spend around our captive herd, I've gotten very good at reading a deer's body language," Sam points out. "I can usually tell exactly what a deer is going to do next. This buck still didn't know anyone was within 20 miles, which is amazing, considering that the wind was blowing directly to him. Seeing that he was still calm helped calm me down, too.

"I was holding the bow in front of my face to hide the whites of my eyes," Sam recalls. "A couple of times he looked right through me. An old bowhunter taught me this trick, and I've done it ever since. It really works. Finally, after several minutes, the buck decided to go to his right, which was my left. He was cutting through some brush at a leisurely walk. I let him get about halfway to a shooting lane before I drew. He was about 10 or 12 feet from it. As soon as he hit the lane, I thought about trying to stop him, but as calm as he was, I decided not to do anything to put him on the alert. Instead, I held my pin right on the center of his shoulder to allow for his walking pace.

"When I released the string, it sounded like someone had smacked the flat side of a boat paddle in the mud," Sam notes. "If you'd been a hundred yards away, you could've heard it. I was stunned. My mind screamed, 'You led him too much! You blew it, you dummy!' My stomach just flopped when I saw how much of the shaft was sticking out. He had wheeled around and was headed back the way he'd come, with half the arrow still extending from his side.

"I was in the right place at the right time. I didn't do anything special… but something special sure happened to me."

"He ran straight away, down through a dip and over a knoll," the bowhunter continues. "About a hundred yards out, he started turning and preparing to jump a fence, but then he piled up right into it. My heart did a back flip. I knew then that I'd gotten better penetration than I'd thought. But just that quick, he jumped right back up and away he went again. This time, he ran about 40 to 50 yards and went down again. Now he was far enough away that it was difficult to see him, but I could make out the fletched end of the arrow moving back and forth — it was sticking straight up from the ground.

"When the arrow stopped moving, I couldn't see it, so I stayed in the stand and watched that direction for 10 more minutes," Sam says. The buck was dead when the hunter got to him.

"I didn't measure him until the following Sunday," Sam notes. (The deer was shot on a Thursday). "All I really cared about was the fact that he was a Booner, and I already knew that just by looking at him. My daughter, Gina, was recording the numbers while I measured. When we got done, she added up the first column and told me the total, I said, 'There must be some mistake,' and I asked her to add them again.

"She looked up and said, 'Dad, I was the first one to ace the math entrance exam at Iowa Wesleyan (a local college). I think I know how to add fractions!' But I had her add them up again anyway. She came up with the same number."

The Colloras' rough total suggested the deer could net around 200, making

Sam Collora's Iowa giant has one of the highest gross typical scores of any bow kill ever.
Photo courtesy of Sam Collora.

him the world's potential No. 2 typical by bow. Soon thereafter, Dave Boland and Mike McKenna, two highly experienced official measurers, green-scored the deer at 202 1/8 net, only 2 3/8 inches lower than Mel Johnson's 204 4/8-point world record from Illinois.

A P&Y panel eventually ruled two points off the top of the rack's right main beam should be deductions. This was a controversial call, as the points in question appeared to many observers to be typical in nature.

However, the panel's ruling was final, and the score fell all the way to 193 3/8.

At the time, that score was still good enough to place the deer in the all-time Top 10 by bow.

Regardless of this deer's ranking, there's no doubt he's one of the true giants in whitetail history. Knowing he's taken such a tremendous buck is plenty to make Sam happy.

"You can't imagine how privileged I feel to have this happen to me," he says. "I truly feel like I didn't do anything other hunters wouldn't have done. I was in the right place at the right time. I didn't do anything special... but something special sure happened to me."

Chapter Eleven

THE BRIAN DAMERY BUCK

---

200 2/8 TYPICAL, ILLINOIS, 1993

A Giant Typical with Far More Inches than Even the World Record

BY DICK IDOL

If you wanted recognition for shooting the world's No. 10 typical whitetail of all time, the fall of 1993 wasn't the time to get him. On Nov. 23 of that year, Saskatchewan's Milo Hanson (Chapter 15) took a giant typical that would go on to be recognized as the official Boone and Crockett world record, at 213 5/8 net points. Once word of that amazing deer got out, the eyes of the hunting world immediately focused on western Saskatchewan and the farmer who'd just shattered James Jordan's longstanding record in the category.

Somewhat overlooked in the buzz over the Hanson buck was the fact that 1,200 miles away and three days prior to the hunt that produced the new No. 1 typical, a hunter in Illinois was shooting what's arguably an even bigger one. In fact, Brian Damery's trophy ultimately would post the highest gross typical score ever recorded for any B&C whitetail, including the Hanson buck.

Although deductions later cost the Illinois deer more than 30 inches of net score, he still was big enough to net over 200. That's nothing short of amazing!

BRIAN DAMERY, ILLINOIS, 1993

	Right Antler	Left Antler	Difference
Main Beam Length	32 0/8	32 4/8	4/8
1st Point Length	9 1/8	8 6/8	3/8
2nd Point Length	12 1/8	13 0/8	7/8
3rd Point Length	11 5/8	11 2/8	3/8
4th Point Length	9 4/8	7 4/8	2 0/8
5th Point Length	5 6/8	4 5/8	1 1/8
1st Circumference	5 4/8	5 3/8	1/8
2nd Circumference	4 4/8	4 4/8	0/8
3rd Circumference	8 2/8	6 0/8	2 2/8
4th Circumference	5 6/8	5 1/8	5/8
Total	**104 1/8**	**98 5/8**	**8 2/8**

Main Characteristics: Unprecedented 92 7/8" total length of main beams and inside spread. Nets over 200" despite heavy deductions.

MISCELLANEOUS STATS

No. Of Points–Right	9
No. Of Points–Left	8
Total No. Of Points	17
Length Of Abnormals	22 5/8
Greatest Spread	30 6/8
Tip To Tip Spread	20 0/8
Inside Spread	28 3/8

FINAL TALLY

Inside Spread	28 3/8
Right Antler	104 1/8
Left Antler	98 5/8
Gross Score	231 1/8
Difference (–)	8 2/8
Subtotal	222 7/8
Abnormals (–)	22 5/8
NET TYPICAL SCORE	200 2/8

At the time of the kill, Brian was 28 years old and working in the fertilizer business in the small town of Blue Mound, in Macon County. He'd begun bowhunting at the age of 16 but never really had gotten into it seriously until the age of 25. Although he now considers himself primarily a bowhunter, he does hunt with a shotgun during Illinois' two short slug seasons.

The story of Brian's giant buck really began in early 1993, when a neighboring landowner's dog dragged a big shed antler to the house. The farmer crossed paths with Brian through the fertilizer business and subsequently showed him the antler. Brian was impressed enough to ask to borrow the shed so that he could show it to his father-in-law, Trent Wilcox, and a couple of other friends. They measured this right antler, which had a 28-inch main beam, and came up with a gross score of 85 inches. If the missing left antler were a close match, the deer would have a gross score of 170 without a spread. From the looks of the shed, his actual spread would have been well in excess of 20 inches, meaning he probably would gross better than 190 typical.

This was a fresh shed, found near the end of March, so the odds were good that the buck would be around for the next season. Brian obtained hunting permission from the landowner where the shed was found and began scouting during the summer, hoping to get a glimpse of what he knew was a monster. But he never managed to see the deer.

As the October bow opener neared, Brian intensified his scouting but still never laid eyes on the ghost buck. However, he did manage to find some huge tracks, which he assumed belonged to this animal. He hoped to take the buck with his bow and hunted hard the entire first week of bow season. Although Brian regularly saw bucks, the one he was after managed to elude him, with not so much as a simple sighting. Was he really there?

Work commitments mounted, and Brian was unable to hunt much during the rest of early bow season. He knew other hunters were also in the area, and he could only hope they wouldn't get "his" buck.

A couple of days before the opening of the mid-November first slug season, Brian decided to move his bow stand across a creek, to a spot he felt might be better. He noticed there were many vines on this new tree he'd chosen, but at the time, he gave little thought to the matter.

"About 1 p.m., as Brian was glassing, he caught sight of moving antlers. He couldn't believe his eyes — the big buck had just stood up from his bed in a grassy waterway about 600 yards from him!"

On opening day of the gun season on Nov. 19, however, Brian gave a great deal of thought to those same vines. Climbing into the tree before dawn, he innocently came into contact with the vines and soon realized they were poison ivy! Before the hunt had even started, Brian's face and hands were itching relentlessly. Soon, one eye was swollen shut. He had no choice but to go to the doctor for relief.

After receiving some medication, salve and an injection, Brian decided to hunt, regardless of the discomfort. He finally crawled into his stand at noon. The wind was howling, and he spotted another hunter across the field from him — indeed this was not starting out as one of his best gun seasons.

Brian's stand was along a line of brushy timber overlooking a tilled corn field and a hay field dotted with a few round bales. Although he'd never seen the buck that had grown the big shed, he felt this area was one of the most likely spots for the deer to be living in.

About 1 p.m., as Brian was glassing, he caught sight of moving antlers. He couldn't believe his eyes — the big buck had just stood up from his bed in a grassy waterway about 600 yards from him! The rack was so big that Brian nearly lost his composure. But for now he could only sit and watch the buck, as there was nothing between them but open field.

A big 8-pointer was also in the vicinity, along with a couple of does. Based on the 8-pointer's actions, one of the does was in heat, and all of the deer looked to be part of a group.

For two tense hours Brian watched the deer. Finally, at 3 p.m., he convinced himself they wouldn't be coming his way, as they hadn't moved far at all during this time. Brian elected to try to close the gap, in hopes they would move at least part of the way to him. The hunter eventually did get somewhat closer, but with the sparse cover and poor wind direction, he finally concluded around 3:30 that he needed to just slip out of there and leave the deer alone until the next morning.

Needless to say, that night brought little sleep, and the next morning Brian was on stand an hour before daylight. Only 10 to 15 minutes after dawn he again spotted the deer, but this time they were in the hay field, slowly working toward the same waterway where they had bedded the previous day. After about 15 minutes of watching, Brian was sure of their direction and knew they weren't going to pass near his stand. He had to make a move.

There was a thin strip of willows and brush along a hedgerow, so he began belly crawling, in hopes of cutting off the buck before the animal could get into the waterway. Brian crawled about 200 yards before he heard antlers thrashing a bush not far ahead.

With his heart in his throat, Brian slowly raised his head, hoping the huge buck would be within range of his 12-gauge pump. Suddenly, the 8-pointer walked across an open willow run, never seeing Brian as he passed.

The grass here was only a couple of feet tall and offered scant cover for Brian to crawl to a final patch of weeds between him and the big buck, which was following a doe toward the waterway. Brian knew the giant was close, and he hardly dared to raise his head above the cover. He lay there in six inches of water for more than 20 minutes, hoping the buck would pass within range.

After what seemed like hours, the hunter finally saw the buck walking broadside at 75 yards. He decided it was now or never!

At the shot the buck bolted, but instead of going the other way, he ran straight at Brian. Panicking, the hunter short-stroked the pump action, jamming the empty shell back into the chamber. In the excitement of it all he stood up, trying to clear the action.

By this time the big buck had actually run to within 20 yards of Brian, who still couldn't fire. The buck veered to the side and was running at 50 yards when the hunter finally got a bead on him again. He missed cleanly, but when the buck was at 80 yards and still running, Brian dropped him with a third shot. As it turned out, the first shot had been fatal, but that was after-the-fact knowledge.

The hunter knew even before he had reached the buck that he'd killed a great trophy, but the deer only got bigger as he grabbed the rack. War whoops soon followed!

This was certainly a mature buck, estimated to be 5 1/2 years old with a dressed weight of 210 pounds. However,

> *"This buck's antler spread is among the widest in the B&C records, and his beams certainly rank with the longest. To have both amazing features on one rack is unheard of."*

The sheer size of the Damery buck's rack is especially evident in this photo, taken shortly after the deer was shot in 1993. Photo by Tom Evans, courtesy of North American Whitetail.

the real story was the rack. Official measurer Dave Boland came up with a gross typical score of 231 1/8 points (inches)! Even after deducting side-to-side differences, the typical frame had a net score of 222 7/8 points, which would have shattered the world record.

Unfortunately, as with a number of other giant typicals over the years, abnormal points knocked the final score farther down the ladder. The rack has a total of five such points, all of which of course had to be deducted from the typical score.

The double brow tines hurt him the most. His extra brow on the right side is 6 4/8 inches, so had it never grown, the buck would have netted 206 6/8 — 5/8

inch above the Jordan buck and trailing only the Hanson buck. And had Brian's buck not grown an "extra" 7 4/8-inch brow tine on the left, he'd have netted 214 2/8, a new world record! As is, the Damery buck nets 200 2/8, which places him firmly among the top handful of whitetail typicals ever.

What sets the Illinois buck apart from perhaps all others is his incredible combination of inside spread (28 3/8 inches) and main beams (32 4/8 and 32 inches). His antler spread is among the widest in the B&C records, and his beams certainly rank with the longest, so to have both amazing features on one rack is unheard of. Without a doubt, this is one of the greatest deer of all time.

Chapter Twelve

THE
KENNY FOWLER BUCK

257 0/8 NON-TYPICAL, KANSAS, 1988

It Wasn't a Doe
After All

BY TODD MURRAY

Too big to be real… was probably the thought going through Kenny Fowler's mind as he again tried to count points on the awesome rack a mere 30 yards away. It was early September, still nearly a month before the opening of the 1988 Kansas archery season, and the Buhler resident was getting in some scouting on a place he'd never hunted.

A friend had obtained permission for Kenny and himself to hunt this property through which the Arkansas River runs. The trophy buck had strolled out onto the edge of a field shortly before dark, quickly removing any doubts Kenny had about bowhunting this new area.

There was another buck with the monster, but Kenny doesn't remember much about him — seems understandable! For nearly 20 minutes the awestruck hunter watched the deer feed. After both bucks wandered off, he drove home and told his wife of his new find. She thought he was trying to "pull her leg." Soon after, when sharing the experience with a friend, he was once again accused of leg stretching.

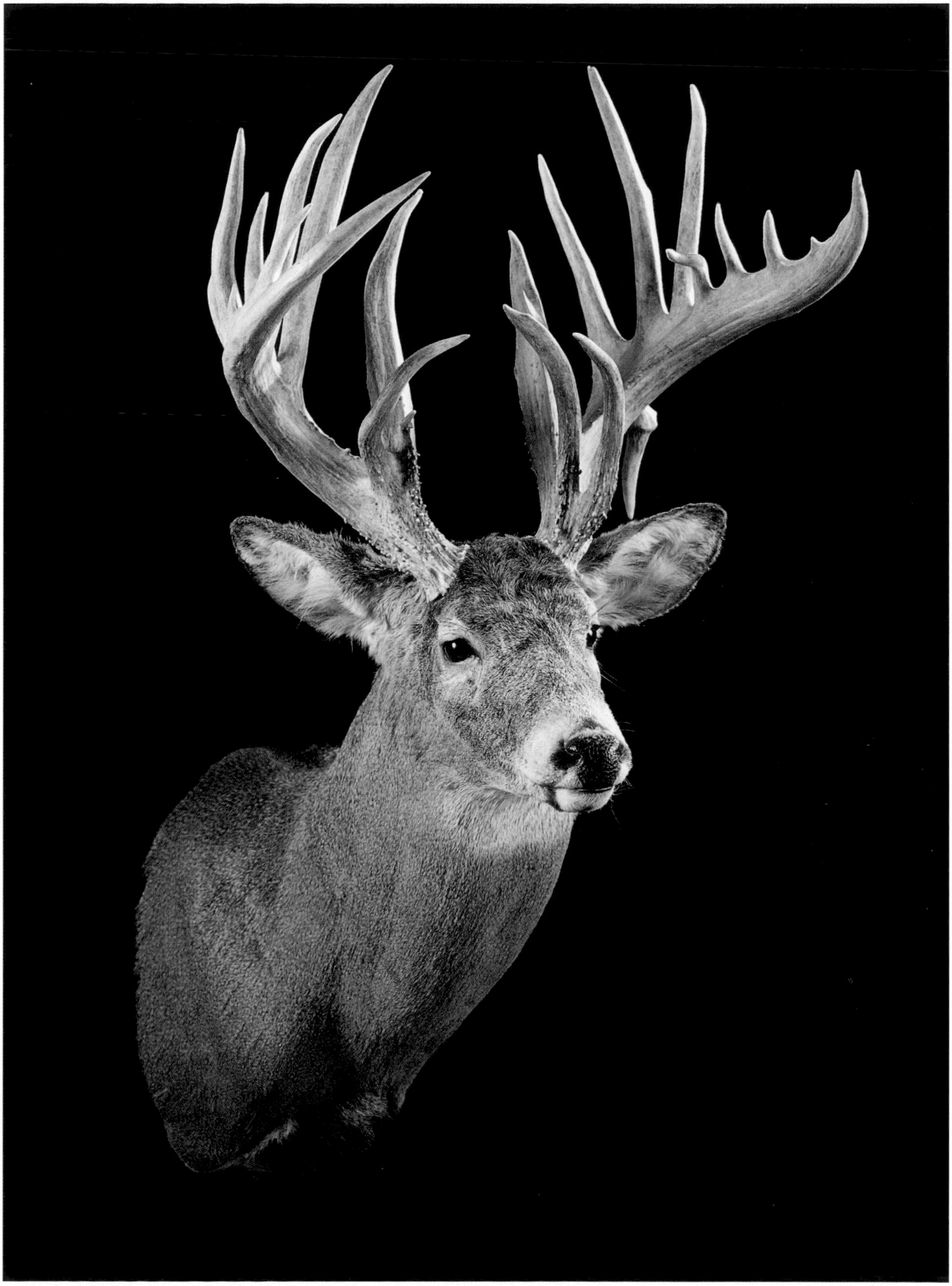

Photo courtesy of Bass Pro Shops.

KENNY FOWLER, KANSAS, 1988

	Right Antler	Left Antler	Difference
Main Beam Length	27 1/8	25 7/8	1 2/8
1st Point Length	10 7/8	8 7/8	2 0/8
2nd Point Length	7 4/8	9 2/8	1 6/8
3rd Point Length	9 0/8	10 4/8	1 4/8
4th Point Length	5 6/8	8 7/8	3 1/8
5th Point Length	7 3/8	3 4/8	3 7/8
6th Point Length	3 3/8	2 7/8	4/8
1st Circumference	5 5/8	6 1/8	4/8
2nd Circumference	6 0/8	6 1/8	1/8
3rd Circumference	9 1/8	7 5/8	1 4/8
4th Circumference	6 7/8	6 7/8	0/8
Total	**98 5/8**	**96 4/8**	**16 1/8**

Main Characteristics: Basic 7x7 typical frame, which is rare. Great mass all the way out the beams.

MISCELLANEOUS STATS	
No. Of Points–Right	12
No. Of Points–Left	11
Total No. Of Points	23
Length Of Abnormals	59 2/8
Greatest Spread	21 3/8
Tip To Tip Spread	14 2/8
Inside Spread	18 6/8

FINAL TALLY	
Inside Spread	18 6/8
Right Antler	98 5/8
Left Antler	96 4/8
Gross Score	213 7/8
Difference (–)	16 1/8
Subtotal	197 6/8
Abnormals (+)	59 2/8
NET NON-TYPICAL SCORE	257 0/8

The buddy became a believer when he saw the buck for himself two weeks later. But while Kenny spent every other evening during September trying to do the same, he never got another glimpse of the great deer.

When the Oct. 1 bow opener finally rolled around, sunrise found Kenny in a stand in the area where he'd seen the deer. Unfortunately, rain finally forced the archer from his stand. It would be the next evening before he could hunt again.

Kenny went out early the following afternoon to do a little looking around, trying to find something that would give away the buck's exact location. He found a very decent rub with two fresh scrapes in an area that had a natural depression — where the trees narrowed somewhat and came close to the river's edge.

Kenny found what seemed to be a good tree to put his wedge stand in, but halfway up he saw a better tree a few yards over, so he set up there instead. What a difference that decision ultimately would make.

After getting settled in, the bowhunter shot a practice arrow into a narrow funnel behind his stand. While this was the opposite side from where he thought any deer would likely come, when he climbed down to retrieve the arrow, he cleared a small shooting lane in that direction, "just in case." Then it was back up the tree to await prime time.

Upon getting settled back in, his thoughts were on the giant buck and where he might be. He hadn't been seen in more than two weeks. Perhaps he'd moved off. Or maybe the worst thing that could happen to a good buck had happened: A poacher had shot him. All Kenny could do was wait and hope.

For this Kiowa Indian, archery seemingly would have come naturally. However, his winnings at local archery tournaments had resulted from a lot of practice. While his choice of equipment was a far cry from that of his forefathers, it was fairly simple by today's standards: a 70-pound compound, a 5-pin sight and aluminum arrows tipped with 4-bladed broadheads he'd sharpened himself.

It was nearly two hours before dark when the bowhunter glanced behind the stand and saw deer legs moving through the underbrush at a fast clip. The deer was going to angle past the stand, so he decided it was as good a time as any to fill his doe tag. Slowly he turned and got ready for the deer to come through the shooting lane he had just cleared.

The archer still could see only the deer's legs and bottom of its chest at this point. When the deer trotted into the opening, it suddenly stopped short — and so did Kenny's heart. It was him.

The monster swung his massive, non-typical rack from side to side, trying to figure out where the human odor was coming from.

Kenny didn't bother trying to count points this time; he drew and shot quickly, before the buck could react. Yellow vanes disappeared high into the chest, angling downward. Immediately the buck jumped and trotted off about 25 yards, hesitated, then took off again.

Knowing there were other hunters in the area, Kenny immediately climbed down. He knew from experience that the buck wouldn't go far. The arrow was covered with frothy blood, indicating a sure lung hit.

Kenny's tree was about 60 yards from the river, and the blood trail headed straight into the water. Kenny trailed the deer to the river's edge, then jumped in. The animal had gone straight across and was lying dead just past the other bank.

Kenny now had time to count all of those points: 12 scorable on the right antler and 11 on the left. But not until Pope and Young measurers scored the deer did Kenny find out just how well the rack would stack up. The initial conservative tally was 252 4/8 points: potentially a state archery record and the world's all-time No. 2 by bow! At P&Y's April 1989 convention in Boise, Idaho, a panel bumped the net score up to 257 0/8, making the buck an even more secure No. 2.

Why was the deer moving so early that early-October afternoon? Could another hunter have spooked the buck? Did the buck just decide it was time to move? Kenny says he doesn't know, nor does he care. "It's my tag on that rack," he says.

Chapter Thirteen

The Fred Goodwin Buck

239 4/8 Non-Typical, Maine, 1949

The Legendary Buck of Silver Ridge

By Dr. Rob Wegner

Fred Goodwin, one of the founding fathers of antler collecting, was born in Silver Ridge, Maine, on Jan. 3, 1909, two years after the Maine Legislature established the state's first "bucks only" hunting restrictions. Fred would go on to become a legendary figure in the outdoors, and throughout the 20th century and even beyond, his name would be synonymous with trophy whitetails.

By the age of 15, he already was well on his way to becoming a deerslayer in the tradition of James Fenimore Cooper's Natty Bumppo. He slept in small tents in the wilderness of Aroostook County, the mecca of Maine deer hunting, while pursuing whitetails with a Winchester Model '94.

In 1936, at the age of 27, Fred started to work as a deer-hunting guide. That year, the Maine season lasted for six weeks, and he received $100 per week for guiding five men. They stayed at Fred's Silver Ridge deer camp, a small, picturesque log cabin in the wilderness of southern Aroostook County. The nearest "town," six miles away, was a place known as "T2R4," which was shorthand for its position on the map: Township 2, Range 4.

Photo by Bryce Towsley.

FRED GOODWIN, MAINE, 1949

	Right Antler	Left Antler	Difference
Main Beam Length	31 6/8	30 0/8	1 6/8
1st Point Length	7 6/8	10 0/8	2 2/8
2nd Point Length	11 5/8	13 6/8	2 1/8
3rd Point Length	11 2/8	12 0/8	6/8
4th Point Length	10 5/8	7 3/8	3 2/8
5th Point Length	4 4/8	2 5/8	1 7/8
1st Circumference	5 5/8	5 6/8	1/8
2nd Circumference	4 6/8	5 0/8	2/8
3rd Circumference	9 5/8	6 1/8	3 4/8
4th Circumference	5 4/8	5 3/8	1/8
Total	103 0/8	98 0/8	16 0/8

Main Characteristics: One of the highest gross typical scores of any whitetail ever, with 6 tines of 10" or more and huge beams.

MISCELLANEOUS STATS	
No. Of Points–Right	9
No. Of Points–Left	11
Total No. Of Points	20
Length Of Abnormals	29 6/8
Greatest Spread	36 0/8
Tip To Tip Spread	15 0/8
Inside Spread	24 6/8

FINAL TALLY	
Inside Spread	24 6/8
Right Antler	103 0/8
Left Antler	98 0/8
Gross Score	225 6/8
Difference (–)	16 0/8
Subtotal	209 6/8
Abnormals (+)	29 6/8
NET NON-TYPICAL SCORE	239 4/8

"I'd furnish a pair of horses to move them (clients) in and out," Fred recalls. "I had a hovel there to keep the horses in so I could take a horse out three or four miles, throw a deer or bear on its back, and lug it back to camp. I also furnished the wood, lugged the water we needed and built the fires. They brought the grub for us and did all their own cooking."

Over his many years in these remote woods, chasing whitetails for weeks on end

every fall, Fred acquired a vast understanding of the animal's ways. In the process, he shot a number of outstanding trophies. But the greatest of them all was a huge-racked Silver Ridge buck he pursued for three years before finally gaining the upper hand.

Fred first learned of the awe-inspiring deer in the fall of 1946, from his brother Edwin. While still-hunting Silver Ridge that year, Edwin jumped the buck and missed him at close range with his .33-caliber Model

A young Fred Goodwin at age 15, already on the deer trail. Photo by Fred Goodwin.

'86 Winchester. That night in deer camp, Edwin told his brother that the buck's rack had an outside spread of three feet!

Knowing well Edwin's inclination to stretch reality into fiction when discussing whitetail antlers, Fred hesitated to believe what he was hearing. In fact, he never gave the incident any more attention until the following summer, when he saw the huge buck while scouting near camp. Sure enough, the deer's rack was as big as Edwin had described!

That observation of the buck, which was traveling with a large doe in a burned-over area of Silver Ridge, was the first of several Fred would make

prior to hunting season. In each case, the buck always was in the company of that same doe.

The 1947 deer season began on Oct. 21 and ran through Nov. 30. However, in all that time, the big buck Fred was pursuing never materialized. Nor did the hunter find either of the deer's shed antlers, despite diligently searching for them after the season. He did discover more than a dozen sheds from other bucks, however. Historically, Fred was finding and collecting shed antlers before most other deer hunters ever thought of doing so. He was an authentic pioneer in collecting antlers, and when he sold his

Fred Goodwin with the Silver Ridge Buck in a field photo of this great animal. Note the old buck's gaunt condition.
Photo by Fred Goodwin.

whitetail collection to Dick Idol in 1982, the assemblage consisted of more than 1,300 trophy racks.

Early in 1948, Fred continued to prowl the cedar bogs to study the movement patterns and home range of the unique Silver Ridge buck. In his daily tramps, he observed that the buck had one rounded right front hoof that clearly distinguished it from the other foot's longer and narrower hoof. This characteristic ultimately revealed the buck's bedding

"That spooky old doe caused me more pain and suffering while I hunted him. I cursed her some, I'll tell you that."

area: a little peninsula that extended into the center of a large bog. A hardwood ridge of beech trees ran along one side of the bog; the other side consisted of a burned-over area with downed treetops and scattered debris. The buck walked along the thin strip of cover to reach a small spruce knoll at the end of the peninsula, where he bedded in a couple of blowdowns.

Fred's detailed observations of the buck's behavior indicated that he left very little visible sign of his presence in and around the bedding area. There were no rubs and only a few scrapes. Fred built a stand in a tall beech tree overlooking the point where the peninsula entered into the bog, but despite countless hours of waiting and watching in this stand during the 1948 season, he never saw the huge buck. Although that season produced a statewide harvest of 35,051 whitetails, the wide-racked deer of Fred's dreams was not one of them.

Time after time over the years, the old doe foiled Fred's attempts to get a clear shot at the Silver Ridge buck. Decades later, in discussing the story with author Bryce Towsley, Fred described the disappointment the buck's lady friend caused on more than one occasion.

"That spooky old doe caused me more pain and suffering while I hunted him," Fred noted. "I cursed her some, I'll tell you that. I don't believe he ever bred her. I never saw fawns. It was, I suppose, a platonic relationship, and I never saw him without her. She would always come by first and check out the area for him. If one small thing wasn't right – and believe me, nothing was too small for her to notice – they left. I thought often of shooting her, but I was afraid he would move out and abandon the area if I did."

The 1949 season began on Oct. 21, and Fred now was more determined than ever to get the Silver Ridge buck. After several failed attempts to reach his stand in the beech tree without disturbing the

buck and doe, Fred decided to circle from the other side of the bog in the dark. Unfortunately, this necessitated his crossing a very deep depression known locally as a "hagus," a virtually impassable area he had to cut his way through.

Long before daybreak on Nov. 23, Fred crawled through the hagus and reached the peninsula. It was still dark as he slowly climbed into his tree stand. In his dreams and in the thick bogs and muskeg swamps of Silver Ridge, the hunter already had followed the trail of this world-class buck for two full seasons, and now the third was only a few days from ending in another defeat. As the hunter stared into the darkness that morning, doubts and frustrations came to mind. He thought about all of the time and energy expended in this quest, thus far without any tangible reward. Getting the elusive Silver Ridge buck had indeed become an obsession.

And then, as the eastern sky turned pink, the old doe was suddenly there, as if she'd come out of nowhere. But there was still no sign of the buck. With the temperature holding at 0°, Fred fought off the pains of chilling numbness as he waited for the buck to show. Finally, a massive rack emerged almost ghost-like from the bog. At last, the buck of Fred's dreams stood before him. A single, sharp report from his Model 99 .300 Savage downed the Silver Ridge buck with a bullet to the neck. The long ordeal had ended in a sunrise of euphoria.

"The rack never had been scored for entry into the Boone and Crockett record book, so Fred looked forward to having it officially measured. Unfortunately, there was now a big problem: his friend had cut each antler off the skull plate!"

Fred Goodwin poses with his awe-inspiring "Buck of Silver Ridge" shortly after the deer was bagged in the bogs of northern Maine in 1949. Photo by Fred Goodwin.

"He was an old bugger with his teeth all worn down," Fred later said of his trophy. "He was haggard and thin and weighed far less then he should have."

Despite the prodigious effort involved in downing this noble deer, Fred sold the 18-point rack to an out-of-state hunting partner for $100. That was a great sum in those days, especially to a man trying to make a living in the wilderness of Silver Ridge. Fred agreed not to mention shoot-ing the deer, but he did put a stipulation on the sale: If he should outlive the new owner, he'd regain possession of the rack.

When Fred's buddy died in the spring of 1994, his family lived up to the old agreement and returned possession of the Silver Ridge buck to Fred. Knowing the rack never had been scored for entry into the Boone and Crockett record book, Fred looked forward to having it official-ly measured.

Unfortunately, there was now a big problem: his friend had cut each antler off the skull plate! Without antlers being naturally attached to the skull, there is no way to be certain of an accurate measurement of the inside spread, so the deer was ineligible for the record book.

That is certainly a shame, because even without a spread figured into his score, the buck would net 214 6/8 non-typical points, almost 20 inches above the B&C minimum for that category! With an estimated 24 6/8-inch inside spread, the rack would have a gross typical score of 225 6/8 to go along with his 29 6/8 inches of non-typical antler.

Despite 16 inches of symmetry deductions off his huge typical frame, the deer's net score still would rank him among the top bucks ever shot in Maine. Although the Silver Ridge buck won't ever grace the pages of the B&C record book, that fact makes him no less legendary in the whitetail world.

"…even without a spread figured into his score, the buck would net 214 6/8 non-typical points, almost 20 inches above the B&C minimum for that category! With an estimated 24 6/8 inch inside spread, the rack would have a gross typical score of 225 6/8 to go along with his 29 6/8 inches of non-typical antler."

As of this writing, Fred still collects antlers and Winchester rifles. In fact, he probably knows more about Winchester firearms than does any other person. In addition to being a renowned gun expert and guide, over his long life he worked as a guide, shopkeeper, logger, truck driver, mill worker, road builder, gunsmith, trapper, bounty hunter and tattoo artist — even photographer.

But perhaps most importantly, Fred always will be regarded as one of the great deer men of the 20th century. For such a person, the Silver Ridge buck was indeed a most appropriate trophy.

❖

Chapter Fourteen

THE HILL GOULD BUCK

---

259 0/8 NON-TYPICAL, MAINE, 1910

From the Land of Moose Came a Buck that Looked Like One

BY DICK IDOL

Τhe romance surrounding big, unusual whitetail racks is nothing short of amazing. And, more and more, it becomes apparent that the fascination with these special trophies has existed for a very long time. In fact, one particularly monstrous palmated set of antlers has been a popular topic in some deer-talk circles for more than 90 years now.

"Record Deer Head of All Time Killed at Grand Lake Stream is the Object of Great Curiosity" was the headline that appeared on the front page of the *Bangor Daily News* on Wednesday, Oct. 19, 1910. According to the story, the buck was believed to have been the largest whitetail ever killed, though no official scoring system existed in those days.

Through a strange twist of fate, the rack disappeared soon after the newspaper article was published, and the trophy stayed out of sight for more than 75 years. Only after its unlikely reappearance did the true story of the hunt slowly begin to unfold.

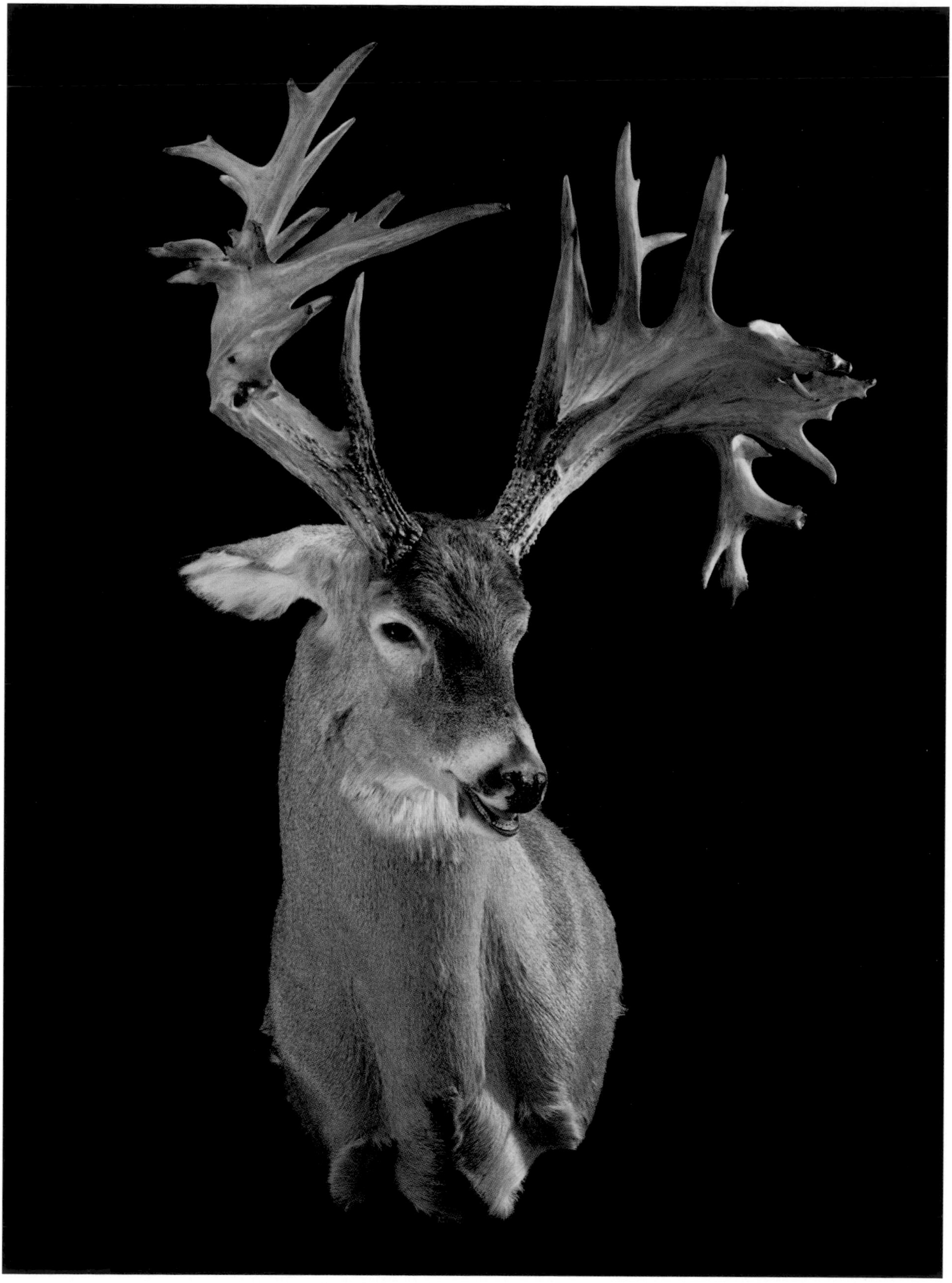

Photo courtesy of Bass Pro Shops.

HILL GOULD, MAINE, 1910

	Right Antler	Left Antler	Difference
Main Beam Length	25 4/8	26 7/8	1 3/8
1st Point Length	6 6/8	8 7/8	2 1/8
2nd Point Length	9 2/8	7 3/8	1 7/8
3rd Point Length	10 1/8	9 0/8	1 1/8
4th Point Length	3 2/8	4 6/8	1 4/8
5th Point Length	1 7/8	3 1/8	1 2/8
1st Circumference	6 1/8	5 7/8	2/8
2nd Circumference	6 5/8	6 4/8	1/8
3rd Circumference	12 0/8	11 0/8	1 0/8
4th Circumference	13 0/8	9 4/8	3 4/8
Total	**94 4/8**	**92 7/8**	**14 1/8**

Main Characteristics: Extreme palmation not unlike a moose rack, with 3 circumferences of 11" or more.

MISCELLANEOUS STATS	
No. Of Points–Right	15
No. Of Points–Left	16
Total No. Of Points	31
Length Of Abnormals	66 1/8
Greatest Spread	28 1/8
Tip To Tip Spread	12 0/8
Inside Spread	19 5/8

FINAL TALLY	
Inside Spread	19 5/8
Right Antler	94 4/8
Left Antler	92 7/8
Gross Score	**207 0/8**
Difference (–)	14 1/8
Subtotal	**192 7/8**
Abnormals (+)	66 1/8
NET NON-TYPICAL SCORE	**259 0/8**

It began in northern Maine in October 1910, when three teenagers from Grand Lake Stream headed into the vast wilderness on a hunting trip. Boys grew into men at an early age in those days, as work, survival and life in the woods were the accepted norm.

Eldon and Hill Gould were twin brothers who often hunted together, and on this particular trip they would be joined by their good friend Leonard "Kizzie" Kennison. Together, they headed off to a hunting camp known as the "Bear's Den," located on the Little River, which flows between West Grand Lake and Big Lake. Their plan was to hunt for a week.

As was customary back then, each boy went his separate way to still-hunt for the day. Late one afternoon, Hill was hunting along the edge of a cedar-and-alder swamp just below Little River Rips, which was known to be a well-used deer crossing. Suddenly, ahead in the alder swamp, he heard sticks break as something moved his way. For a moment, Hill thought it might be Kizzie, who'd begun his afternoon hunt along a ridge only 100 yards above where Hill had started. But soon he caught movement of a huge, dark animal with a gigantic set of antlers.

Ah ha… a moose, Hill thought as he raised his .38/55 Win. to his shoulder. It was legal to shoot two deer and a moose at the time, and moose meat was welcome table fare. Hill fired, and the animal dropped dead in his tracks.

Even at the age of 16, Hill was well known around those parts as a crack shot. Several buddies had witnessed his shooting feats and could attest to his skills.

Once, as he and some friends stepped from a shed behind Hill's house, they noticed a buck standing in an apple orchard well over 100 yards away. Immediately the buck ran, and Hill fired just as the buck cleared a fence with his flag raised. Everyone was certain he had missed, but Hill calmly put the rifle back in the shed, dug out his knife and stone and began touching up the blade. Someone in the group finally asked why he was sharpening his knife, and he replied, "Why, to dress out the deer, of course." They all got a good laugh out of it, but when they walked to the fence and looked on the other side, the buck was lying dead only a few yards from where he had cleared the fence!

After the shot on the "moose," Hill worked his way though the alders and puckerbrush to get a look at his kill. To the boy's great surprise, he'd shot not a moose, but a tremendous whitetail with a gigantic,

> *"…after some stumbling around in the alder swamp, finally found the animal where he'd left it. Kizzie and Eldon gasped in awe as the light reflected off the huge, webbed beams. They counted 52 points and measured bases that were more than 7 inches in circumference."*

webbed set of antlers and a body as large as he'd ever seen!

Hill knew darkness was almost upon him, so he quickly dressed out the buck, grabbed the heart and liver and headed for the Bear's Den.

When he arrived, Kizzie and Eldon were seated at the table, deep into a card game. Hill plunked the heart and liver in the middle of the table and asked, "What do you think of *that* for a deer?"

Both were sure the organs certainly belonged to a moose, and Hill simply couldn't convince them otherwise. To settle the claim, they finally lighted their carbide lamps and headed downriver to have a look.

Hill followed a game trail that took them close to the buck, and after some stumbling around in the alder swamp, finally found the animal where he'd left it. Kizzie and Eldon gasped in awe as the light reflected off the huge, webbed beams. They counted 52 points and measured bases that were more than 7 inches in circumference. They had a lot to talk about at the Bear's Den for the rest of the night!

The next morning the work began, as the boys prepared to get the huge buck out of the woods. Fortunately, the deer was lying close to the river, so they decided to walk back to Grand Lake Stream and borrow a canoe. Eldon and Hill lived near the mouth of Grand Lake Stream, so they put the canoe in there and paddled to a point nearest the downed buck.

Finally, they dragged the stiff deer out of the swamp and got him loaded into the canoe. After another long haul back down the river, they eventually reached their house along the shore just before darkness set in. It certainly had been a long, hard day.

Later that night, the deer was quartered and the meat divided. Unfortunately, the huge buck was never weighed, as there were no scales in town. To travel to another town with scales would have meant a long, slow trip by horse and wagon. All we know is that Kizzie was quoted some 61 years later as saying, "That buck of Hill's was by far the heaviest deer I've ever seen, and I've seen a bunch of them."

As news of the great buck spread, Frank Ball, who owned a set of sporting camps (hunting camps/lodges) in Grand Lake Stream, eventually bought the rack from Hill for $10. Frank had it mounted at Bangor's S. L. Crosby Co., a prominent taxidermy firm in that day.

For a while the mounted head hung in Frank's lodge, which in later years was called Weatherby's Fisherman's Resort. Eventually he sold the head for $200 to an unknown sportsman. During the next few years, it appeared publicly at several locations in the Northeast. For several years it was exhibited at the Boston Sportsman's Show in the old Mechanics Building, and reportedly it hung in a men's club or museum in New York for another period of time.

Then, at some point many, many years ago, the buck disappeared from public view, not to be seen again for many decades. Several photos from the early days were in existence, including two that had accompanied the newspaper article of 1910, but the whereabouts of the head remained a secret.

Rumor has it that some time around 1984, a widow had employed a handyman to clear out her garage after her husband's death. The deer head was buried in an obscure corner and subsequently was given to the handyman, as the widow had no interest in such things. The rack reportedly was discovered in Hancock County, Maine, and had been killed in Washington County, where Grand Lake Stream is located.

Eventually, the antlers ended up in the hands of Larry Emerson of Ellsworth, an official scorer for the Maine Antler and Skull Trophy Club. He would disclose only that the buck had been in a private home for several decades. The rack was scored by Jean Arsenault, an official scorer for the Boone and Crockett Club, at 259 net points. That score made it a new state-record non-typical, surpassing Flora Campbell's 228 7/8-pointer from 1953. Hill's great Maine buck eventually had become a state record — 75 years after the animal had been killed!

It's incredible that a rack can change owners several times and endure the potential perils of fire, vandals, knife makers, floods and various other elements for so long; however, the rack is in near perfect condition and looks as if it were grown last year.

Such antler mass isn't normally found in Maine — or anywhere else, for that matter. Hill's buck was a true wilderness dweller, shot in a country of cedar swamps, alder bogs and dark, murky streams. In those years logging may have helped the food supply by prompting new growth, but agriculture was non-existent for many miles around.

Still, an occasional wilderness buck defies the odds and grows a rack one would expect to see only in crop-rich farmlands. It makes me wonder what kind of rack Hill's buck would have grown if he had lived in farmland. Because wilderness bucks normally

"Hill's great Maine buck eventually had become a state record — 75 years after the animal had been killed!"

aren't hunted so heavily that most of the superior animals are taken, antler growth as a benefit of older age and superior genetics often offsets the inferior quality of the feed.

Hill's buck was magnificent, regardless of his habitat. Early accounts reported him to have 52 points, a 28-inch spread and 7-inch bases. Again, he was thought to be the "largest buck in the world" at the time, although no scoring system existed then.

He does have 52 "points," but only 31 are an inch or more in length. But the rack's most unusual feature is the incredible webbing on both antler beams. The bases are exceptionally heavy, at 6 1/8 and 5 7/8, and the circumferences just get bigger from there on out! This is undoubtedly one of the most attractive and spectacular webbed racks in existence.

Although the Hill Gould buck is obviously a non-typical, his underlying frame is actually very typical. His right side typical-ly totals 94 4/8 and his left 92 7/8; adding in the 19 5/8 inches for inside spread gives a total typical score of 207 0/8 before deductions. After subtracting 14 1/8 inches of side-to-side difference, he has a net typical frame of 192 7/8 points. His 19 abnormal points total 66 1/8 inches.

Everyone wants a buck that's "high, wide and heavy," but such deer are extremely rare. Even fewer bucks have the looks and the score. Incredible palmation with long, forked drop tines, a beautiful shape and a 259-point state-record score — what more could you ask for?

And on top of that, there are almost no legends to match the one surrounding this magestic whitetail. After all, few bucks go back to 1910 with an existing newspaper article describing both the hunter *and* the hunt. Yes, only a handful of bucks ever taken qualify on all of these counts, and Hill Gould's "moose" is among them.

Chapter Fifteen

THE MILO HANSON BUCK

213 5/8 TYPICAL, SASKATCHEWAN, 1993

The Shot Heard 'round the Whitetail World

BY GORDON WHITTINGTON

For years, the town of Biggar, Saskatchewan, had only one claim to fame: a clever sign proclaiming, "New York Is Big, But This Is Biggar!" The farming community west of Saskatoon never had experienced what could truly be called a moment in the limelight.

But that was before Nov. 23, 1993, when Milo Hanson fired the shot heard 'round the whitetail world. Milo's hunt that morning produced the Boone and Crockett world record in the typical category, an achievement definitely rare enough to put any hunting spot on the map.

The story of Milo's historic hunt is an exciting one — not merely because the end result was a record-shattering deer, but also because the hunter and his friends were hunting *that* specific deer, against difficult odds. When Milo got the buck, it was the final piece in a story that had taken almost a year to unfold.

During the last days of the 1992 rifle season, local school bus driver Jim Angelopoulos kept returning to the coffee shop with tales of a huge buck he'd been

MILO HANSON, SASKATCHEWAN, 1993

	Right Antler	Left Antler	Difference
Main Beam Length	28 4/8	28 4/8	0/8
1st Point Length	6 5/8	6 0/8	5/8
2nd Point Length	12 4/8	13 1/8	5/8
3rd Point Length	13 6/8	14 0/8	2/8
4th Point Length	11 4/8	11 5/8	1/8
5th Point Length	5 0/8	7 0/8	2 0/8
1st Circumference	4 6/8	5 0/8	2/8
2nd Circumference	4 2/8	4 2/8	0/8
3rd Circumference	4 3/8	4 2/8	1/8
4th Circumference	4 2/8	4 2/8	0/8
Total	**95 4/8**	**98 0/8**	**4 0/8**

Main Characteristics: Classic combination of tine length, beam length and spread. Broke world record because of symmetry and lack of abnormal points.

MISCELLANEOUS STATS	
No. Of Points–Right	8
No. Of Points–Left	6
Total No. Of Points	14
Length Of Abnormals	3 1/8
Greatest Spread	29 0/8
Tip To Tip Spread	24 3/8
Inside Spread	27 2/8

FINAL TALLY	
Inside Spread	27 2/8
Right Antler	95 4/8
Left Antler	98 0/8
Gross Score	220 6/8
Difference (–)	4 0/8
Subtotal	216 6/8
Abnormals (–)	3 1/8
NET TYPICAL SCORE	213 5/8

seeing on his route. While Jim wasn't a deer hunter, everyone figured he must have observed something impressive.

Late the next summer, neighbor John Kowalchuk told Milo of a huge buck he'd been seeing in a small patch of timber: "bush," as it's called in Canada's prairie provinces. John actually had spotted the buck in daylight near his home, and he gave Milo a detailed description of the antlers, which at that point were just coming out of

velvet. Naturally, Milo hoped he would be the lucky hunter to hang the rack on his wall, but many other local folks shared his same dream.

Milo and his wife, Olive, are full-time farmers, and that year weather problems had the harvest running behind schedule. By the time they had their farm duties wrapped up, the Nov. 15 rifle opener was just around the corner. The big buck hadn't been shot by anyone in the early muzzleloader or bow seasons, so there still was hope. When Milo joined forces with Walter Meger, Adam Evashenko, Walter Gamble and Gerry Yaroshko before dawn on the Monday opener, the objective was clear: bag the big one.

Fate is a mysterious force that favors some and tosses others aside. Nobody knows that better than Dwayne Zagoruy. On opening morning, he nearly stamped his own name on whitetail history.

Around 8 a.m., Dwayne spotted the buck going into a large "bluff" (woodlot). The deer was alone, but Dwayne decided he dare not try to slip up on him for a shot; there was simply too much cover.

He pulled out and went to the home of friend Bill Litwinow, who wasn't yet home from working the night shift at a nearby salt mine. Once Bill arrived, Dwayne told him what he'd seen, and the men quickly organized a drive.

The drivers went into the cover, and the buck ran out. Dwayne's shot was a difficult one. He missed, and the buck ran onto a nearby tract of posted land. Dwayne's chance at history was gone.

At the time, Milo and friends were in the same general area, hoping to find the buck they'd heard plenty about but had never seen. Finally, in the late afternoon, they had their first sighting, as Walter Meger glimpsed him at long range on the posted land. Now they at least knew for sure he existed.

Milo and his friends prefer to sit on high vantage points in the first minutes of legal shooting light, not only hoping to get shots at unspooked bucks but also looking to spot distant deer that can be approached later in the day. The rolling prairies are dotted with drainages, the steeper portions of which remain

uncleared of brush. Area hunters will often glass for deer or their tracks in the snow, then plot strategy for how to get close enough for a shot.

First light on Tuesday morning turned up no trace of the buck, so the hunters went to the edge of the posted ground and searched for clues that he'd moved off it during the night. When they found a set of fresh tracks heading from the posted ground toward Rene Igini's unharvested rye field, they hoped the trail was that of the trophy deer. But they couldn't be sure — the track wasn't that impressive. "It wasn't a big track at all," Milo recalls, "which is one of the reasons this buck was so hard to hunt. You'd think a buck with a rack like that would be really big-bodied, but he wasn't. His track was about the size of a large doe's."

The men were able to follow the tracks to Rene's field. Once there, however, things began to get complicated. The field was full of deer tracks, making it impossible to sort out this buck's rather ordinary prints from those of many other deer. The trail eventually was lost.

"We didn't know where to go from there," Milo says. "There were lots of other hunters out, and we couldn't seem to get on the buck's track, so we just moseyed away to some other areas we have permission to hunt. Walter Gamble ended up shooting a nice 4-pointer (an 8-pointer by Eastern count)."

On Wednesday morning, Nov. 17, Walter Meger again spied the buck of their dreams, but only for a moment and at great distance. Once more the buck was heading for Rene's uncut rye field, and just as before, he got there ahead of the hunters and threw them off in that maze of tracks.

On Thursday, Adam and Gerry left to hunt moose in a distant area. But on Friday, Rene Igini and John Yaroshko returned from moose hunting and joined the "deer party." But things didn't look good. The countryside was still crawling with hunters, many of whom had the same buck in mind. What's more, the weather was making things tough; the skies refused to yield any more tracking snow, and there wasn't even enough wind to cover old tracks. When Milo looked up early one morning and saw that a neighbor's dog had followed him to his stand, the prospects hit rock bottom.

Sunday is by law a non-hunting day in Saskatchewan, but by then everyone needed the break. The weather hadn't improved, and Milo had chores to do. Even when Monday rolled around again, and everyone else in the hunting party once more headed into the bush, he declined, deciding to finish up some business at the local grain co-op. He didn't miss anything, however; no one in the party saw the big buck that day.

Monday night, Milo was standing at the crossroads of his deer-hunting career. Some farm work remained undone. But, the weather had changed — a sprinkling of new snow and some wind to cover old sign. Milo phoned his friends and made plans to go with them on Tuesday.

The next morning, Walter and Rene went out to glass from a high vantage point at first light, while Milo waited for John to arrive at his house. The plan was for them to rendezvous with Walter and

"Any time a world record of any species is taken, it's an occasion worth celebrating. When it happens that the most legendary of all deer records comes tumbling down, it's even more special."

Rene later in the morning, at which time a strategy could be put together. When Milo and John met up with their buddies not long after daybreak, there was good news to be shared: Walter and Rene had seen the buck again!

According to the two hunters, the buck was with a couple of does — the first time anyone had known him to be with other deer. But he didn't appear to be trailing either doe. All the men knew at that time was that they were zeroing in on the local legend.

Rene, one of the best trackers in the party, got onto the buck's trail and followed it into heavy willow cover. The buck was heading north, away from posted ground. To try to ensure that he didn't loop back against the flow and return there, Milo posted at the south end of the willows, with John off to his southeast and Walter to the northwest.

Almost as soon as Rene went into the south end of the willows, the buck started out the north end, flagging all the way. "I could see him over the willows from where I was, maybe a half-mile away," Milo says. "I figured it couldn't be him, flagging like a doe, but it was. By the time he came into view, he was a long way from me, and nobody could get a good shot at him. But he was making a mistake, going north all the time. That was putting him into an area we all had hunted a lot and knew well."

The men moved ahead to where the buck had entered another small bluff. Rene once more took up the track, which eventually led him to an old road, where several sets of fresh tracks had crossed. But did any belong to the buck? After a close look, the hunters finally decided that the buck had indeed crossed there. Now he was heading once again for Rene's uncut rye field, which even after a fresh snow was likely to be full of confusing tracks. This didn't look good.

Thus began a tense two hours of looking for the buck in Rene's pasture, hoping to catch at least a glimpse of him so another drive could be conducted. Milo finally went to the road circling the area and saw there were no fresh tracks leading out. That buck was still in there.

"Walter suggested we go around the area again and keep looking," Milo notes. "We didn't know what else to do. Finally, at about 10:30, we saw the buck again, heading onto a tract of land I own. The buck ran into 30 or 40 acres of willow and small poplars (aspen), an area we've always called The Willow Run. I'm sure he had been in there before, because it's thick and hard to hunt."

Another drive was organized. "John and I were on the north side of the run, while Walter was on the west side," Milo recalls. "Rene stayed on the track and went into the run, hoping he could get the buck to bust out.

"If the deer had wanted to hide, I don't know that we could have gotten him to come out," Milo admits. "But he wanted to get out of there and loop back around to a similar patch of willows on my neighbor's land. He came out, trying to get over there, but he spotted me standing there. Before I could get off a shot, he turned back to the north. Now he was about 150 yards from me, broadside but running flat out. I missed him, and so did John."

The next push turned up no sightings of the buck; he apparently had slipped through that bluff and on to the next one before the drive even started. But Rene kept dogging the track, and on the next push, the buck made his final mistake: He headed west, right toward Milo and his Winchester Model 88.

"The buck came out and turned, giving me only a shot at him running straight away," the hunter explains. "He was probably only about 100 yards from me when I touched the trigger. As soon as I shot, I could see steam pouring off of his back. That's when he went down onto his knees, and I thought he was dead. John was pretty close to me, and he yelled, 'You got him!' We both put our guns down; in fact, I didn't even bother to eject the shell. But just then, the buck got up and took off again."

(In retrospect, the buck's rack might actually have been hit by the shot that knocked him down; to this day a big chunk of lead is still embedded in the back of the right beam, just below where the G-2 tine is attached. Milo thinks the 150-grain bullet hit the top part of the rib cage at an angle, deflecting part of it upward into the antler. Fortunately, while there's a chip out of the back of the beam and a small crack on one edge of the bullet hole, the beam didn't break. Had it done so before being panel-measured by B&C, the buck would have been unscorable!)

Milo wasted no time in getting to a high lookout position in the next bluff, where he spotted the buck below him. The next shot caught the animal in the neck and angled back into the shoulder, and a final bullet placed at the juncture of the head and neck ended the chase.

As the tired but happy group of hunters converged to check out their prize, they were as excited as one might imagine — but not because they realized that a new No. 1 buck had just hit the ground. "We knew he was the biggest deer we'd ever seen, and he was for sure the one that everybody around here had been talking about, but we never thought about him being a world record," Milo points out. "We thought he'd go maybe 190, even 200 Boone and Crockett, but we never put a tape on him ourselves."

Later that day, the buck was hung up at the Hanson farm, and word began to spread. Even in Saskatchewan, high-racked 6x6 bucks with outside spreads of nearly 30 inches aren't exactly common, and so a parade of wellwishers started to file in. For several days the deer hung there in the unlocked shop, and for part of that time, neither Milo nor Olive was around. Looking back on it, Milo says it makes him nervous to think that the deer could have been stolen or the rack broken during that period.

The first hint of just how big the buck was came on the evening of Sunday, Nov. 29, when Adam Evashenko, now back from his moose hunt, came to the Hanson home for supper. Adam is a former measurer for the Biggar Wildlife Federation, the local sportsman's club, and he wanted to stretch a tape over the big rack.

The procedure went without fanfare until the totals were added up. When the measurer saw his final score, he assumed he'd made a big mistake. He studied the figures again and said, "I don't know."

"What's the matter?" Milo asked.

"Here," Adam said, "go through my figures and see if the fractions add up."

There had in fact been some minor misfiguring of the measurements, but nothing significant. Even after the math was corrected, Adam's unofficial net score came to 214 Boone and Crockett points — way above the Jordan buck's longstanding world record of 206 1/8! Now, for the first time, Milo realized that he was in possession of a serious threat to the world record. "Everybody turned white, and we broke out the rum for a little celebration," he recalls.

The next day, neighbor Bruce Kushner, current measurer for the local wildlife federation, returned from a moose hunt in eastern Saskatchewan, where he'd heard about Milo's buck. Bruce's information was that the antlers already had been officially scored for Saskatchewan's Kelsey Club at around 190 net points. That was plenty big enough to get Bruce interested in taking a look. But what he found was a deer far bigger than that.

When Bruce finished up his measuring and totaled the numbers, he began to look confused. "We have to go back and re-measure the rack," he said.

"Why?" Milo asked.

"Because I came up with 215 points," Bruce replied, feeling certain he had made a mistake. But no major blunder had occurred. After checking his math, Bruce actually ended up with a net score of 214 6/8, only slightly off from what Adam had calculated.

Later that evening, Bruce relayed the news to Jim Wiebe, habitat coordinator for the Saskatchewan Wildlife Federation, who lives perhaps 20 miles from the Hansons. According to Bruce, Jim's reaction was somewhat predictable: "He didn't believe me."

The Hanson buck shattered James Jordan's world record for typicals and turned Milo into a whitetail icon.
Photo by Cindy Moleski.

Jim abruptly changed his mind the next evening, when he put a tape to the antlers himself.

And so it was that the next morning, I answered the phone at *North American Whitetail* magazine and found myself talking to Jim. Naturally, things started to happen at warp speed from that moment forward. Publisher Steve Vaughn and I raced to the airport to catch a flight to Saskatoon, and the next morning, Jim

led us to Milo's farm for a look at the deer we'd all been waiting years to see.

Any time a world record is taken, it's an occasion worth celebrating. When the most legendary of all deer records comes tumbling down, it's even more special. The fact that a serious hunter pulled the trigger is the icing on the cake, for Milo Hanson is a man who fully appreciates both the animal and the close friends who helped him get it.

Chapter Sixteen

THE ELISHA HUGEN BUCK

182 3/8 TYPICAL, IOWA, 1996

*One of the Highest-Scoring
4 x 4 Typicals Ever*

BY BILL WINKE

Because both halves of Iowa's split shotgun deer season fall after the rut, almost nobody who goes afield at that time counts on natural movement to bring a big buck their way. Instead, deer drives are the order of the day, and some of them involve enough logistical maneuvering to make a four-star general envious.

On Dec. 14, 1996, opening morning of the second season, Elisha and Brad Hugen joined Brad's father, Lyle, and brother, David, as well as Elisha's cousin, Greg Carpenter, for a day of group hunting near the Hugens' home in Knoxville. Greg got a nice 8-pointer in the morning, but that was the sum total of the day's action. The next day, they'd hunt an uncle's farm farther south.

This farm consists of a pastured valley with a creek bottom running through the middle and narrow, brushy draws extending up the slopes on both sides. Underbrush is limited, but a large number of cedars make up one portion of the farm and serve as security cover. There's also a narrow band of trees following the creek itself. Another

Photo by Kirsten Lyons.

Main Characteristics: Among the top 4x4 racks of all time, thanks to great height, width and mass.

Elisha Hugen, Iowa, 1996

	Right Antler	Left Antler	Difference
Main Beam Length	27 7/8	26 6/8	1 1/8
1st Point Length	7 6/8	8 1/8	3/8
2nd Point Length	14 7/8	15 0/8	1/8
3rd Point Length	12 4/8	12 3/8	1/8
4th Point Length	—	—	—
5th Point Length	—	—	—
1st Circumference	5 5/8	5 7/8	2/8
2nd Circumference	5 0/8	5 0/8	0/8
3rd Circumference	5 0/8	5 1/8	1/8
4th Circumference	4 1/8	3 6/8	3/8
Total	**82 6/8**	**82 0/8**	**2 4/8**

Miscellaneous Stats	
No. Of Points–Right	5
No. Of Points–Left	5
Total No. Of Points	10
Length Of Abnormals	3 3/8
Greatest Spread	26 2/8
Tip To Tip Spread	23 4/8
Inside Spread	23 4/8

Final Tally	
Inside Spread	23 4/8
Right Antler	82 6/8
Left Antler	82 0/8
Gross Score	**188 2/8**
Difference (–)	2 4/8
Subtotal	185 6/8
Abnormals (–)	3 3/8
Net Typical Score	**182 3/8**

party actually hunted the farm hard during the first season, which had recently ended.

On the day of the Hugens' hunt, the temperature was in the low 30s but without snow cover. Brad and Elisha were doing the "dog work" on the morning's first drive when Elisha's incredible story began to unfold.

"We were about three-fourths of the way through when I saw a coyote standing on a fallen log, unaware of me," she says. "I was deciding whether or not to shoot when he

disappeared over a hill. I was proceeding cautiously, hoping to get a shot at him on the other side, when I heard a noise in a ditch. To my surprise, a nice buck jumped up and took off out of the ditch. I shot once as he went up the bank. He ran another 40 yards and stopped and fell over backwards. He was the biggest buck I had ever shot."
(He wouldn't be for long.)

Iowa allows "party" hunting, meaning that if at least one person in the group has an open tag, every member can continue to hunt. So, after taking what was — to that moment — her biggest buck, Elisha didn't lay down her gun.

A bit later, following another drive, the Hugens heard a volley of shots. They later learned that Lyle had seen a huge buck coming toward him down the creek but had missed. The buck then had run past Greg, who'd also taken a couple of shots but likewise had failed to connect.

Elisha and her monster 8-pointer. Photo by Bill Winke, courtesy of Elisha Hugen.

"Brad and Lyle went to the other side of the farm to go on stand," Elisha says. "They were near the heavy grove of cedar trees and figured that was probably where the big buck had run after Greg shot at him."

After the two men got into position, another drive commenced from the point where the shots had been fired. The area is a sidehill pasture with grass-covered ridges separating three narrow fingers of brush running down to the creek bottom. After walking over the first open ridge, Elisha was about to cross one of the narrow draws when she heard shots above her on the hill.

"David had shot at a doe and missed, and Greg had dropped her," she says. "I started walking up the ditch to see if they needed any help, and then I looked over and saw the big buck lying in a pile of old logs. He was watching me out of the corner of his eye, hoping I wouldn't see him."

"I took a quick shot," Elisha recalls, "but in my excitement, I missed. He jumped up and ran into a huge sticker bush. This time my slug connected, and he fell. He got back

up and ran down the ditch (toward the creek). I took another shot as he went over the back of the small creek, hoping and praying I wouldn't hit his rack. I didn't see him go up or down the creek, so I moved in quietly. He was lying on the other side. I let out a few hoots and hollers, bringing David and Greg running down the ditch. I met them, saying, 'He's big and he's down!'

"I was so excited that I didn't want to leave the buck, so when David and Greg went on to finish the drive, I stayed behind," she notes. "While I was waiting, a nice 9-pointer came trotting right to where I was standing. I waited for a good shot and fired. He went down. Of course, the drivers didn't know a buck had doubled back, and they were surprised when they got back and found two bucks beside me!" Elisha had shot the three biggest bucks of her life, all in one day, while the rest of her group could muster only a single doe!

"After loading the deer into the truck, we were so impressed with the size and mass of my big buck that we decided to get it mounted," she says. "We called taxidermist Marlin Hoch and asked if he would mount a big 8-pointer for us. He agreed, and when we showed up, he was amazed."

"After looking at the rack carefully and taking some measurements, Marlin exclaimed, 'You folks don't know what you've got here. This is big!'"

Big indeed — as in one of the world's highest-scoring basic 8-pointers of all time!

Chapter Seventeen

THE TODD HURLEY BUCK

256 7/8 NON-TYPICAL, ILLINOIS, 1995

A World-Class Whitetail His First Time in a Deer Stand... Ever!

BY LES DAVENPORT

Tina Corbin had thoughts of refusing when her boyfriend, Charles Hoffman, popped the question. "Will you walk a standing corn field toward me and try driving this monster buck out?" he asked. The thought of sharing the close quarters of a corn field with a "monster" didn't set well with Tina, a non-hunter. But her devotion to Charles ultimately prevailed, and she reluctantly agreed to help.

The drive would be Charles' last-ditch effort to arrow the buck before the November 1995 Illinois shotgun season. He'd spotted the non-typical twice before, but no shot had been offered either time. Both times the deer had come out of the field, leading Charles to think he might be bedding among the tall stalks.

When Tina's day of reckoning arrived, she dutifully walked up and down the rows while Charles waited nearby, bow in hand. However, their efforts went unrewarded. Had the buck sneaked out of the corn in a different direction? Or had he possibly decided to bed elsewhere with a "hot" doe?

Photo by Les Davenport.

Main Characteristics:
A record-class
8-pointer with 22
non-typical points
that added 91 3/8"
of score.

TODD HURLEY, ILLINOIS, 1995

	Right Antler	Left Antler	Difference
Main Beam Length	26 6/8	26 3/8	3/8
1st Point Length	8 4/8	9 2/8	6/8
2nd Point Length	11 3/8	10 4/8	7/8
3rd Point Length	7 6/8	10 4/8	2 6/8
4th Point Length	—	—	—
5th Point Length	—	—	—
1st Circumference	5 0/8	5 0/8	0/8
2nd Circumference	4 7/8	4 5/8	2/8
3rd Circumference	6 0/8	6 3/8	3/8
4th Circumference	4 0/8	5 5/8	1 5/8
Total	**74 2/8**	**78 2/8**	**7 0/8**

MISCELLANEOUS STATS	
No. Of Points–Right	16
No. Of Points–Left	14
Total No. Of Points	30
Length Of Abnormals	91 3/8
Greatest Spread	27 7/8
Tip To Tip Spread	13 3/8
Inside Spread	20 0/8

FINAL TALLY	
Inside Spread	20 0/8
Right Antler	74 2/8
Left Antler	78 2/8
Gross Score	172 4/8
Difference (–)	7 0/8
Subtotal	165 4/8
Abnormals (+)	91 3/8
NET NON-TYPICAL SCORE	**256 7/8**

Charles was disappointed but not discouraged. A veteran hunter, he knew his odds would improve during the gun season a week later. And even if he couldn't connect with this awesome buck, maybe his new hunting partner, Todd Hurley, would have luck on his side.

Later that week, only a half-mile from where Charles hunted, P.D. Kropp was traveling down a county road in his grain truck, while his son, Kent, followed on a tractor. Suddenly, Kent began flashing his lights and pulled off to the side. P.D. wheeled the grain truck to the shoulder as well.

"Scoot over and let me drive!" Kent said excitedly as he ran up to the truck. "I want to show you the biggest buck I've ever seen! He's lying in the ditch 100 yards back!"

Kent got into the truck, turned it around and drove well past the spot before about-facing a second time and heading slowly toward the idling tractor.

"When I pull over, Dad, look in the weeds along the ditch," Kent said. "The buck will probably bust out when we stop to look at him."

As the truck slowed to a halt, P.D. could barely believe his eyes. Points jutted in every direction from the bedded buck's heavy main beams! But he refused to flinch.

"Do you think he could have been hit by a car?" Kent questioned.

"It's possible," P.D. replied.

"I'll honk the horn and see what he does," Kent said.

Not surprisingly, neither man had noticed the doe lying beside the buck in the brush. As if launched from a rocket, at the horn's blast the two deer bolted into a nearby woods.

On Nov. 16, the eve of the gun opener, Roger McNeff was returning home from nearby Quincy when the huge deer crossed the road in front of him. This sighting occurred very near where the Kropps had seen the animal. Roger reported to relatives Rob and Bob McNeff that the buck was the biggest he'd ever set eyes on. "He looked like a small moose," Roger claimed.

Nov. 17, opening day of slug season, would be Todd's first-ever deer hunt. While the 32-year-old was an experienced hunter of small game, he'd never strongly considered hunting deer until constant talk about whitetails at work took its toll on him. An invitation from Charles was all the impetus Todd needed to give deer hunting a try, and he bought a leftover either-sex permit.

Charles and Todd were optimistic as they headed out before dawn on opening day. Weeks earlier, Charles had placed Todd's tree stand along a brushy fence line. Rubs

Todd Hurley's 30-point giant was shot on opening morning of the 1995 slug season in Adams County, Illinois. Photo courtesy of Les Davenport.

and scrapes were scattered along the narrow strip, which linked open ground to thick timber. Charles would be watching a creek crossing 300 yards away.

Todd had worked the night before, but his excitement kept him alert as dawn broke. He'd already decided that any deer offering a good shot was fair game.

A half-hour after dawn, Todd noticed movement out of the corner of his eye. A large buck had jumped a pasture fence 75 yards away and was meandering in his direction! Shouldering his 12-gauge, the hunter picked an opening through which to shoot.

The buck stopped and stuck his nose into the air. Had he smelled trouble? Fortunately, a quick tail wag later the deer resumed his advance. Todd let him walk within point-blank range before pulling the trigger, and the giant dropped. A follow-up shot ended all movement.

Having heard horror stories regarding bucks' seeming ability to "rise from the dead," Todd held tight, gun in hand, and watched the deer. After-the-fact buck fever hit, and the rookie hunter started to shake uncontrollably.

"I shot something as big as a horse!" Todd shouted when he saw Charles walking up a few minutes later.

It wasn't much of an exaggeration. At the time, the buck's net score of 256 7/8 Boone and Crockett points ranked him as the No. 3 non-typical in Illinois, as well as the second-biggest whitetail shot in North America during the fall of 1995. Not bad for a guy's first deer hunt!

Chapter Eighteen

THE BRUCE JAMESON BUCK

248 1/8 NON-TYPICAL, KANSAS, 1989

A Giant that was Literally "Down in the Dumps"

BY BRUCE JAMESON

As all serious hunters know, shed antlers of world-class whitetails are rare finds. So, what are the odds that sheds off the same giant non-typical would be found for three straight years — and then, for that deer to be arrowed by a local bowhunter?

During the fall of 1987, my dad found a single 8-point shed that mice had chewed slightly since being dropped in the spring. As it turned out, that same fall my brother, Johnnie, shot a 205-point Pope and Young non-typical three miles from where the antler was picked up. Despite the distance, because the shed somewhat resembled the antlers of Johnnie's trophy, some of us thought it could have been from that deer.

Two months later, however, we realized there was a second monster out there. While walking through a pasture in the section of land where my dad had found the shed, my cousin found a freshly dropped antler. Then, a week later, a farmer found the match in a field about a quarter-mile away. Together, these two antlers formed a 22-point rack that would score well over 200 non-typical.

Main Characteristics: Amazing rack height, due to beam angle and length. 50 5/8" of mass measurements.

Bruce Jameson, Kansas, 1989

	Right Antler	Left Antler	Difference
Main Beam Length	27 5/8	28 3/8	6/8
1st Point Length	7 1/8	8 2/8	1 1/8
2nd Point Length	9 5/8	10 7/8	1 2/8
3rd Point Length	9 7/8	8 3/8	1 4/8
4th Point Length	4 7/8	2 3/8	2 4/8
5th Point Length	—	—	—
1st Circumference	7 7/8	7 2/8	5/8
2nd Circumference	7 3/8	6 4/8	7/8
3rd Circumference	6 4/8	5 4/8	1 0/8
4th Circumference	4 7/8	4 6/8	1/8
Total	**85 6/8**	**82 2/8**	**9 6/8**

Miscellaneous Stats	
No. Of Points–Right	14
No. Of Points–Left	12
Total No. Of Points	26
Length Of Abnormals	69 5/8
Greatest Spread	24 5/8
Tip To Tip Spread	14 3/8
Inside Spread	20 2/8

Final Tally	
Inside Spread	20 2/8
Right Antler	85 6/8
Left Antler	82 2/8
Gross Score	**188 2/8**
Difference (–)	9 6/8
Subtotal	178 4/8
Abnormals (+)	69 5/8
Net Non-Typical Score	**248 1/8**

In the fall of 1988 I was busy opening an archery and taxidermy shop in the nearby town of Pittsburg, so I had little time to bowhunt. However, when I did, I hunted the non-typical's area. He was seen a couple of times that fall, though not by me. Eventually, I arrowed a 165-pound 8-pointer and called it a year.

Rifle season passed without any word of the non-typical being killed, so there was still hope. Sure enough, in February 1989, more

fresh sheds surfaced. A neighbor boy found one of the antlers and began to show it around. The response he got from everyone caused the boy to look for the other side, and he picked it up about 80 yards from where he'd found the first.

The antlers, which would score in the 240s, were such a conversation piece that I decided to mount them on a cape to display at my shop. Soon, the massive 23-point rack had become part of every local bowhunter's dreams. Unfortunately, the boy who found the sheds eagerly revealed the location, putting even more pressure on the area the buck traveled.

In August 1989, I started my scouting. After several evenings of driving local roads, I spotted several obvious P&Y bucks. One evening, as I drove past where the most recent sheds had been found, and within a quarter-mile of where the previous year's sheds had been picked up, I spotted him. The buck was about 150 yards away, and I glassed him for about 30 seconds before he vanished.

"The buck bounded along the top of the pit dump, coming back toward me. I followed him with my bow, looking for a hole in the brush to shoot through. The buck ran past, broadside. It was shoot now or not at all."

I knew the area well, having hunted and fished there since I was a kid. However, as I started spending some time there, I quickly became discouraged. The widespread knowledge of the monster's whereabouts had created tremendous traffic in the area. This part of southeastern Kansas is all mile-sectioned county-maintained gravel roads, and people constantly were driving around the three or four sections where the buck was known to be. With so much traffic in the area, all deer became harder to find.

I've found hunting for big whitetails to be unproductive in my area in early season, so I didn't even try for the buck until October was winding down. However, in talking with several other local bowhunters, no one had seen the big buck since the season had opened.

Everyone had their own ideas of where the buck was hiding. Where I thought he was staying was a section of strip-mine pit dumps a half-mile wide by a mile long. (Strip-pit dumps are large areas of land where open-pit coal strip-mining has been done). The pits are the large areas dug deep to reach long veins of coal. Pits range from 20 feet wide and 10 feet deep to 200 feet wide and 40 feet deep. Over years these pits filled with water. The pit dumps are the large piles of dirt dumped by the steam shovels or draglines along the sides of the pits. A dump can range from 8 to 45 feet high, with steep slopes.

The pit dumps in our area are mostly covered with large cottonwood trees and thick dogwood underbrush, along with scattered oaks. The oaks do provide acorns, but a lot of the strip-pit dumps are surrounded with wheat, soybean and milo fields, giving the deer multiple feeding areas.

Owning an archery shop with an indoor range, I had great confidence in my equipment and shooting skills. A bowhunter never can practice making a shot with his adrenaline pumping, or with the anxiety and pressure he feels when shooting at a big buck, but if you practice good shooting form long enough, it does become automatic. I was just hoping to get a chance to prove it on the non-typical.

Feeling he'd gone nocturnal, I believed my only chance was to invest time in the area and learn where the deer were moving. Presumably, the rut would bring the buck out in daylight.

I couldn't get permission to hunt the strip-pit dumps where I felt he spent most of his time, so I picked a spot about a half-mile away. This area was right at the edge of a mile-long stretch of pits and dumps that had been dug by horse-drawn equipment. Strip mining with horses usually left a lot more strips of water between the dumps, and the water tends to keep deer from going through the center. If a buck were going to do some traveling in this area, he'd probably walk just inside the edge of the dumps.

During the rut, shortcut trails are made by big bucks as they cover territory in their search for does. These trails are difficult to find in the timber, because there might be only one or two deer using them, but normally the soft shoulders of a gravel road will display the tracks of a large buck if one crossed. So, I decided to look for some of these trails.

It rained once in early November, and I was able to find a large set of buck tracks crossing a road. The tracks entered the section twice but didn't exit there. Perhaps this was the non-typical's route, but I couldn't be sure.

That Monday morning, I pulled my stand from another area, so that I could put it up in the section where I'd found the big tracks. I parked my truck, and as I grabbed my stand out of the back, I looked across the field and saw a large buck. As soon as my binoculars hit the deer, I knew it was the non-typical!

He never looked up; instead, he just ran around in circles, sniffing the ground like a coon dog on a hot trail. Then he made up his mind in which direction he was going and took off along the inside edge of the strip pits.

It was just before 8 a.m., and I knew the buck was out on a doe search. I also knew that if he were going in that direc-

tion, he might use the shortcut trail I'd found. I immediately jumped into the truck and drove to the other side of the section, stopping about 150 yards from the trail. Grabbing my bow, I ran down the road to within 30 yards of the trail, then headed up into the strip pits.

Once the trail got into the pits, it was hard to tell just where it went, but usually the deer follow the contour of the dumps. I ran down the top of one of the dumps and set up. I was thinking that if the buck came through, it would be on the two pit dumps to my left.

After I'd been sitting there for about 10 minutes, my hopes of intercepting the buck started to fail. Then I caught movement four pit dumps to my right. There he was, coming fast, about 50 yards away. The wind was good, and the buck seemed unaware of my presence. He walked until he was perfectly broadside. I knew, however, that because of the brush there was no way to get an arrow to him.

All of a sudden, the buck stopped. He stood there for about 10 seconds, as if he sensed something was wrong. He then turned and walked over the dump and out of sight.

My hopes dropped to almost nothing. To have a buck of a lifetime so close and not get a shot is a bowhunter's nightmare. With an arrow still nocked, I began to stalk to where I'd last seen him. I at least wanted to get a good look at his tracks, so I could compare them to those I had been seeing. As I got to where he had stood, I saw his tracks and immediately realized they were the ones I'd seen.

Thinking that I might as well follow him for a ways, to see where he was going, I walked to the top of the next pit dump. Standing there, combing the area, I wondered where he could have gone.

All of a sudden a loud crash sounded, and I saw the monster jump up about 35 yards away! My bow automatically came to full draw and anchor. The buck bounded along the top of the pit dump, coming back toward me. I followed him with my bow, looking for a hole in the brush to shoot through. The buck ran past, broadside. It was shoot now or not at all.

I touched off my release, and the next thing I knew my arrow was flying right on target. The buck took several more jumps before I could see him again. I got another good look before he went out of sight.

I drove to my dad's house and told him what had happened. I then called my brother, Richard, and told him to meet us out there. We waited for an hour, then went in to see what things looked like. We walked along the top of the pit dump. The buck had been running down the side of the dump when I shot him.

When we reached the area where I had shot, we saw a large splotch of foamy

Bruce Jameson's massive Kansas non-typical was arrowed in an area with extremely high hunting pressure. Several of his huge sheds had been found. Photo courtesy of Bruce Jameson.

blood. After examining it, we felt confident about the shot. We took a few moments to look for my arrow and found it floating in the water just below the dump.

Blood could be seen for several yards in front of us. We followed a good blood trail for 50 yards along the top of the dump. There the buck changed direction and went over the top of the next dump. As my brother topped it, he yelled that he'd found the deer. The giant lay not more than 70 yards from where I'd hit him.

The broadhead had cut the liver and the back of his left lung, then the center of his right lung.

The buck field-dressed 243 pounds, which is exceptional, but the massive 26-point rack was even more impressive. The deer ultimately was scored at 248 1/8 net non-typical, which at the time would have made him No. 3 in Kansas.

To have shot such a great whitetail under any circumstances would have been a thrill. But to have done so after having spent so many hours looking at his mounted sheds on my wall was nothing less than a fantasy come true.

Chapter Nineteen

THE KRUEGER-KEETON BUCK

235 3/8 NON-TYPICAL, SOUTH DAKOTA, 1965

A Day to Buck the Odds

BY J.D. ANDREWS

In 1876, after the battle of the Little Bighorn in Montana, General George Crook's cavalry command slipped into western South Dakota in desperate search of provisions. En route, the general's command ran smack into a village of Sioux Indians encamped near a prominence of pine-clad bluffs known as the Slim Buttes. One of the most significant battles of that year occurred immediately thereafter.

Every fall now, another "army" converges on the Slim Buttes area, but this one wears blaze orange instead of blue. They're deer hunters, and though they're primarily after big mulies, every so often a super whitetail also is taken.

Starting in 1963, the South Dakota Game, Fish and Parks Department tried an experiment there in eastern Harding County, to see if more trophy deer could be produced. In previous years, the area had been open to non-selective hunting. Beginning with the 1963 season, only bucks with a minimum of four points on at least one side could be taken in this special unit, with the gun season running only 11

Main Characteristics: Unique "hook" points sweeping upward toward beams. Bullet hole through right brow tine.

KRUEGER-KEETON, SOUTH DAKOTA, 1965

	Right Antler	Left Antler	Difference
Main Beam Length	21 7/8	22 6/8	7/8
1st Point Length	5 7/8	5 7/8	—
2nd Point Length	11 3/8	11 7/8	4/8
3rd Point Length	6 4/8	10 5/8	4 1/8
4th Point Length	2 6/8	7 1/8	4 3/8
5th Point Length	—	—	—
1st Circumference	6 2/8	6 0/8	2/8
2nd Circumference	8 2/8	9 6/8	1 4/8
3rd Circumference	4 7/8	5 3/8	4/8
4th Circumference	3 5/8	4 1/8	4/8
Total	**71 3/8**	**83 4/8**	**12 5/8**

MISCELLANEOUS STATS	
No. Of Points–Right	13
No. Of Points–Left	10
Total No. Of Points	23
Length Of Abnormals	71 3/8
Greatest Spread	23 5/8
Tip To Tip Spread	21 4/8
Inside Spread	21 6/8

FINAL TALLY	
Inside Spread	21 6/8
Right Antler	71 3/8
Left Antler	83 4/8
Gross Score	176 5/8
Difference (–)	12 5/8
Subtotal	164 0/8
Abnormals (+)	71 3/8
NET NON-TYPICAL SCORE	**235 3/8**

days. This policy continued through 1967, and evidently it helped produce big bucks — including the one featured here.

On the second day of the 1965 season, Dr. John Krueger was hunting with his young brother-in-law, Russell Keeton. After failing to score on opening day, the men were getting anxious. Several friends were hunting farther west, but John and Russell decided to hunt on a ranch just south of the Slim Buttes, in some smaller hills known as the

Sheep Buttes. As the two men drove toward a creek bottom that morning, they passed through a seemingly endless sea of prairie grass and sagebrush. Finally they neared a fence line, parked and started walking down toward the creek.

About 100 yards from the fence was a small clump of buckbrush (western snowberry). As the men climbed over the fence, the twanging noise made by the barbed wire was picked up by three pairs of radar-like ears hidden in the brush. And branching out wide over one of those pairs of ears was the largest known set of whitetail antlers ever produced in western South Dakota!

As the buck raised his head to investigate the noise, John spotted the massive rack and exclaimed, "There's a big buck!" Quick as a flash, each man drew down on the deer with his bolt-action .270. They fired at the same time, and apparently missed!

The non-typical and the two does with him immediately were up and wasting no time "gettin' out of Dodge!" The buck was making for the security of the creek bottom; however, he still had a hill to go over before reaching it, and the two hunters were ready for him when he did.

Hearts pounding, John and Russell each fired again at almost the same time, this time bringing down the buck in spectacular fashion. One bullet drilled through the right antler; the other hit the buck in the hindquarters. The two excited men ran toward their trophy, and John finished him off with another shot.

While the deer wasn't exceptionally heavy, the antlers were. The 23 points reached out in "spread-eagle" fashion, looking much like limbs on a cottonwood tree!

John, a dentist in Wessington Springs, hung the mounted head in his office. There it was admired by many local residents; however, the rack's true significance remained a mystery. Finally, Boone and Crockett measurer Dave Boland put a tape to it and came up with a net non-typical score of 235 3/8. At last the world knew just how great a buck this really was.

One drop tine off the right beam met and almost grew into a long abnormal point

growing downward from the beam. However, the rack's most unusual feature is the bullet hole drilled neatly through the center of the right antler's double brow points. You can look right through it, much like a rifle peep-sight. It was a most "lucky" unlucky shot, as a mere fraction of an inch either way would have blown off both brow points, drastically reducing the score.

But perhaps the strangest part of this story occurred later on the day the deer was shot. Once he'd been loaded into the vehicle, John and Russell joined the other hunters in their party. After they'd done so, more deer were spotted, and as the men were walking over a stock dam to try to get a shot, one stepped on a huge non-typical antler in the grass. When John had a look at it, he felt certain it had been dropped by the buck he and Russell had just shot! John began looking for the other side, and unbelievably found it a few yards away!

As the sheds were still brown and in perfect condition, they must have been from the 1964 season. They were found less than a mile from where the buck had been killed. Given the same inside spread as the 1965 rack, this rack would score 199 0/8, meaning it had grown around 36 inches from one year to the next. How much bigger it eventually would have become we'll never know, but even at 235 3/8 this is one of the top whitetails in state history.

Think of the chances of killing a buck that scores as high as this; of firing a shot through two antler points without breaking either of them; and of finding not one, but both of his shed antlers — all in one day! These two South Dakotans truly "bucked the odds" on that hunt!

Chapter Twenty

THE DALE LARSON BUCK

264 1/8 NON-TYPICAL, KANSAS, 1998

The Hunt for a Deer of a Lifetime… A Buck Named Dagger

BY DALE LARSON

As an avid trophy bowhunter, I like to drive the roads in my hunting area in late afternoon, looking for big bucks. My wife, Connie, and I usually start doing so in mid- to late July, as that's a good time to check out the number and size of bucks here in northeastern Kansas.

During the summer of 1998 we were especially eager to begin scouting, as we hoped to spot one special buck: a great non-typical I called "Dagger." So named because of a long drop tine on his left antler, he'd been seen several times in recent years. Also, we'd found his sheds while turkey hunting in early 1998, so we knew he'd survived the previous deer season.

But all through July and August our search for the buck came up empty, and I couldn't help but wonder if he was still alive. Maybe old age had taken him, though we'd estimated his age the previous season to be only 5 1/2.

Maybe he'd died of hemorrhagic disease. Maybe he'd relocated to a better food source for the summer, in which case he'd likely return during the rut. Or maybe he'd simply become nocturnal.

Dale Larson, Kansas, 1998

Main Characteristics: Outstanding spread and world-class beams. Drop tine of 13 2/8" longest of 19 abnormal points.

	Right Antler	Left Antler	Difference
Main Beam Length	29 6/8	31 0/8	1 2/8
1st Point Length	7 1/8	6 3/8	6/8
2nd Point Length	9 3/8	8 2/8	1 1/8
3rd Point Length	11 2/8	11 3/8	1/8
4th Point Length	11 4/8	9 2/8	2 2/8
5th Point Length	6 0/8	4 1/8	1 7/8
1st Circumference	6 1/8	5 7/8	2/8
2nd Circumference	4 6/8	4 7/8	1/8
3rd Circumference	4 7/8	5 1/8	2/8
4th Circumference	4 7/8	4 7/8	0/8
Total	**95 5/8**	**91 1/8**	**8 0/8**

Miscellaneous Stats

No. Of Points–Right	14
No. Of Points–Left	17
Total No. Of Points	31
Length Of Abnormals	61 1/8
Greatest Spread	26 1/8
Tip To Tip Spread	18 3/8
Inside Spread	24 2/8

Final Tally

Inside Spread	24 2/8
Right Antler	95 5/8
Left Antler	91 1/8
Gross Score	**211 0/8**
Difference (–)	8 0/8
Subtotal	**203 0/8**
Abnormals (+)	61 1/8
Net Non-Typical Score	**264 1/8**

The area we hunt is largely cattle country, but there are small amounts of cultivated cropland. The landscape consists of tallgrass prairie on the flat-topped hills, with red cedars scattered over the long, steep slopes.

Hardwood timber occurs in irregular blocks along the drainages and sidehills. These woods consist primarily of bur and chinquapin oaks, hickory, walnut, hackberry, green ash and American elm, as well as the cedar.

After bowhunts for bighorn sheep and elk in Colorado in early fall, I returned home to focus on deer season. The October bow opener was fast approaching, still with no sightings of Dagger. I was almost to the point of conceding that he might not be coming back. But my hunting partner, Perry Smith, kept saying that the buck would show up in early November.

After the evening hunt on Election Day, Nov. 3, Connie and I headed to the polls. It was still barely light enough to see as we headed out, and en route, Connie spotted a big deer in our hunting area. I drove on to the next corner, turned around and drove back to the pasture to put my binoculars on the buck.

Visibility was poor, but I could tell the deer's rack was huge. He had a big typical frame with kickers and stickers, plus a long drop tine on the left beam. I told Connie, "If that's Dagger, his typical frame has really grown! But if it isn't him, we have another whopper to hunt!" Needless to say, that sighting really fired me up. But I still had some doubts that the deer was Dagger, because trying to identify a buck with a quick look is so difficult. In any case, I knew the deer Connie had spotted was a keeper, and I began making plans to hunt him.

Dagger got his name during the 1995 hunting season, when we started seeing a big 5x5 with a single drop tine extending back and down below the left G-2 tine. From then on, Dagger was distinguishable by his drop tine. From a 10-point typical frame in 1995, he went to a 9-point frame with an additional small drop tine on his right beam in 1996 to a 10-point frame with a single forked drop tine in 1997. But nobody ever managed to get a shot at him.

On Nov. 5 my stepson, Matt, and I were returning from an errand in the early evening when we noticed several deer on a neighbor's field. As we glassed them in the fading light, one caught our attention. The lighting was so poor that making a positive identification was impossible. The deer was facing away, but I could see he carried a wide rack with a long drop tine on his left beam. I was pretty confident it was Dagger.

On Saturday afternoon, Nov. 7, I decided to hunt a stand on a flat-topped ridge that connects daytime bedding areas with nighttime feeding areas. This travel corridor has been used for years by both deer and hunters. The point of the ridge had been one of Dagger's known bedding areas, and my position on this hunt was between there and the feeding area where we'd last seen him.

The whole day was overcast with light drizzle, and the temperature was in the low 40s. Moisture was accumulating on the tree branches and then falling as "raindrops," hitting the fallen leaves in a sporadic rhythm. These conditions can provide good background noise for concealing any unnatural sounds a hunter might make while on stand.

I'd spent an uneventful 90 minutes listening to these "raindrops" when I noticed a flick of a deer's tail and caught a glimpse of an antler. The buck was about 90 yards away, heading east, which meant he was traveling at a right angle to my position. He was heading to another feeding area and wasn't using the travel corridor I was hunting. But I still didn't know which buck it was.

Retrieving my True Talker grunt call from under my rain suit, I gave a couple of tending grunts; however, by this time I couldn't see the deer through the brush. I grunted a couple more times with more volume, then put the call away to see what would happen.

The view I had of the deer's possible approach route was obscured with brush and trees. As I was placing the grunt call back inside my rain suit, I caught some movement with my peripheral vision about 25 yards to my right. It was Dagger, and he was coming hard! In just a fraction of a second he was right below me, casting his head one way and then another, trying to locate the buck he thought he'd heard!

Here was the buck we'd been trying for so long to tag, a great trophy with antlers sticking everywhere, standing 12 feet directly below me. I knew from 30 years of calling experience with various types of animals that when you start calling, you'd better be ready to shoot. Unfortunately, I hadn't fully prepared myself for this turn of events. Dagger had caught me with my pants down; my Jennings bow was still hanging in the tree, and I was leaning against a limb!

The deer took a couple of steps west to look down the sidehill. It was now or never. I slowly put my hand into the bow sling and in one slow movement stepped back away from the limb and drew.

I expected that when I finally got the monster in my peep sight I'd see him looking up at me, but instead he had continued angling away. He hadn't even noticed my movement! I settled my 20-yard pin behind his shoulder and let instinct take over.

When the arrow hit, the deer bolted over the rimrock and out of sight, as if shot from a cannon. At first I could hear his retreat; then, all was quiet.

I started playing back what had just happened. Was my shot as good as it had looked? Or was that impact I'd heard the sound of my arrow hitting brush? It's funny how at such times your mind tries to play tricks on you.

"Unfortunately, I hadn't fully prepared myself for this turn of events. Dagger had caught me with my pants down; my Jennings bow was still hanging in the tree, and I was leaning against a limb!"

I sat down and thought about how lucky I was to have been given such a chance. I'd had everything in my favor: the noise made by the dripping water; Dagger's interest in finding the other buck; his move to look down the sidehill. I'd definitely had a 5-gallon bucket of luck on this hunt. However, I still couldn't be sure that I'd actually killed the deer.

I sat in the stand until dark, then quietly climbed down and headed to the truck. When I got there, Perry had just arrived. I told him that I'd just shot Dagger.

"Sure you did," he said, thinking that I was kidding.

"No, I really did shoot him," I insisted and gave him a play-by-play report. Then we went back to the house to get Connie and Matt and flashlights.

Despite all of the nagging questions that plague a bowhunter after the shot, I was confident I'd made a good hit, and with the conditions (light rain and everything on the ground being wet), we were anxious to start trailing.

We returned to the stand and found half of my arrow behind where the buck had been when I'd shot. There was an obvious blood trail leading down the hill, and as we approached the bottom of the steep slope, a flashlight beam caught the form of a big-bodied buck with huge antlers. Dagger was dead, having fallen so that his 13 2/8-inch drop tine was holding his head almost upright.

My excitement largely had subsided after the shot, but now, as I looked at this incredible buck, I felt something I hadn't

The author (right) and friend Perry Smith pose with the giant non-typical a number of Kansas hunters had been pursuing for years. Photo courtesy of Dale Larson.

felt before. I'd arrowed other big deer, but this one was different. I felt amazed, happy, sad and appreciative all at once. We all just looked at the deer for some time. Every hunter there had had visions of harvesting him, but he'd always escaped. Now that one of us had been fortunate enough to get the 31-pointer, in a way we all felt strangely sad that it was over.

After the required 60-day drying period, I gave Connie (who, like me, is an official P&Y measurer) the honor of scoring Dagger. Fellow P&Y measurer Tom Bowman assisted her with the process, which took several hours. Once they were done, they'd come up with an entry score of 267 7/8 net points. My buck looked to be the world's highest-scoring P&Y buck in the 36 years since Del Austin had arrowed his 279 7/8-point world record in Nebraska (featured in *Legendary Whitetails*).

By the time the next P&Y panel met to measure entries in 2001, shrinkage and minor differences in judgment calls had dropped Dagger's final score to 264 1/8 points. What's more, by then Randy Simonitch had shot a 269 7/8-point non-typical in Missouri to claim the No. 2 spot in P&Y. Thus, my buck was pronounced P&Y's new No. 3 whitetail, as well as the new Kansas bow record by 7 1/8 inches over Kenny Fowler's 1988 trophy (Chapter 12). Not bad for a deer I had doubted I'd ever see again!

Chapter Twenty One

THE DUANE LINSCOTT BUCK

259 5/8 NON-TYPICAL, MISSOURI, 1985

*A Five-Hour Wait
for the
Shot of a Lifetime*

BY DICK IDOL

When my phone rang one day in early 1984, the excited voice of a hard-core hunting friend from Kansas City began to relate some wonderful news. "Dick," he said, "you won't believe the pair of sheds that has just been found over here! They're freshly dropped and in perfect condition. They're massive, with a ton of points, and they score 238 non-typical! One of my buddies even saw the buck this season, but he never could get a shot."

Soon enough, our conversation had drifted on to the deer's huntability and conjecture about who would be hunting him the following season. I even contemplated going after the buck myself, but as it turned out, a number of proficient hunters already were planning to pursue him.

The buck lived in a large northern Missouri wildlife refuge that allowed only limited deer hunting; however, he occasionally had been seen outside its boundaries. In fact, one shed had been found inside the refuge by Clark Milligan, a local conservation officer, and the other had been picked up outside its boundaries by David Lentz.

Photo courtesy of Bass Pro Shops.

DUANE LINSCOTT, MISSOURI, 1985

	Right Antler	Left Antler	Difference
Main Beam Length	26 7/8	26 7/8	0/8
1st Point Length	7 0/8	8 0/8	1 0/8
2nd Point Length	10 5/8	11 0/8	3/8
3rd Point Length	9 6/8	10 5/8	7/8
4th Point Length	8 1/8	9 0/8	7/8
5th Point Length	5 5/8	5 2/8	3/8
6th Point Length	—	3 0/8	3 0/8
1st Circumference	6 0/8	5 4/8	4/8
2nd Circumference	5 3/8	5 4/8	1/8
3rd Circumference	6 2/8	6 2/8	0/8
4th Circumference	5 5/8	5 6/8	1/8
Total	**91 2/8**	**96 6/8**	**7 2/8**

Main Characteristics: Heavy mass throughout rack. Multiple drop tines.

MISCELLANEOUS STATS	
No. Of Points–Right	14
No. Of Points–Left	13
Total No. Of Points	27
Length Of Abnormals	58 4/8
Greatest Spread	25 6/8
Tip To Tip Spread	8 0/8
Inside Spread	20 3/8

FINAL TALLY	
Inside Spread	20 3/8
Right Antler	91 2/8
Left Antler	96 6/8
Gross Score	**208 3/8**
Difference (−)	7 2/8
Subtotal	**201 1/8**
Abnormals (+)	58 4/8
NET NON-TYPICAL SCORE	**259 5/8**

You'd have figured that during an entire bow and gun season in an area of fairly heavy hunting pressure, someone would have put a tag on that monster in 1984. However, big bucks have a way of beating the odds, and the season ended without anyone killing the deer.

Meanwhile, another character was about to enter this drama: Duane Linscott, an evolving trophy hunter who frequently hunted just outside the refuge. He knew nothing of the discovery of the sheds, nor of the presence of this buck, but persistence and fate were to deal him a winning hand.

Duane grew up in farming, making him very comfortable in the woods. At 31, he'd farmed for several years in and around the refuge, so he knew the countryside in detail and had access to the majority of private ground in the area.

During the previous few years, Duane had taken some small and medium-sized bucks, but he'd decided to hold out for something bigger in 1985. His cousin took a nice buck with a bow early in the season, prompting Duane to make the statement, "This year, I'm going to get one big enough to mount."

As in other years, Duane spent as much time as possible in the woods during bow season. He alternated among several tree stands he used regularly, his exact choice depending upon time of season, crops, etc. But while he'd seen some huge tracks and other exciting sign, he'd observed no good bucks.

When the Nov. 16 gun opener rolled around, heavy rains that had fallen during the last few days caused Duane to change his hunting plan. The ground beneath the stand he'd initially chosen was under two to three feet of water, so he decided to try another spot just outside the refuge. A creek that passed through the heart of the refuge was completely out of its banks, and Duane hoped the high water might move some of the deer onto huntable land.

Like those in most other areas, Midwest deer — especially bucks — are prone to living in standing crops when available. The stand Duane was hunting that morning was strategically located between the refuge boundary and several acres of standing corn and unpicked soybeans mixed with sunflowers. As usual, Duane walked to his stand about 45 minutes before daylight.

It seemed the high-water theory had some merit, as by 9 a.m. Duane had seen several does and a couple of small bucks. That was more than he normally saw from this stand. As much as he hated to do it, however, he had to leave at 9 a.m. in order to get home by 10. Wife Barbara

had a special affair to attend, and Duane had to babysit their three kids. He dared not be late.

After climbing down, the hunter slowly made his way along the treeline that separated the cropland from the refuge. He hadn't gone far when he saw a decent buck walking across the picked corn stubble from the direction of the standing crops.

As Duane watched this buck "nosing around," he caught a glimpse of movement and saw a huge buck coming across the stubble. The hunter immediately began preparing for a shot, but as he did, the smaller buck let out a loud snort and headed for the brush. The big one followed, and both disappeared before a shot could be fired.

Hoping to cut them off in a smaller patch of brush before they could cross the levee, Duane sprinted through the heavy mud to a crossing. The woods were silent for several minutes; then, Duane heard a couple of grunts coming from across the water.

After peering into the 50-yard-wide strip of timber for several exasperating moments, the hunter finally picked up some antler movement. However, just as quickly as it appeared, it disappeared.

Although Duane was sure the larger buck hadn't seen him, he finally decided they were gone. He slowly eased forward another 30 yards, then again caught the movement of antler tips. Now the hunter understood where the big buck had gone. He was bedded just 30 yards away!

It was 9:15 a.m., and Duane could do nothing but wait. Fortunately, the wind was steady and perfect in direction. The mound of dirt on the levee kept the buck's body invisible to the hunter; nor could he get across the chin-deep water for a shot. And so, for a solid hour Duane hardly blinked an eye as he waited for the buck to make the next move.

At 10:15, the giant buck rose to his feet and immediately began hooking an overhanging branch with his rack. Duane twisted his body back and forth as he desperately looked for a shooting lane, but none was there. His heart pounded in his throat as the buck browsed briefly, then bedded down again!

For the next hour, Duane only could sit and ponder his dilemma. Would the wind change direction in the buck's favor? Would the two smaller bucks feeding off to his side get his wind and spook? How annoyed would Barbara be that he wasn't home?

Amazingly, at 11:15 a.m. and again at 12:15 p.m., the buck performed his "get up and lie down" act, as though he were wearing a watch. And each time the heavy brush prevented Duane from having any reasonable shot. His nerves were becoming frayed, but there was nothing else to do but keep waiting.

It was a cold day, and the hunter shivered as he continually worried about someone driving or walking too close, which surely would spook the buck. Duane realized his 6mm Ruger was a bit light for this situation, but he only could hope the buck eventually would present a clear target.

By 2 p.m., Duane had experienced cramps, shivers, nervous fits, illusions, daydreams and everything else that pos-

> *"By 2 p.m., Duane had experienced cramps, shivers, nervous fits, illusions, daydreams and everything else that possibly could result from watching the antler tips of a 260-class non-typical at 30 yards for nearly five hours without being able to shoot."*

sibly could result from watching the antler tips of a 260-class non-typical at 30 yards for nearly five hours without being able to shoot. Talk about frustration!

Finally, though, the giant rose to his feet again and began to feed toward the weary hunter. This time, the buck fed up the side of the levee and exposed most of his body. Duane put the cross hairs on a small opening and quickly fired before the body could move out of view again.

As the bullet found its mark, the surprised buck humped up, took a few steps and fell out of sight.

Duane dismissed the idea of trying to cross directly to where the buck lay, as the water there was likely over his head. He slopped through the mud for a quarter-mile to a spot he knew the water was only chest deep. Here he quickly waded across and headed back toward the buck.

The 40-degree air was cold, but Duane hardly noticed as he reached the buck. He couldn't believe his eyes, as he'd had no inkling the rack was so large and non-typical; most of his views had been through a wall of brush.

Now Duane had to figure out how to get the buck home. Once gutting chores were done, he headed for the house and dry clothes. Somehow, he managed to get changed without seeing his wife. It's safe to say that her finding that pile of wet, muddy clothes on the floor didn't contribute any points toward his popularity around the house that day — especially in light of the fact that he'd returned home and then left again!

It didn't take Duane long to get a cousin and a small johnboat to help retrieve his trophy. After much effort, they finally loaded the buck into the pickup. He took the deer to the check station and finally arrived home around 6 p.m. — slightly later than the 10 a.m. he and his wife agreed upon.

To say Barbara was a little irritated would be a fair statement, but she did soften up after seeing the buck and the commotion it was causing. "A coffee-and-donut stand would have done great around here the next morning," she lightly points out.

Tremendous mass and multiple drop tines make the Linscott buck one of Missouri's best. Photo courtesy of Dick Idol.

After the initial excitement died down, Duane took his buck to a nearby locker plant for caping and butchering. Taxidermist Anthony Eddy of Slater, Missouri, then did an excellent job of mounting the magnificent trophy.

Check-station personnel estimated the buck's age at 5 1/2 years. Presuming that was correct, the buck was 3 1/2 years old when he grew the 1983 antlers, which were found as sheds in the spring of 1984. Some might find that hard to believe, thinking a buck must be 5 1/2 or older to be a "trophy," but I'm convinced many record-class deer are only 3 1/2 or 4 1/2 years of age.

This rack's most striking features are its mass and multiple drop tines. But the antlers also have great beauty and symmetry, a rare combination in non-typicals. Duane's buck has an appearance equal to its score.

A few days after this giant was shot, Duane learned that at noon on opening day, a local boy who had permission to hunt the same area had started to drive his pickup to a point very near where Duane was sitting. Only the thought of the high water changed his mind and stopped him from probably spooking him out. Consider also the likelihood of the water being so high, or the fact that the wind direction held steady for five hours, or even the fact that the buck finally stepped into view.

These are the types of "chance" factors every hunter must depend upon occasionally, but they aren't the primary reason Duane killed this buck. He paid his dues with hard scouting, hunting every spare minute of bow season and learning where the big bucks hung out. Doing the right things in the right places as often as possible is what allows a hunter to "make his own luck," and the strange story of the Linscott buck is a perfect example.

Chapter Twenty Two

THE
ROOSEVELT LUCKEY BUCK

198 3/8 TYPICAL, NEW YORK, 1939

A Legendary Deer from a Legendary Deer State

BY DICK IDOL

New York is rarely the first place to come up in a discussion of big deer. But decades ago, it was at the forefront of interest in trophy hunting, and one of its finest trophies holds a truly special place in the pages of whitetail history.

In a simpler era, New York was home to Theodore Roosevelt and many of the other men who founded and built the Boone and Crockett Club. Through at least the first half of the 20th century the state was a hub of activity regarding the outdoors in general, and it was home to many related businesses, including sporting publications, fur traders, trapping suppliers and a variety of manufacturers of outdoor products. Not surprisingly, New York also was one of the first states to establish an organization primarily responsible for locating, measuring and documenting top deer racks.

In New York, the roots of "whitetail organization" go back to the 1930s, when Clayton Seagers, a wildlife biologist with the game department, began locating, documenting and publicizing big bucks. He undoubtedly was influenced by his good friend Grancel Fitz, one of several men responsible for developing the modern B&C scoring

Photo by Charles Alsheimer:

ROOSEVELT LUCKEY, NEW YORK, 1939

	Right Antler	Left Antler	Difference
Main Beam Length	29 5/8	29 4/8	1/8
1st Point Length	3 0/8	3 0/8	0/8
2nd Point Length	10 4/8	11 6/8	1 2/8
3rd Point Length	13 0/8	14 1/8	1 1/8
4th Point Length	11 1/8	12 3/8	1 2/8
5th Point Length	7 1/8	5 7/8	1 2/8
1st Circumference	4 6/8	4 6/8	0/8
2nd Circumference	4 6/8	4 6/8	0/8
3rd Circumference	6 5/8	6 3/8	2/8
4th Circumference	6 3/8	5 4/8	7/8
Total	**96 7/8**	**98 0/8**	**6 1/8**

Main Characteristics: Exceptional beams that almost overlap. 6 tines of 10 4/8" or longer. Former B&C world record.

MISCELLANEOUS STATS

No. Of Points–Right	6
No. Of Points–Left	8
Total No. Of Points	14
Length Of Abnormals	8 4/8
Greatest Spread	21 0/8
Tip To Tip Spread	4 2/8
Inside Spread	18 1/8

FINAL TALLY

Inside Spread	18 1/8
Right Antler	96 7/8
Left Antler	98 0/8
Gross Score	**213 0/8**
Difference (–)	6 1/8
Subtotal	**206 7/8**
Abnormals (–)	8 4/8
NET TYPICAL SCORE	**198 3/8**

system. Grancel and Clayton lived in the same part of the state and shared a passionate interest in trophy animals.

Clayton began his documentation of New York's big deer with a simple pamphlet that accompanied the big-game license in 1941. Based on strong and positive response to that, he followed up with the release of the "Ten Best Heads" of New York, published in various issues of the game department's Conservationist magazine over the next

20-plus years. Once Clayton retired, though, a full nine years passed before anyone else emerged to take on such a chore.

Fortunately, along came Bob Estes, an official B&C measurer from Caledonia and an avid fan of trophy whitetails. Bob once again began publicizing New York's finest bucks. He held scoring seminars, put together trophy displays for county fairs and continued to collect information on many of the state's biggest deer.

It wasn't until 1972, however, that Bob's dream of a New York State Big Buck Club became a reality. The club was the result of the hard work of Bob, newspaper writer John Brown, Herb Daig and Wayne Trimm of the Department of Environmental Conservation and various other interested parties across the state. The club is still going strong today, and even though Bob stepped down as president after serving in that capacity for the first 15 years, at this writing he continues to be a guiding light and staunch supporter.

Much of the identity of the New York State Big Buck Club is married to its star attraction, the Luckey buck, and the sheds from that deer. And rightly so. How could any club whose primary objective is to locate, score and honor the state's biggest bucks not place on a pedestal a former world-record typical that still ranks among the greatest ever? This buck has truly become a unifying symbol for all who love New York's trophy whitetails.

The story would seem to begin with Roosevelt Luckey, a garage owner and Ford dealer in Hume, New York. He was, in fact, a very good deer hunter; he'd shot his first buck in 1926 and over the years had taken several more, including a big 8-pointer that netted 132 B&C points. Raised in Allegany County, about 50 miles southeast of Buffalo in the western part of the state, he annually trekked to the distant Adirondack Mountains to pursue whitetails.

"At the time Roosevelt killed his buck, the current B&C system of scoring hadn't yet been created. But in 1952, just two years after the system was implemented, Grancel Fitz officially measured the rack at 198 3/8 net typical points. It soon thereafter was declared North America's new No. 1 typical."

The reason for doing so was simple: Roosevelt's home county of Allegany hadn't had an open deer season since the turn of the century. But that all was set to change in 1939, when the 38-year-old hunter would get to hunt the woods around home for the first time in his life. After four decades of closure, deer hunting would be allowed again that fall.

Years later, Roosevelt would pass along his version of that season's events to Bob, who fortunately recorded the tale for posterity. The hunter himself passed away in 1991 after a long life, but he left with us the following description of his fateful hunt:

"It was the year November 1939 that the deer season was opened for the first time in Allegany County. On the second day of the season, which was cool but a very nice day for hunting, five men — my brother Alden Luckey, Gerald Thomas, Richard Gayford and another friend and myself — struck out to try their luck. In the afternoon, we had put on two drives, and the other men had seen and shot at the big buck. Prior to this, no one was known to have seen the big deer. His home was in a woods about seven miles long and one mile wide, surrounded by farmland in Hume, New York.

"On a third drive I was on watch, taking what was left and feeling like there was no chance for a deer to come by, as I had hunted for many years," Roosevelt recalled. "I stood in a bunch of thorn apples and caught a glimpse of a deer coming my way. There was an opening he would go through. The big buck was taking 20-foot leaps. My first impression was that the deer had caught some brush on his antlers. I took a fast shot at the heart and lung area. When my 12-gauge automatic shotgun reported and sent the rifled slug 100 yards, the big buck's front legs sprawled in the center of the clearing. The next second, he collected himself and was out of sight.

"I knew he was hit, and we found blood and tracked the deer for what seemed to be a half-mile," the hunter continued. "At 4:30 p.m. we found the buck, with a massive set of antlers! He had been shot through the heart, and the bullet had blown it completely apart.

"The deer was brought and hung behind my house in Hume. The hometown buzzed with excitement that night, and anyone interested in hunting came to see the big deer. It weighed 195 pounds dressed out. I knew right away I would have the deer head mounted," the hunter told Bob.

At the time Roosevelt killed his buck, the current B&C system of scoring hadn't yet been created. But in 1952, just two years after the system was implemented, Grancel Fitz officially measured the rack at 198 3/8 net typical points. It soon thereafter was declared North America's new No. 1 typical. It remained in that lofty spot until 1964, when John Breen's great Minnesota buck (featured in *Legendary Whitetails*) was given a final score of 202 0/8, displacing the Luckey buck as the world record. Even then,

> *"Joe reached down to pick up a branch to chuck at the horse, for a little 'friendly persuasion.' But to Joe's amazement, the 'branch' was actually a deer antler — and a big one at that!"*

Roosevelt's deer remained at No. 2 until the 206 1/8-inch James Jordan buck was officially measured as yet another world record a few years later. The B&C record book still lists the Luckey buck as New York's No. 1 typical.

In 1976, new attention was focused on the buck when Ray Minnick and Grant Shattuck uncovered a set of sheds from the same deer. When the story finally came to light, it turned out that a 13-year-old farm boy named Joe Merwin had picked them up in April 1938. Joe had been sent to the pasture to bring in the horses and cows. As he was herding them, a horse ran some of the cows away from the gate. Joe reached down to pick up a branch to chuck at the horse, for a little "friendly persuasion." But to Joe's amazement, the "branch" was actually a deer antler — and a big one at that!

Fortunately, Joe realized that the other antler might be lying nearby, and he eventually found it perhaps 50 yards from where the first one lay. He took the antlers home, drilled a hole between the burr and brow tine of each and then mounted them on a board and hung them in a barn, where they remained until 1976. It's a miracle they weren't chewed up by rodents or simply lost in that span of nearly four decades.

When the sheds were first scrutinized, many refused to believe they'd come from the Luckey buck. But it turned out that they'd been found just a half-mile from where Roosevelt had killed his deer two autumns later. And besides, the racks were nearly mirror images of each other, right down to the bumps on the beading. Finally, everyone was convinced that the sheds had indeed come from the Luckey buck.

In the early 1950s, the hunter donated his mounted buck to the Department of Environmental Conservation, which then had a policy of making it available to exhibit at local shows and fairs. The head was shown many times over the years. Then, in 1978, Bob Estes put together a Big Buck Club display of trophies for the Erie County Fair in western New York. The actual Luckey mount was unavailable for display at the time, but Bob was able to include in the exhibit the matched sheds, which had been found in the barn only a couple of years earlier.

When Bob went to pick up the trophies at the end of the fair, he was shocked to discover that the sheds, as well as a mount of a solid-white buck, were missing! Bob searched for the missing antlers relentlessly for many years, but nothing materialized.

Then, in March 1994, an anonymous phone call came in to the game department. The caller said that "a big pair of deer horns" was tied to a particular stop-sign post in a snow bank, and if the game warden would go there and check it out, he'd like what he'd find. An officer was dispatched to the location, where he

"With a net score of 198 3/8, the Luckey buck certainly is one of the most outstanding typicals ever. But his sheds are even more intriguing — because the year he grew them, he would have scored even better!"

immediately discovered Joe Merwin's missing sheds of the Luckey buck! An investigation revealed that a security guard at the show had swiped them, and many years after the fact, his conscience finally had forced him to turn them in.

Unfortunately, Joe had passed away in 1993, so he went to his grave not knowing the antlers ever would be recovered. Joe's family now has donated the sheds to the wildlife department, so the buck's actual rack and sheds once again will be together. (As of this writing, the stolen white deer mount remains missing.)

With a net score of 198 3/8, the Luckey buck certainly is one of the most outstanding typicals ever. But his sheds are even more intriguing — because the year he grew them, he would have scored even better! The sheds show that in 1937, the deer had a basic 7x7 typical frame with only one abnormal point. Given the same inside spread the deer had when he was killed, the sheds would have netted 205 6/8! And that's making no allowance for the nearly 40 years of shrinkage that affected the sheds before a measuring tape ever was put to them.

No matter how you analyze the Luckey buck, the bottom line is that he was one of the greatest ever. A bigger New York typical someday might come along, but even if he beats this deer's mark, he isn't likely to top his story!

Chapter Twenty Three

THE JERRY MARTIN BUCK

183 4/8 TYPICAL, KANSAS, 1999

A Switch of the Wind Reaps a World-Class Whitetail

BY BRENDA VALENTINE

Jerry Martin of Springfield, Missouri, is fully aware that to kill big deer, you must hunt where they live. As an employee of Bass Pro Shops, which owns one of the world's major collections of high-scoring whitetail racks, Jerry knows which areas consistently produce monsters and which ones don't. Because many of the bucks in the Bass Pro collection are from Kansas, in 1999 Jerry applied for a rifle tag there. As it turned out, he beat tough odds and drew a permit for the southern part of the state. Now all it would take to complete his dream was the right guide... and, of course, the right deer. Enter Larry Konrade, a local guide working in conjunction with George Taulman's U.S. Outfitters.

In June, Larry noticed five hefty bucks hanging together, and glassing them in a nearby alfalfa field became an afternoon ritual. All of the bucks were trophies, but one wide, massive typical was particularly impressive.

The monster buck's core area was roughly a square mile of thick tamarack brush edged by the alfalfa. A dry creekbed with crooked cottonwood trees curved through

JERRY MARTIN, KANSAS, 1999

	Right Antler	Left Antler	Difference
Main Beam Length	27 2/8	29 0/8	1 6/8
1st Point Length	10 1/8	6 4/8	3 5/8
2nd Point Length	10 7/8	11 5/8	6/8
3rd Point Length	10 1/8	10 0/8	1/8
4th Point Length	4 7/8	7 0/8	2 1/8
5th Point Length	—	—	—
1st Circumference	5 4/8	5 3/8	1/8
2nd Circumference	5 2/8	5 1/8	1/8
3rd Circumference	6 6/8	6 2/8	4/8
4th Circumference	5 0/8	5 7/8	7/8
Total	**85 6/8**	**86 6/8**	**10 0/8**

Main Characteristics: Super mass and spread give the rack great eye appeal. 5 tines of 10" or more.

MISCELLANEOUS STATS

No. Of Points–Right	6
No. Of Points–Left	6
Total No. Of Points	12
Length Of Abnormals	4 1/8
Greatest Spread	27 0/8
Tip To Tip Spread	22 7/8
Inside Spread	25 1/8

FINAL TALLY

Inside Spread	25 1/8
Right Antler	85 6/8
Left Antler	86 6/8
Gross Score	197 5/8
Difference (–)	10 0/8
Subtotal	187 5/8
Abnormals (–)	4 1/8
NET TYPICAL SCORE	183 4/8

the tamarack, forming a virtual fortress for the buck. With food, water, cover and many does close at hand, there was no reason for him to travel far or expose himself in daylight. He certainly wouldn't be a pushover.

On Nov. 30, George Taulman met Jerry and cameraman Ray Moulton at the airport to transport them and their gear to Larry's camp. En route, George filled Jerry in on the buck and his habits, as well as the lay of the land. Although a conflicting schedule would give Jerry only two days to hunt the super buck, he opted to go after the monster, rather than simply try to take a respectable deer on camera for Bass Pro Shops' Outdoor World television show.

The next morning found Jerry and three other hunters posted in various spots, but while some young bucks were seen, no big ones appeared. For the afternoon hunt, Jerry and Ray made a ground blind. They weaved prairie grass through strands of barbed wire in a corner of the alfalfa field, then set up behind the thatch, hoping for a glimpse of the big guy.

Amazingly, the hunter and his cameraman were rewarded with not just a glimpse but a long, agonizing look. Sadly, though, when the buck came out, it was eight minutes past the end of legal shooting hours!

Long before dawn the next day, Larry and George took the four rifle hunters to the edge of the bedding area. They theorized that all of the deer would still be feeding in the field, making one of the travel routes a productive ambush site. But no one saw the giant that morning.

Around midday, the breeze began to blow from the southeast, which was unusual. This new wind direction might let Jerry set up behind the staging area and catch the buck en route from his bedding spot during legal hours. It was a long shot, but this was the 11th hour. The fat lady was humming.

Jerry and Ray meticulously scrubbed down, put on their scent-absorbing suits and in early afternoon began creeping up the dry creekbed. Instinct and experience guided Jerry to "the place" — a widening of the creekbed with a short range of view under the canopy of cottonwoods. He told his companion to set the camera low and lie on his belly in the rocks. Jerry followed suit, getting into the prone position with his Remington .280 Mountain Rifle.

Hours passed; a few does meandered past on their way to the alfalfa. But minutes

Jerry Martin took his Kansas trophy at the last minute. Photo courtesy of Brenda Valentine.

later, a truck driven into the field by a guy checking gauges on an oil well sent the deer bounding back to safety.

As dusk neared, one by one the does eased back into the field. However, with just 10 minutes of legal light left, there was still no giant. Doubts grew, and the rocks got harder by the second.

Suddenly, Jerry caught movement. It looked to be a tree swaying — but it wasn't swaying, it was marching! Although there was no body visible, the hunter recognized the moving mass of heavy branches as a huge whitetail rack!

The buck was close and coming closer, but still antler was all Jerry could see. Softly, the hunter whispered into the wireless microphone linking him to Ray's earphones: "It's him… start the camera… don't move a muscle… he's right on top of us."

The deer was walking down a shallow wash that funneled into the creek bed right below the men. He was so close that peeping outside the scope was the only way to follow his progress.

The top of the deer's head appeared, then more and more of the body until the chest came into view. In an instant, Jerry aimed and fired. The animal fell in his tracks — just 10 yards from the end of the gun barrel!

Despite heavy deductions, the buck's wide, massive rack nets 183 4/8 points, making it one of the best basic 10-pointers ever taken in Kansas. Yeah, that was worth drawing a tag for!

Chapter Twenty Four

THE RONALD MARTIN BUCK

249 7/8 NON-TYPICAL, NEW BRUNSWICK, 1946

The Mile-Wide Monster from Canada

BY JIM SHOCKEY

I t's doubtful that any one of the drivers swerving to miss the mounted deer head had any idea what they were looking at. The year was 1984, and though it hadn't been planned that way, the buck was making his first public appearance ever — in the middle of a highway!

Before we look at the bizarre events of that day, let's head back another 38 years, to 1946. A lone hunter was making his way through the New Brunswick wilderness, near the headwaters of the New River in Kings County. As he slipped along, he noticed a large animal moving slowly along an adjacent ridge. When the beast lifted its head at a range of 50 yards, the man knew he was looking at something strange. One shot from the hunter's .30/06 ended their brief encounter.

The man pulling the trigger was Ronald Martin, a woodsman without equal in that area and in that age. Ronald's gone now, and with him went many details of this story; however, local legend has it that he mistook this whitetail for a woodland caribou. If so, he could hardly be blamed — the rack had an outside spread of 37 inches, with massive growth out toward the end of each main beam!

Photo courtesy of Bass Pro Shops.

RONALD MARTIN, NEW BRUNSWICK, 1946

	Right Antler	Left Antler	Difference
Main Beam Length	26 5/8	25 6/8	7/8
1st Point Length	5 2/8	5 0/8	2/8
2nd Point Length	10 3/8	8 2/8	2 1/8
3rd Point Length	9 1/8	8 4/8	5/8
4th Point Length	3 1/8	3 7/8	6/8
5th Point Length	—	—	—
1st Circumference	4 1/8	4 2/8	1/8
2nd Circumference	4 3/8	4 5/8	2/8
3rd Circumference	8 6/8	8 1/8	5/8
4th Circumference	6 2/8	7 1/8	7/8
Total	**78 0/8**	**75 4/8**	**6 4/8**

Main Characteristics: Outside spread of 37", one of the widest on record. 22 points on left antler alone.

MISCELLANEOUS STATS

No. Of Points–Right	12
No. Of Points–Left	22
Total No. Of Points	34
Length Of Abnormals	79 5/8
Greatest Spread	37 0/8
Tip To Tip Spread	23 1/8
Inside Spread	23 2/8

FINAL TALLY

Inside Spread	23 2/8
Right Antler	78 0/8
Left Antler	75 4/8
Gross Score	**176 6/8**
Difference (–)	6 4/8
Subtotal	170 2/8
Abnormals (+)	79 5/8
NET NON-TYPICAL SCORE	**249 7/8**

"Now, I had shot a lot of deer in my day, but this one, well, it was different," Ronald said years later. "I had never in my life seen anything like it. I thought there was something wrong with the deer, having a rack like that. I checked the meat; it seemed all right, so I dressed the deer out and left the rack there in the woods."

Left the rack there in the woods? Yes. Ronald, like nearly all other hunters of that era, was after meat. Antlers were something to talk about, but nothing to waste energy on by dragging home.

Fortunately, though Ronald had no intentions of keeping the rack, he knew it was special, so he hung the skull in a tree. Weeks later the hunter happened to pass the spot again, and apparently only because he was on his way home, this time he took the antlers with him.

But even then, Ronald afforded the deer little more than passing thought. The rack ended up hanging on the side of the garage. And it was there it might have stayed permanently, had not interested parties begun to offer money for it. In the beginning, most of the offers were around $5 cash or a case of beer. Then they started climbing. When one looker offered Ronald $50 the hunter declined politely; however, he decided such a valuable object should be better preserved, so he moved it to his attic. There the rack stayed for the next 3 1/2 decades, slowly forgotten by antler aficionados.

Ronald Martin and his New Brunswick trophy, taken with his .30-06 Winchester Model '54. Photo courtesy of George Chase & Billy Hanson.

Enter George Chase of Grand Bay: outfitter, outdoorsman and, most importantly, whitetail devotee. The early 1980s had seen the beginning of trophy awareness in New Brunswick, and George was among the leaders in that movement.

"I was working in my gun shop one day when Mr. Martin walked in," George explains. "He said he had a buck for me to score, but I was busy, so I tried to get him to leave it." But Ronald wouldn't leave the rack at the shop, so George and his son, Paul, went out to the hunter's car for a look.

"The rack was in his trunk, with a garbage bag over each side," George remembers. "When I looked at it, I figured there were two or three racks in the bags, and I wasn't really all that interested in scoring them." But when Paul pulled off one of the garbage bags, he turned to his father and exclaimed that it was in fact only covering half of one rack!

"When I scored the buck, I'm sure it gave Ronald 10 extra years," George says. Ronald didn't want to sell the rack, but his wife had said she would sell it for $100. "I told him that it was worth something more than that and asked if Paul could mount the buck."

Ronald agreed, and he also told George he could show the buck at big-buck contests across the province. "There were four or five shows to attend in 1984, and I assured Ronald his buck would win every category it could be entered in," George recalls.

The day before the first show, George and Paul loaded the buck into the back of their open pickup truck and took off.

"I don't like to dawdle when I drive, so I was headed down the highway as usual when one of those big vans passed in the opposite direction," George relates. "Next thing I knew, there was no rack in the back of my truck!"

And that's the story of how the mount came to be lying face up on the centerline of a highway. Beyond belief, the rack was 100 percent intact; the cardboard box around the head had absorbed all of the punishment, and the mount had ended up sliding along the asphalt on the thick wooden plaque Paul had attached to the back.

As of this writing, the Martin buck remains the No. 1 non-typical in New Brunswick, at 249 7/8 net points. You know, he wouldn't have been a bad caribou!

Chapter Twenty Five

THE NEIL MORIN BUCK

279 6/8 NON-TYPICAL, ALBERTA, 1991

The Rack as Big as a Willow Bush

BY TODD LOEWEN

When you're a teenager, the best way to spend Saturday morning is always a serious question to ponder. But on Friday, Sept. 15, 1991, Neil Morin found it especially difficult to decide. Should the 17-year-old central Alberta farmboy travel with his parents to the city, or instead pursue the biggest whitetail he'd ever seen?

Earlier that fall, Neil had spotted a huge buck while doing some field work. However, Neil's parents were going to the nearest city on the 16th, so if he went with them, he'd miss opening morning.

As it turned out, the boy's decision to join his parents on their trip wasn't as tough as you might assume. The hunting pressure in this area was hardly noticeable around the opener; plus, gun season would run for another 2 1/2 months. In fact, the best part of it likely would be much later, during the rut. So, Neil headed to the city with his parents.

Photo by Jamie Boardman.

Main Characteristics: Stunning brow tines with 5" circumferences. Basic 5 x 4 typical frame grosses 189 2/8".

NEIL MORIN, ALBERTA, 1991

	Right Antler	Left Antler	Difference
Main Beam Length	27 6/8	26 0/8	1 6/8
1st Point Length	13 3/8	14 2/8	7/8
2nd Point Length	12 2/8	12 0/8	2/8
3rd Point Length	9 0/8	10 7/8	1 7/8
4th Point Length	1 4/8	—	1 4/8
5th Point Length	—	—	—
1st Circumference	6 0/8	6 0/8	0/8
2nd Circumference	5 1/8	4 7/8	2/8
3rd Circumference	5 7/8	5 3/8	4/8
4th Circumference	4 0/8	3 2/8	6/8
Total	**84 7/8**	**82 5/8**	**7 6/8**

MISCELLANEOUS STATS	
No. Of Points–Right	13
No. Of Points–Left	14
Total No. Of Points	27
Length Of Abnormals	98 2/8
Greatest Spread	27 2/8
Tip To Tip Spread	18 4/8
Inside Spread	21 6/8

FINAL TALLY	
Inside Spread	21 6/8
Right Antler	84 7/8
Left Antler	82 5/8
Gross Score	**189 2/8**
Difference (–)	7 6/8
Subtotal	181 4/8
Abnormals (+)	98 2/8
NET NON-TYPICAL SCORE	**279 6/8**

While on his way home from the city, the boy's mind was on the big buck. Thus, Neil was particularly alert as the family's vehicle neared the place where he'd seen the deer. Sure enough, moments later the boy spotted a deer feeding far out in the standing wheat. It was probably a half-mile away, but Neil felt there was a strong possibility it was the buck he'd seen.

Neil was back to the spot shortly thereafter, carrying his rifle, but to his surprise, the deer wasn't in sight. As the boy scanned the field, he saw only a small willow bush out in the wheat.

Now, willows aren't uncommon in this part of Canada, but Neil knew the area well, and this one just didn't fit in. And so, the boy stalked this misplaced "bush." He crouched low and moved slowly through the standing wheat, which provided excellent cover. The closer Neil got to the "bush," the more it appeared that his suspicions were correct.

That "willow" was looking more and more like antlers! Neil's heart was beating quickly with excitement. Covering ground in a low crouch was strenuous and also taking its toll on him. His hands were trembling.

When Neil was only 100 yards from the buck, the huge animal stood up. Neil immediately dropped fully to the ground. He was far too shaky to risk an offhanded shot at this distance, and he knew it. He held his position and waited. Something was bothering the deer, but Neil was unsure of what it was.

The hunter waited for what seemed an eternity as the buck lifted his head high and tested the wind. The non-typical looked around in all directions… and then lay down again!

"The boy felt fully prepared, but what happened next caught him by complete surprise. Instead of standing up, as he'd done before, the buck exploded from his bed at a dead run."

Neil couldn't believe his luck; he took a couple of deep breaths and started the stalk again. This time, he crept to within an incredible 30 yards from the bedded buck! At this point, the young hunter felt confident that the buck was his. All he had to do was wait for the deer to move. When the giant stood up, the hunt would be over.

The boy felt fully prepared, but what happened next caught him by complete surprise. Instead of standing up, as he'd done before, the buck exploded from his bed at a dead run.

The hunter's gun immediately was up and following the deer. The first shot brought no reaction from the deer, but the second shot put him down.

Neil carefully approached the deer, which had covered 50 yards in those few seconds and had fallen stretched out in an area of stubble. Part of one antler had been buried in the dirt by the force of the fall. As the hunter pulled up the head and marveled at the great antlers, he knew the buck was one that would attract attention.

The following day, Neil contacted me at my taxidermy studio in nearby Valleyview. He described his deer as having 27 points and said it seemed as big as any he'd ever seen in a magazine. Sure enough, when the young hunter showed up that evening and brought the buck out of the back of his van, I nearly fell to the ground. The rack was enormous! I quickly got the antlers into good light and started measuring.

Two aspects of this rack set it far apart from others I've seen. One of them is the drop tines — five in all. Two are huge knobs with velvet still on them. At the largest point, one is 5 inches in circumference and the other 6! The other feature that jumps out at you is the brow tines. They're 13 3/8 and 14 2/8 inches in length, making them the longest points on the rack. And their smallest circumferences are 5 inches!

The first official scoring of this massive rack turned out a score of 278 7/8 non-typical Boone and Crockett points. That was easily high enough to earn Neil's deer an invitation to the 21st Big Game Awards, held by B&C in Milwaukee, Wisconsin, in June 1992. There, the panel of measurers raised the final score to 279 6/8 points.

This made him the official Canadian record, nudging out the 277 5/8-point monster Doug Klinger shot in Alberta in 1976. It also made the Morin buck a new No. 5 in B&C, and No. 3 ever taken by a hunter: a true giant for the ages!

Chapter Twenty Six

THE KEVIN NAUGLE BUCK

197 1/8 TYPICAL, ILLINOIS, 1988

Too Many Points to be the World Record

BY ERNEST D. RICHARDSON

Back in the late 1980s, western Illinois was one of those trophy hotspots few hunters other than local folks knew about. One of the bucks that put it on the map was the first deer ever to wear Kevin Naugle's tag — and what a buck it was.

Going into the 1988 season, Kevin never had been deer hunting. However, that year several close friends coaxed him into giving it a try, so he applied for and received a full-season shotgun permit for Macoupin County.

Kevin's initiation into whitetail hunting was on Friday, Nov. 18, opening day of the first slug season. Friend Russell Rhoads had on several occasions seen a monster buck in his hunting area, and Kevin chose to hunt a ground blind close to where Russell twice had spotted the deer.

As the day dawned, Kevin sat in his chosen position with high hopes. This was a new adventure for him, and excitement filled his veins. For several hours he sat quietly as he watched the woods rodents scurrying about in search of tidbits on the forest floor. Then, he heard something moving on the deer trail he was watching.

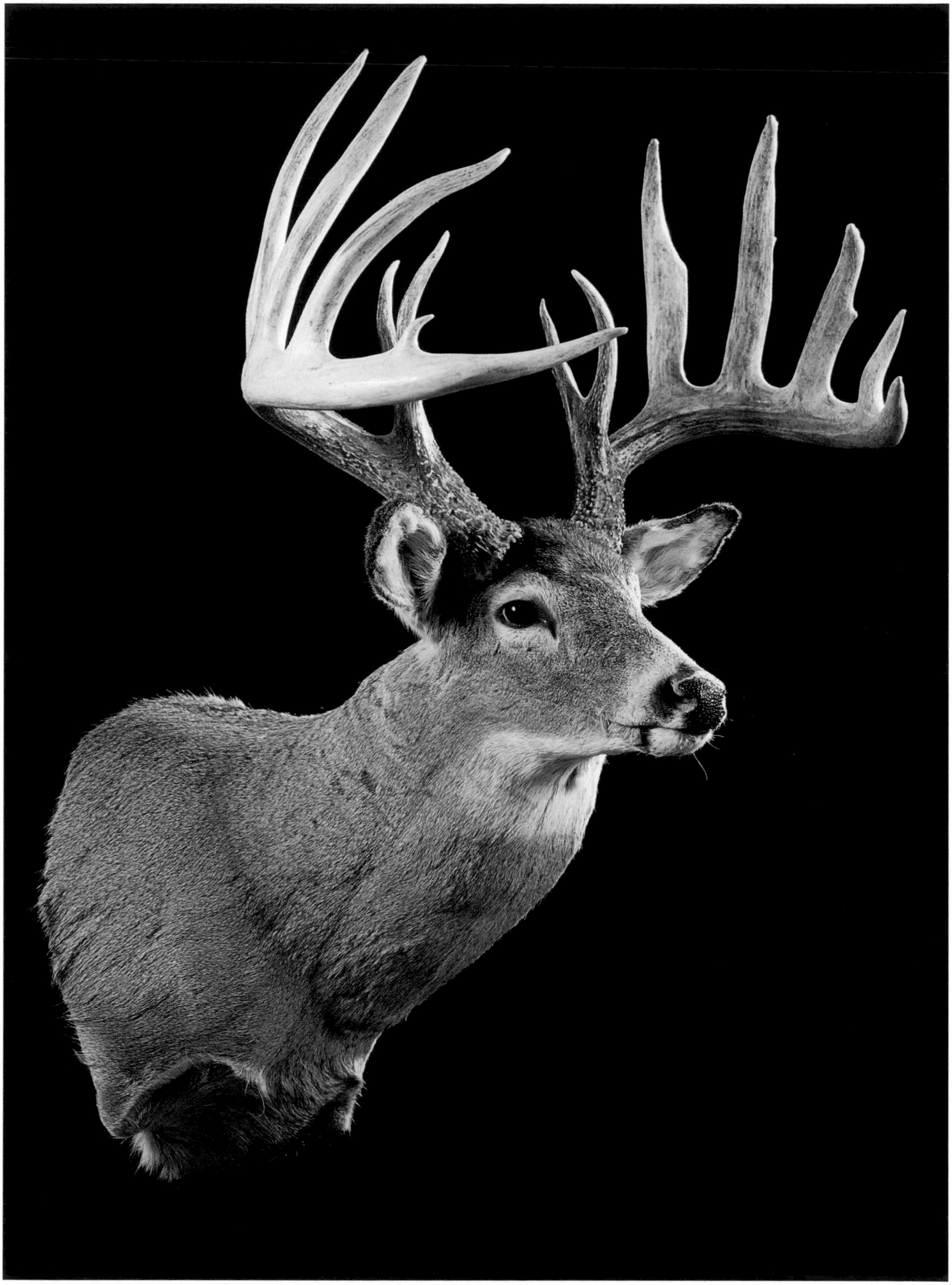

Photo courtesy of Bass Pro Shops.

KEVIN NAUGLE, ILLINOIS, 1988

	Right Antler	Left Antler	Difference
Main Beam Length	31 0/8	29 7/8	1 1/8
1st Point Length	8 0/8	7 4/8	4/8
2nd Point Length	12 7/8	11 4/8	1 3/8
3rd Point Length	11 7/8	12 6/8	7/8
4th Point Length	10 1/8	10 2/8	1/8
5th Point Length	1 6/8	4 4/8	2 6/8
1st Circumference	6 1/8	6 5/8	4/8
2nd Circumference	5 2/8	5 2/8	0/8
3rd Circumference	6 0/8	5 3/8	5/8
4th Circumference	5 0/8	5 2/8	2/8
Total	**98 0/8**	**98 7/8**	**8 1/8**

Main Characteristics: Classic 6x6 with ultra-long beams and 6 tines of 10 1/8" or longer. Double brow tines cost it the world record.

MISCELLANEOUS STATS	
No. Of Points–Right	7
No. Of Points–Left	7
Total No. Of Points	14
Length Of Abnormals	12 7/8
Greatest Spread	23 7/8
Tip To Tip Spread	11 0/8
Inside Spread	21 2/8

FINAL TALLY	
Inside Spread	21 2/8
Right Antler	98 0/8
Left Antler	98 7/8
Gross Score	**218 1/8**
Difference (–)	8 1/8
Subtotal	**210 0/8**
Abnormals (–)	12 7/8
NET TYPICAL SCORE	**197 1/8**

Kevin turned to the sound and saw four fat does coming up the trail, about 30 yards from the stand. The young hunter was shaking as he took his gun off safety to attempt his first-ever shot at a whitetail. But though Kevin shot twice as the does quickly departed down the trail, neither shot cut a hair.

The excitement he felt during the encounter had hooked him on big-game hunting, though. He spent all of his available time during the next two days of the first gun season trying to get a deer, but while he did see several more, none offered a good, clean shot. Kevin wasn't at all discouraged, however. He'd never hunted deer before, but he came from a long line of hunters, and he had hunted small game in Illinois for 10 years. He'd try again during the second gun season a couple of weeks later.

But before that happened, Kevin decided, he needed to improve his shooting. Ditching the shotgun and generic ammo he'd used in the first season, the hunter and his uncle, Terry Goodman, bought Winchester slug shells, and they practiced with them for about 1 1/2 hours. Kevin now had switched to a 20-gauge Remington 870 pump shotgun, and its performance was very good. He was now grouping shots well at up to 90 yards.

Kevin scouted the area between slug seasons and saw where a buck had recently rubbed a pine measuring almost 8 inches in diameter. Being an observant outdoorsman, Kevin knew by this that a big buck was around. This rub was close to his friend Gary's tree stand, which Kevin had been given permission to hunt.

Before daylight on Dec. 9, Kevin returned to the area to again try his luck. He and Terry were on their stands long before the deer began to move along the trails. Kevin was seated in Gary's bow stand as he awaited dawn.

After a long, fruitless vigil, at 8 a.m. he saw four does on the trail only about 30 yards away. Kevin's heart began to pound — he wanted to kill a deer! But, because the does were in thick brush, he decided to pass up the possible shots. He hoped a better shot would present itself later. This turned out to be one of the best decisions in Kevin's young life. Little did he know what was soon to come.

Terry had hunted Gary's stand in the past, and he'd always vacated it by 9 a.m. So, Kevin had no idea what to expect in terms of deer movement in late morning — especially during cold, unpredictable December. As the clock ticked on, he sat quietly in the elevated stand. The freezing cold tore at his body. He was uncomfortable, but he still sat with high hopes.

Kevin grew restless and looked at his watch. It was 10:30 a.m., and he was just about to call it a morning. Then, he heard a disturbance on the trail behind his stand. He turned and peered down the trail and saw what he at first thought to be five big does coming straight up the deer trail. The deer in the lead was bigger and darker than the rest, and walking with a longer stride. However, Kevin thought it was just a large doe, because all he could see on its head was large, white ears. Then, the deer looked back, and Kevin noticed the treelike antlers on the lead deer's head. It was a buck… and what a rack!

How could I have mistaken this buck for a doe? Kevin thought as he watched the giant whitetail tilt his huge rack to view his lady friends. The rack had blended in so well with the dead tree limbs above him, due to the great mass and many tines, that Kevin at first had not realized what he was seeing!

Now Kevin's hands began to shake; this mammoth rack was breathtaking! The huge-racked monster swung his rack forward, away from the does that followed him, and started along the trail toward Kevin. His massive rack swayed from side to side as he continued along the trail.

> *"The deer in the lead was bigger and darker than the rest, and walking with a longer stride. However, Kevin thought it was just a large doe, because all he could see on its head was large, white ears. Then, the deer looked back, and Kevin noticed the treelike antlers. It was a buck… and what a rack!"*

It looks like a tree, Kevin thought to himself as the big boy walked along. Kevin was now a living heartbeat and a bundle of nerves as he raised his 870 pump and prepared to make the shot of a lifetime. The buck was only 20 yards distant and was walking toward Kevin with each giant step!

I don't see how he can hold his head up! the hunter thought as he clicked the 20-gauge Remington off safety. This was it, the moment of truth! As the deer walked past at less than 20 yards, Kevin took careful aim the best he could with his shaking hands and fired.

After faltering for a second, the deer quickly regained his composure and took off running along the ice-covered creek near Kevin's stand. The giant crashed through the ice in his attempt to get away from whatever had stung his hide, but as he attempted to get up the opposite bank, the well-placed shot took its toll.

As the deer suddenly went limp and slid back into the edge of the water, Kevin breathed a sigh of relief. He knew he'd just killed the largest buck he'd ever seen. While Kevin had never hunted deer, he was an avid outdoorsman and had seen his share of big bucks in the woods. He knew this one was special!

Kevin lowered his shotgun from the stand and then climbed down on wobbly legs. After stretching and flexing his legs for a few minutes, he picked up his shotgun and walked the 60 yards to the place where his prize deer lay dead on the opposite bank. Even from across the creek, the hunter could see why the buck had died so quickly — the shot had gone through the lower part of the neck and down into the lung and heart area. It had been a beautiful shot on a beautiful buck.

Unfortunately, Kevin couldn't wrap his meat hooks around the buck's antlers just yet. The hunter was on one side of the creek and the buck was on the other. The buck lay dead at the water's edge, but the creek was wide and deep, and it was a very cold day. Kevin knew better than to try to wade or swim to his buck. He was a good outdoorsman, but no Eskimo. And so he just stood there, admiring his prize from afar, as Terry approached. After a few handshakes and congratulations, Terry and Kevin decided that Kevin should drive home and get his johnboat to retrieve the buck. Terry would stay and guard the deer until he returned. As Kevin left the scene, Terry sat down on a log to rest and admire the great buck.

Kevin was pulling out of his yard with his johnboat in tow as his brother Brian and friend Daren Behme pulled in. "Hey, Kevin, you can't hunt deer with a johnboat," joked Brian.

"Yes I can!" Kevin replied. "We need some help. Jump in and come along with me and I'll show you guys what a real deer looks like!"

Brian and Daren gasped when they saw what Kevin had killed. They soon had the deer in the boat and brought him across the icy creek. Soon they had both the buck and the boat safely loaded and were heading for the check station. They were all very excited when they finally pulled the boat and antlered cargo into Kevin's yard.

There was hardly anyone at the check station to admire the buck. It was a cold day, and most other deer hunters in the area had filled their tags during the first November season or had given up altogether.

Despite being quite run down from the rut, the buck field-dressed 204 pounds. In October or early November, this buck would have surely weighed a bit more.

Kevin told his father he didn't know if he ever wanted to kill another world-class buck. "All I did for three days after that hunt was to answer the door or the phone constantly," he explains. At least 125 people came to his home to see the trophy. "Deer hunters are really appreciative individuals," Kevin says. "In three days' time, they almost shook my hand off! I met a lot of folks during this adventure, and they all told me that I had killed the buck of a lifetime!"

Kevin took his buck to taxidermist "Tank" Jenkins, where I unofficially scored the rack at 197 net typical Boone and Crockett points. After the 60-day drying period, the official score came in at 197 1/8, placing the buck firmly among the world's elite typicals. In fact, at the time, he was the biggest typical taken in Illinois since Mel Johnson's world record by bow, which had been killed in Peoria

Kevin Naugle, who went on to become a policeman after taking this great buck, holds up a replica of the trophy. Bass Pro Shops now has the original mount on display. Photo by Gordon Whittington.

County a full 23 years earlier.

But neither that standing nor the net score does justice to Kevin's deer. You see, had the buck knocked off just one of his two abnormal points — one on each brow tine — he'd have netted around 203 typical.

Had he knocked off both he'd have netted 210, making him the unquestioned world record! At that time, the No. 1 typical in B&C was James Jordan's 206 1/8-inch buck from Danbury, Wisconsin, which had been shot in 1914.

What could a hunter possibly do for an encore after taking one of the world's top bucks in his first season? Kevin admits that only after he'd spent many more years in a deer stand did he come to realize just how great a buck he'd shot on that cold day in 1988.

Suffice it to say no more world-class typicals have worn his tag in the years since. But even if he never shoots another deer to match that first one, he'll still have one more monster to his credit than most other hunters ever will.

Chapter Twenty Seven

THE RON OSBORNE BUCK

238 6/8 NON-TYPICAL, OHIO, 1986

A Taste for Apples Proved to be his Downfall

BY RON OSBORNE

I went into the 1986 Ohio bow season hoping to shoot a huge 10-pointer I'd missed the previous November. However, by mid-October I was getting down in the dumps over not being able to find him, so I expanded my search across a broader portion of my hunting area.

One Thursday evening, I checked out a small hickory woods connected to a corn field. Scouting the woods, I found approximately 20 fresh scrapes. In addition, a number of tracks were going to and coming from the woods across a plowed field.

I had only about an hour of daylight left, so I climbed into an oak in a tree line running between the wood lot and other woods that had been logged out, which I referred to as "the cuttings." From this tree I was able to see quite a distance across a field which had not been used for farming recently and had grown up with high weeds and briars. I figured I would watch just the surrounding area until dark, in hopes of spotting the 10-pointer.

The sun had fallen below the trees, and visibility was diminishing. I was sitting on a big limb, figuring yet another evening had been wasted, when along a distant tree

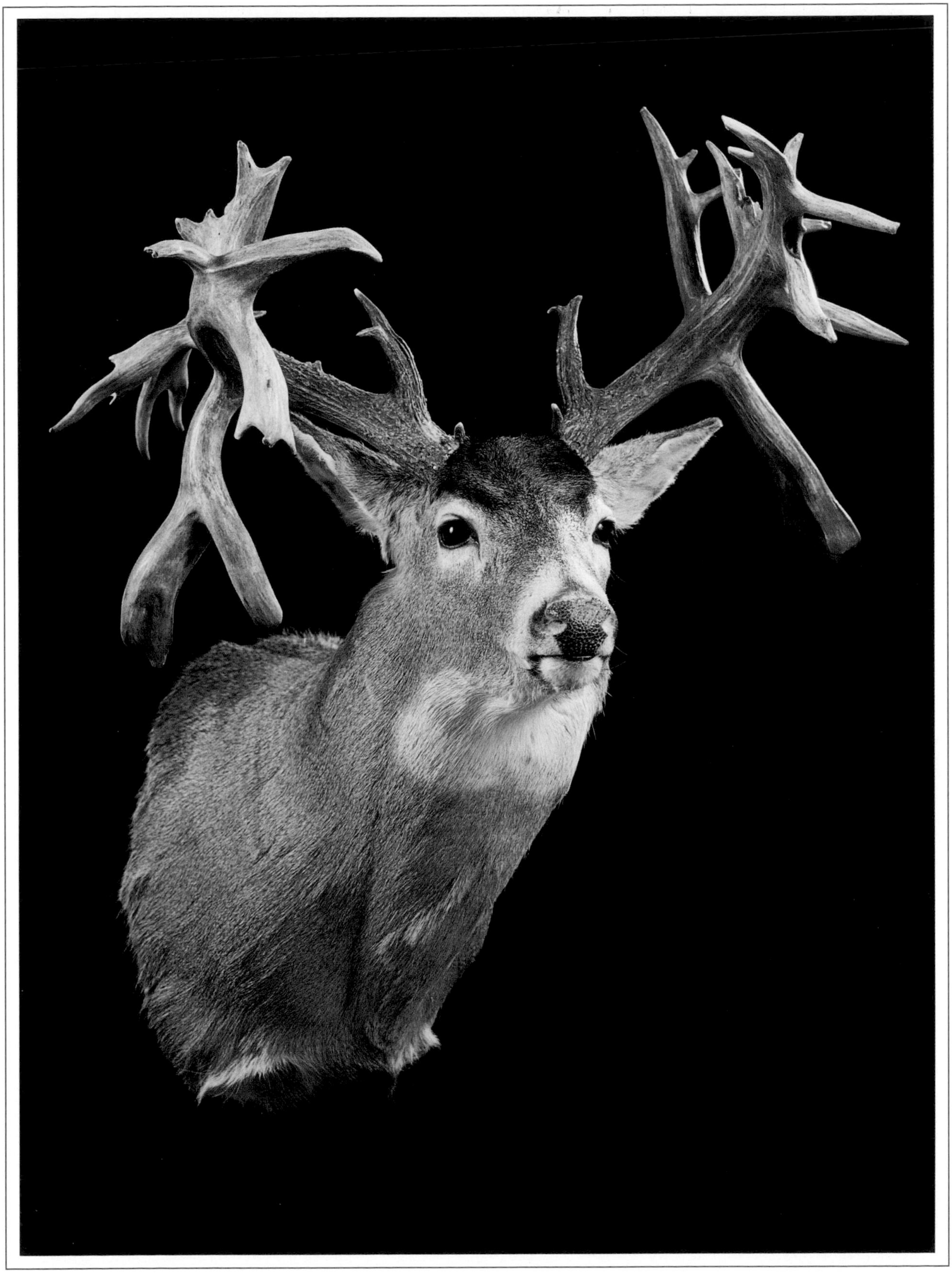

Photo courtesy of Bass Pro Shops.

Main Characteristics: Among only a handful of bucks to have over 100" of abnormal growth. Forked drop tines similar to the "Hole in the Horn" buck.

Ron Osborne, Ohio, 1986

	Right Antler	Left Antler	Difference
Main Beam Length	22 6/8	22 2/8	4/8
1st Point Length	5 5/8	4 7/8	6/8
2nd Point Length	8 5/8	9 1/8	4/8
3rd Point Length	5 4/8	4 6/8	6/8
4th Point Length	—	1 2/8	1 2/8
5th Point Length	—	—	—
1st Circumference	5 2/8	5 0/8	2/8
2nd Circumference	5 0/8	4 7/8	1/8
3rd Circumference	5 2/8	5 3/8	1/8
4th Circumference	4 3/8	4 4/8	1/8
Total	**62 3/8**	**62 0/8**	**4 3/8**

MISCELLANEOUS STATS	
No. Of Points–Right	18
No. Of Points–Left	15
Total No. Of Points	33
Length Of Abnormals	100 3/8
Greatest Spread	30 0/8
Tip To Tip Spread	11 6/8
Inside Spread	18 3/8

FINAL TALLY	
Inside Spread	18 3/8
Right Antler	62 3/8
Left Antler	62 0/8
Gross Score	142 6/8
Difference (–)	4 3/8
Subtotal	138 3/8
Abnormals (+)	100 3/8
NET NON-TYPICAL SCORE	**238 6/8**

line bordering a hay field I saw movement. As my binoculars came into focus, I could see big antlers moving. I continued watching the rack until darkness came but never could see the deer's body. All I knew for certain was that the antlers were huge — and that they didn't belong to the buck I'd been after.

The following two evenings I couldn't hunt. Then came Sunday, the day I generally scouted and moved stands. (Sunday deer hunting was illegal in Ohio). The tree I'd

been in when I'd seen the big buck seemed to be in a good spot, because of the tracks I'd found. My portable tree stand wouldn't fit onto the oak, due to the trunk's great size, so on Sunday I built a stand in it.

After several unproductive afternoon hunts there, I got out fairly early in the afternoon to do a little more scouting. I noticed an apple tree at the corner of the cuttings and found some good-sized tracks and an open section in the fence there. Having a bit of time before I figured on going to the oak stand, I climbed a fair-sized pine about 15 yards from the apple tree and trimmed out some limbs.

I hunted out of the oak that evening and watched an 8-pointer come right under my stand from the field and enter the wood lot. I was tempted to shoot but held off. We had only one buck tag per season, and I wanted to use mine wisely.

The sun was setting below the tree line and the light slowly fading when I spotted movement along the tree line at the edge of the cuttings. I reached for my binoculars, but then realized they were still in my pickup. As I watched the edge of the cuttings, I could see huge antlers moving toward the pine I'd trimmed out, approximately 100 yards down the tree line from me.

When the deer got to the pine I no longer could see him, and I just watched to see if he entered the field of high weeds. I figured he was eating apples, because I should have been able to see those antlers had he crossed the field.

I thought about getting out of the stand and stalking the buck; the wind was in my favor, and I might be able to sneak along the tree line toward the apple tree and get a shot. However, I finally decided against it. I continued watching until dark but unfortunately saw nothing more.

The following day I was off work, so well before daylight I walked to a stand some distance from where I'd seen the big buck. This stand overlooked a creek, and I'd seen several deer out of it in the mornings. There was a scrape about 20 yards away that had been active a few

days earlier, so I thought I might have some luck there. When I entered the area near this stand, I noticed a buck had torn up several young crabapple trees and had rubbed a good-sized maple since my last visit there.

About 8:30 a.m., a doe and three fawns came right under my stand. They browsed on young tree buds and grass and ate some apples. After about 45 minutes, they headed toward a bedding area I'd spotted earlier in the season. Another hour or so passed, and I was about to call it quits for the morning when across the creek and up over the bank came a nice buck, following along the same path the doe and her fawns had taken.

As the buck approached my stand, I counted points. He had 12 on what was a very nice-looking rack, and I was tempted to shoot. But in the back of my mind I kept thinking of that huge non-typical, and I let the 12-pointer pass.

I hiked back home and told the family about the buck I'd seen, and they couldn't understand why I hadn't shot. Still, I knew I'd never be satisfied if I didn't at least try to hunt that giant buck again. My dream was to get a buck that would qualify for the Pope and Young record book. I think most guys figured I was crazy when I'd tell them about the different deer I'd seen but hadn't tried to shoot. Some would ask, "What are you waiting for?" and laugh.

I ate lunch, then secured my portable stand in the pine and scouted in the cuttings before evening approached. I found several deer trails branching off into more trails, which led me to several beds.

"This was the closest look I'd had of him, and those antlers seemed to go every which way."

There also was a small, secluded pond over to one side of the cuttings, with many deer tracks around the water's edge. There were a few rubs here and there along one particular trail leading back toward the area I'd seen the big buck come from.

I found a well-used trail going out of the middle of the cuttings across the field of high weeds to the tree line I'd first seen the big buck walking. The more I looked over the cuttings, the more convinced I was that he was bedding and spending a good amount of time there.

The next week went by without my seeing the big deer again. I decided I was overhunting the area, so I went back to some stands in another area in which I'd spotted the 10-pointer earlier. But bad weather then set in for about four days; we had a lot of rain, mixed with some snow. I hunted every evening and got a bad cold that cost about four more days. I was too sick to hunt.

Perhaps 10 days now had passed since I'd last seen the big buck. The scrapes in the hickory woods hadn't been touched in that span, and I was beginning to think I'd never see him again. Then, as I was getting into my stand in the oak one afternoon, I saw something moving across the field of high weeds from me. It was the non-typical!

It appeared that the buck had come from the direction of the apple tree, and I watched as he entered the hickory woods. This was the closest look I'd had of him, and those antlers seemed to go every which way. I quickly climbed into the oak and tried rattling, but only a 6-pointer responded.

On Saturday, Nov. 22, I noticed some fresh scrapes that had been made just at daybreak. (We'd had a heavy frost overnight, and the ground was white. However, the dirt and leaves beside the scrapes had no frost covering them). The sight of the fresh scrapes brought new hope. However, I then spent all morning stalking through the hickory woods without seeing anything.

I spent early afternoon watching the Ohio State-Michigan football game on television. Then, at around 4:00 p.m., I got my bow and practiced a few shots in the back yard, as I always do to bolster my confidence and loosen up my arms before hunting. After checking the wind, I decided to hunt the pine.

I'd been on stand only about a half-hour when out of the cuttings stepped the big buck, coming in my direction. When he was about 70 yards away the sun shined on those huge antlers, making my heart start pounding a mile a minute. I began to shake all over. Ducking back into the pine branches, I grabbed my bow, which was hanging from a limb. I realized that if I didn't calm down, I'd never be able to shoot.

The buck now was about 40 yards away, coming right to my tree. Before I knew it, he'd stopped right under me. As he stood there, looking around, I began to think of what might go wrong. I thought for sure he'd continue on past my stand and go through the break in the fence and across the field, which would give me no shot at all. I absolutely hated the thought of a making a straight-down shot, but it seemed that might be my only opportunity.

Fortunately, the buck helped me out; he half turned and took six to eight steps toward the apple tree, giving me a quartering-away shot at about 10 yards. By

Ron Osborne's non-typical bears a striking resemblance to the "Hole in the Horn" buck, which came from only a few miles away. Photo by Keith Benoist, courtesy of North American Whitetail.

this time I'd calmed myself considerably but still was shaking some. When the deer lowered his head to eat an apple I pulled the bow back, centered my 10-yard pin just behind his right shoulder and let go.

The awesome buck suddenly jumped forward and ran past the apple tree down along the fencerow about 50 yards, then turned around and just stood there, looking back. Finally, he began to stagger, then fell. He did get back up, but then stumbled and fell again.

The buck continued swinging his head back and forth, then lay still. Finally, after another 10 minutes I climbed out of my stand and slowly approached him, not knowing for sure if he was dead. Sure enough, when I was only about eight feet from him, he lifted his head and started to get up and come toward me, but then fell backwards. I shot him again, through the chest.

I hadn't started the year with any idea that a world-class non-typical even lived in my area, much less that I'd manage to shoot one. All I'd wanted was another chance at that big 10-pointer. But as I stood there, looking down at Ohio's new at-that-time No. 1 archery whitetail, that other deer was the farthest thing from my mind.

Chapter Twenty Eight

THE RICHARD PAULI BUCK

267 3/8 NON-TYPICAL, ILLINOIS, 1983

Illinois' Amazing Barnyard Buck

BY JACK EHRESMAN

It was opening day of the first Illinois firearms deer season, and Dunlap resident Richard Pauli, hunting from a big oak on his property just northwest of Peoria, suddenly found himself staring at the most massive buck he'd ever seen. But at the moment, he could do nothing about it.

"When I looked down he was standing exactly underneath me, about 15 feet away," Richard says. "All I could see was his ears and his antlers. I had laid my gun on limbs to my right and was trying to figure out how I could get to it without making any noise, 'cause he was awfully close."

"I moved a little bit, and when I did, my foot knocked a piece of bark off the tree, and it hit him," Richard recalls. "I thought all I'd see was his tail up and he'd be gone, but he didn't move. He soon disappeared under a big limb, and I couldn't see him any more, so I just didn't move."

A few minutes later, after what must have seemed an eternity to Richard, the world-class buck again appeared, now about 20 yards away. By this time, the hunter held his shotgun.

RICHARD PAULI, ILLINOIS, 1983

	Right Antler	Left Antler	Difference
Main Beam Length	25 4/8	28 2/8	2 6/8
1st Point Length	6 0/8	4 5/8	1 3/8
2nd Point Length	11 6/8	11 6/8	0/8
3rd Point Length	8 4/8	11 7/8	3 3/8
4th Point Length	7 2/8	9 0/8	1 6/8
5th Point Length	1 0/8	—	1 0/8
1st Circumference	6 5/8	6 3/8	2/8
2nd Circumference	5 2/8	5 6/8	4/8
3rd Circumference	5 0/8	5 5/8	5/8
4th Circumference	6 1/8	5 3/8	6/8
Total	**83 0/8**	**88 5/8**	**12 3/8**

Main Characteristics: Double beam on right antler, much less non-typical on left. Outstanding mass.

MISCELLANEOUS STATS	
No. Of Points–Right	18
No. Of Points–Left	7
Total No. Of Points	25
Length Of Abnormals	88 1/8
Greatest Spread	29 1/8
Tip To Tip Spread	15 7/8
Inside Spread	20 0/8

FINAL TALLY	
Inside Spread	20 0/8
Right Antler	83 0/8
Left Antler	88 5/8
Gross Score	191 5/8
Difference (–)	12 3/8
Subtotal	179 2/8
Abnormals (+)	88 1/8
NET NON-TYPICAL SCORE	**267 3/8**

"He was moving crossways with the wind, like he always did, and was moving away from me," Richard says. "He turned just a little to his left to look. Then, he turned to his right. When he did this, he exposed his neck to me. That's my favorite shot," the hunter says with a smile.

The rest is history. The hunter's 25-point buck scores 267 3/8 Boone and Crockett points, making him the largest non-typical ever recorded in Illinois — a state well known for world-class whitetails.

"At the time I never realized how big he was," Richard says of his giant buck. "Even after I had checked him in, I really wasn't as excited as everybody else was. It took a couple of days before it hit me."

Richard is a soft-spoken sportsman who says bagging a deer of such proportions is 99 percent luck. However, he's no stranger to big bucks. In fact, in 1968 he harvested one that dressed out at 263 pounds, much heavier than his 197-pound non-typical. As of this writing, only twice since deer seasons resumed in Illinois in 1957 has the guy failed to bring home venison, and in neither of those years did he get to hunt.

Prior to the 1983 season, Richard had been aware that a big buck occasionally passed through his 105-acre property. "I knew it was him, because of his foot-prints," the landowner explains. "I had seen him twice from a distance while bowhunting and got a closer look one night when I was out checking on the cattle. But I never did get a really good look at his antlers, and never knew how big he really was."

While bowhunting, Richard was able to catch only a glimpse of the trophy. "In 1981, I was in a deep washout when I heard something about 15 feet behind me," he recalls. "I was in a position where I couldn't turn around, and there was no way I could shoot left-handed. All I could see was his tail. He just walked to the top of the hill and then came out in plain sight.

"Then, another time in the same creek bed, I noticed a maple tree was down. I was gonna be smart and cross over the creek on it. He bolted from the brush and was gone. It scared me more than it scared him — it was the only time I ever caught him bedded down."

The best look Richard had at the big deer before shooting him came about a month before the 1983 shotgun season. The hunter and his wife, Donna, had been to a relative's house for supper that night. It was dark when they arrived home, and they went out to the pasture to drive their cattle to another field before retiring for the night.

"She drove the car down to the pond, so we could use headlights to see, and the beams hit him," Richard says. "He was

drinking at the pond. He turned around and looked at us. He looked up, turned his head around over his shoulder and just walked off. He never did break stride or change his pace. He acted like he was king of the hill.

"It was a once-in-a-lifetime thrill just to see a deer like that," Richard admits. "In the headlights he looked like that big deer Hartford Insurance uses in its advertising."

Bow season had already started, so Richard was eager to go after the big animal. But despite his searching, he never saw this monster buck again until the opening day of the first slug season.

It was still dark that November morning when Richard took off for his hunting spot, which was on the north side of his farm. But plans changed soon after he stepped through the gate in the field about 30 yards behind his home.

"I was about half asleep, but I sensed there was something in the field with me," the hunter recalls. "I looked up, and this big buck was in the same field. He had been crossing my path, 20 to 25 yards ahead of me. We saw each other about the same time, and we just looked at each other a while. I just stood there and relaxed, and he walked off. I thought that was the end of him, that he would go bed down somewhere for the day."

After the big buck disappeared, Richard stood there for another 10 to 15 minutes before moving, then headed for the place he'd planned to hunt. "But the more I walked, the more I thought," the hunter says. "He went southeast, and he had a bad habit of always going cross-ways with the wind. So, I figured he would go straight west. I was playing a hunch. I thought if I saw him it would be in the most unlikely spot, because I always saw him when I least expected."

It's worth repeating that Richard had noticed the big deer liked to move crosswind, and that this knowledge caused him to change his hunting plans this day. "I wanted to get in the biggest tree in the direction I thought he might go, and the only one I could think of was on a high hill in the middle of nowhere, in an old pasture surrounded by timber," he says. "And that's where I went."

Richard experienced difficulty climbing the tree, but finally he managed to find a comfortable limb and settle down. "About 7:05 I heard a shot to the west of me. I thought, 'Things must be moving.'

"I had been facing the southeast, where I thought he might come from, so I turned around to see if anything was coming from the direction the shot came from. Nothin'.

"I just sat there and relaxed and set my gun up over two limbs," Richard continues. "I never keep it in my hands. I figure if the shot is not good enough where I can take my time, I don't want it anyway."

Another shot came from the west. Richard turned again, but there was no movement, so once again he relaxed.

"About 10 to 12 minutes later I hear a sound behind me," he says. "A deer's got a peculiar walk and sounds kinda like a person. I knew something was back there, but I didn't know what. I didn't want to turn around, so I just sat there. About 15 minutes later I looked down, and there he was."

> *"I fired one shot, and as soon as he went down, he got the second one. Then I sat down and had my usual cup of coffee."*

Richard was using a Browning Sweet 16 shotgun with a Polychoke on slug setting. "I fired one shot, and as soon as he went down, he got the second one. Then I sat down and had my usual cup of coffee. I don't like to get out of a tree for at least 10 to 15 minutes after dropping a deer.

"I was still sittin' up in the tree when my cousin came walking up. He had heard my shootin'. I didn't know he was out that morning. He told me he was coming the next day, but he took off work a day early. He had gotten a buck — a 6-pointer — and he says, 'What'd you do, miss?' I said, 'Yeah, he's lying right there on the ground.' He couldn't believe the size when he saw it."

Richard dressed out his big buck, then helped his cousin with his. They got the tractor and hauled both deer from the field. It was all over by about 10 a.m. that opening day.

Richard observes sign closely, but in chatting with him for several hours, you soon realize patience is his trump card as a deer hunter. He also is an excellent shot. "I can sit in a tree all day," he says. "I don't even get down for lunch. I take no breaks, and it can be tough, especially when it's cold. I've spent a lot of hours sitting with a shotgun. I take a Thermos of coffee, a few candy bars and some old-fashioned crackers… and I'm good for the day." In addition, he says he can put three slugs inside a 2-inch circle at 100 yards with his Sweet 16.

He never uses prepared scents when hunting but leaves home long before legal shooting time begins, so his ground scent

The double beam on the Pauli buck's right antler suggests he might have injured that side of his developing rack. Photo by Dick Idol, courtesy of North American Whitetail.

isn't still fresh when daylight arrives. "I always climb into a tree," he adds. "I prefer a cedar if I can find one. If it's raining or snowing, I can stay dry. I also think it helps mask scent, and it provides good visibility. I can move around."

Amazingly, one of North America's most recognized bowhunting trophies — Mel Johnson's Pope and Young world record typical, which nets 204 4/8 points — was taken in 1965 just five miles away from Richard's land, on property owned by his aunt. It would be an understatement to say the deer herd in that part of Peoria County has good genetics!

In addition, Richard's giant 4 1/2-year-old buck lived among the richest agricultural land in the nation. The Illinois River valley is heavily farmed, and it yields not just prime crops but prime venison.

"You could cut the T-bones from him (the record buck) with a fork," Richard says. "My wife loves venison. If she has a choice between venison and beef, she'll take venison. There are never any complaints from her when I want to go hunting. She wants me to go," he says.

Some guys are lucky in more ways than one.

Chapter Twenty Nine

THE STAN POTTS BUCK

193 4/8 TYPICAL, ILLINOIS, 1983

Huge Success on a Tiny Piece of Land

BY BRENDA POTTS

We are surrounded by a wealth of whitetail-hunting knowledge. Books, magazines, videos, the Internet, you name it — someone has written about nearly every hunting tip or technique imaginable. Even so, one obvious point often is ignored: to be successful at taking a trophy buck, you must hunt where such deer live. Even if you have access to several thousand acres, your chances of getting a big buck are non-existent if none walks that property. On the other hand, even if all you have access to is a 10-acre tract, if it is the right 10 acres, you just might shoot the buck of a lifetime.

This is exactly the situation in which Illinois bowhunter Stan Potts found himself back in the early 1980s, when he harvested one of the largest typicals ever arrowed. Stan and two friends had obtained permission to hunt a 10-acre tract of private land near Clinton Nuclear Power Plant, which later was to become famous for its innovative trophy-management program. (See Chapter 31 for more on this great area).

"Lots of guys said they could have killed plenty of big bucks too, if they could have hunted that same place," Stan says. "Well, it wasn't as easy as everyone thought.

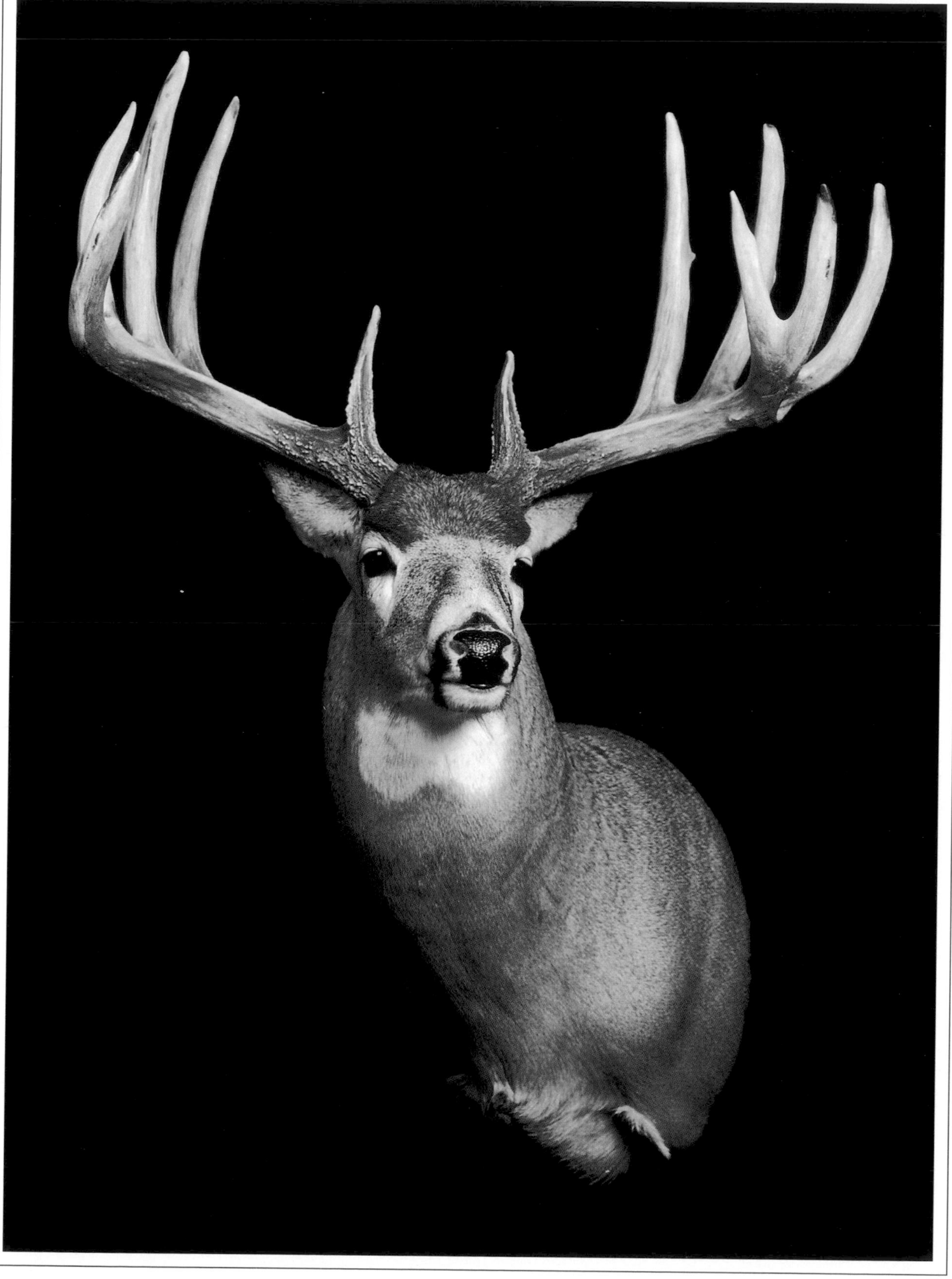

Photo courtesy of Locie Murphy.

Stan Potts, Illinois, 1983

	Right Antler	Left Antler	Difference
Main Beam Length	26 2/8	25 5/8	5/8
1st Point Length	5 5/8	5 0/8	5/8
2nd Point Length	12 6/8	13 0/8	2/8
3rd Point Length	11 7/8	11 3/8	4/8
4th Point Length	8 7/8	9 1/8	2/8
5th Point Length	—	5 6/8	5 6/8
1st Circumference	5 7/8	5 7/8	0/8
2nd Circumference	5 0/8	5 0/8	0/8
3rd Circumference	6 2/8	5 5/8	5/8
4th Circumference	5 4/8	5 1/8	3/8
Total	**88 0/8**	**91 4/8**	**9 0/8**

Main Characteristics: Great width and height to go with exceptional mass in beams and tines.

Miscellaneous Stats

No. Of Points–Right	5
No. Of Points–Left	6
Total No. Of Points	11
Length Of Abnormals	0
Greatest Spread	27 6/8
Tip To Tip Spread	23 0/8
Inside Spread	23 0/8

Final Tally

Inside Spread	23 0/8
Right Antler	88 0/8
Left Antler	91 4/8
Gross Score	202 4/8
Difference (–)	9 0/8
Subtotal	193 4/8
Abnormals (–)	0
Net Typical Score	193 4/8

A number of big bucks outsmarted us."

During those early years, these bowhunters certainly were served up many slices of humble pie. In fact, one huge-bodied, heavy-beamed buck they nicknamed "Wally" gave them a heaping helping of humility right from the start.

A heavy frost greeted hunters on the opening day of the 1981 waterfowl season. Because it was so cold, Stan wore a heavy stocking-type mask with holes cut for his eyes, but none for his mouth or nose. That mask turned out to be anything but helpful.

"Clinton Lake was just a few hundred yards from my stand," Stan recalls. "I could hear duck calls and shotgun blasts all morning. All the commotion down by the lake must have influenced Wally to change positions, because before long, he was headed in my direction. His dark rack was enormous, with six tines on the left, and five on the right. I field-judged that buck as a 190-inch typical. Every step brought him closer to my stand."

The closer Wally came, the more unnerved Stan grew. Buck fever definitely was getting a grip on his emotions. "Wally paused behind a bush on a nearby ridge, standing motionless," the hunter says. "Suddenly, he broke into a trot that would bring him directly under my tree stand. In an instant I was at full draw.

"Back then, I used to whistle at deer to stop them for a shot," Stan continues. "When he stepped into the open, I whistled. At least, I tried to. The heavy face mask muffled any attempt I made at whistling this deer to a stop."

With adrenaline flowing and a trophy buck on the run, Stan wasn't thinking clearly. He followed the deer with his sight pins and touched the release. The arrow plunged into the ground several feet behind the deer. ("Today, I make a sound like a buck grunting to stop a deer for a shot," Stan notes.)

"Four days later I had another nerve-rattling experience with some different bucks," he says. "This time my friend, John Piatt, was along for the afternoon. I got into the stand on the south side of the corn field, and he was on the west side."

Soon, a nice 135-class buck came out, but too far to attempt a shot. As the buck fed quietly, another one jumped the fence. Soon, he was followed by yet another. Then, moments later, two more entered the field! A farmer was combining beans in the next field.

No amount of grunting would bring the bucks into bow range, and neither hunter had rattling antlers with him. As they watched, before long a doe jumped the fence between them. For some reason the biggest buck, a 170-inch 10-pointer,

lowered his head and rushed her. She jumped the fence directly under John's stand, but even as the archer prepared for a shot, the buck stopped 50 yards short of his tree. The buck watched the doe until satisfied that she was gone, then went back to feeding.

Within minutes, the doe popped back over the fence — and again the buck sent her racing back out under John's stand! Unfortunately, the buck once more pulled up far out of shooting range. This game of cat and mouse went on for quite awhile, with the buck always too far for a shot. In the end, despite all of this wild activity, neither hunter got a shot.

A year later, the hunters returned to this 10-acre "field of dreams." This time, their main target was a buck they had nicknamed "Whitey."

"His rack was snow-white with super-long tines," Stan says. "Another friend of mine, Doug Tilley, and I were in our stands when I heard a buck ripping a tree to pieces. I could see a tremendous white-horned buck rubbing his antlers on a tree as big as my leg."

The monster started toward Stan but soon raised his head and stared in his direction. "It wasn't until later that I realized my stand placement had me silhouetted against the sky," Stan explains. "He didn't blow out of there, he just backed up while never taking his eyes off me."

Whitey turned and headed in Doug's direction. At the sound of a bowshot, Stan saw Whitey bolt into an opening, stop and look around, then slowly walk off. As it turned out, Doug's arrow had glanced off a twig and completely missed.

"Back then, we didn't clear much in the way of shooting lanes," Stan admits. "I learned my lessons, though. Now I always clear shooting lanes in the off-season. And, I position my stands so they are not silhouetted in the tree."

Stan returned to the 10 acres a day or two later. Even though several small bucks presented shot opportunities, he decided to hold out. That determination seemed to pay off when a big buck emerged from the timber.

"I looked him over with my binoculars," the bowhunter says. "He was about 400 yards away, and I decided to try for him. I slammed the rattling antlers together as loud as I could, trying to get his attention. There was some commotion in the brush directly behind my stand, and I knew another buck was coming. I stashed the antlers in the tree and grabbed my bow. The buck's antlers looked like a giant rib cage!"

Just as the buck was about to step into the shooting lane, however, he suddenly turned and disappeared into the thicket. "I didn't know what to do, so I reached over and bumped the rattling antlers, hoping to draw him back in. I didn't know the buck was only a few yards away. He bolted out of there, and my spirits took a nose-dive," Stan says.

To make matters worse, by now the hunter had forgotten about the first buck. "When I finally came to my senses, he was only 60 yards away and closing fast," Stan recalls. "I had to square back around to get a shot. When I turned in the stand, I accidentally bumped the rattling antlers — only this time, they fell out of the tree! They slammed against the

stand and dropped onto the fence below. There they hung, rattling together as they swung in the breeze. Of course, the buck was gone in a flash." Make that one more lesson learned at the 10 acres.

It wasn't until an unusually warm November day that this hunter's luck finally changed. Stan's favorite stand was in a tree that was home to several hundred honeybees. Normally that wouldn't have been a problem in the latter half of November, but the 70-degree weather had caused the bees to become active.

> *"Stan's favorite stand was in a tree that was home to several hundred honeybees. Normally that wouldn't have been a problem in the latter half of November, but the 70-degree weather had caused the bees to become active."*

"I considered going to another stand, but something told me not to," Stan recalls. "Maybe it was some kind of intuition, but something persuaded me to climb into that stand. The platform of the stand was positioned above the bees' entrance into the tree, so I climbed past them as slowly as possible. Once I got above the bees, they settled down and forgot about me."

Stan waited 15 minutes for the bees to calm down, then began to rattle. "The winds were light, so the sounds of rattling antlers would carry a long way," he explains. "I started with a loud, aggressive 90-second sequence, then hung up the antlers to wait. After 10 minutes with no action, I tickled the antlers together."

After an hour had passed with no response, Stan rattled again. As soon as he finished this sequence he stood up, bow in hand. Suddenly, a twig snapped. At first Stan thought it was a squirrel, but when the noise was repeated, he thought it just might be a buck.

"I looked as cautiously as I could in the direction of the noise," he says. "A huge buck was heading my way! This deer was even more impressive than Wally or Whitey. It was the biggest-framed typical I had ever seen."

This immense 11-pointer is one of the biggest typicals ever rattled in. Photo by Brenda Potts.

The bruiser came in looking for a fight, swiveling his head from left to right as he searched the areas for his rivals. Somehow, the bowhunter kept his nerve as the giant skirted the thicket behind him.

"The buck was walking along a run that was 20 yards from my stand," Stan remembers. "The shooting lanes were already cleared, and I was ready for the shot. When the buck went behind a bush, I came to full draw. The buck paused and I held my breath, waiting for him to make a move. Finally, he stepped into the opening and gave me a quartering-away shot. I put the 20-yard pin on his vitals and touched the release."

Although Stan felt sure he had made a good hit, he wanted to be cautious. By the time he returned to the woods with John Piatt and Kirby North, it was getting dark. The three split up after the blood trail ran out. Kirby and John fol-lowed a fence to see if the buck had jumped it, while Stan decided to look downhill. As he started swinging his light back and forth, a big scrape caught his attention. When he shined his light in that direction, he saw the right side of the buck's antlers sticking up over the grass.

"It was a very emotional time for me, and I spent a few moments alone with the buck, thinking back over hunts with my father," Stan says. "When I called out to John and Kirby, I remember their flashlights bobbing up and down in the dark as they ran down the hill in my direction. They were almost as excited as I was!"

Stan has taken numerous other Pope and Young-class bucks in his career, but none compare to this one. The wide, massive 11-pointer's net score of 193 4/8 placed him second in the state and comfortably among the top 10 archery typicals of all time. Only Mel Johnson's 204 4/8-inch archery world record, which had been shot in Peoria County 18 years earlier, outranked him on the Prairie State list.

Now, who says you need a lot of land to be a trophy hunter?

Chapter Thirty

THE
JAMIE REMMERS BUCK

---
257 1/8 NON-TYPICAL, KANSAS, 1997

The Biggest Non-Typical
Whitetail Ever Taken
by a Woman

BY BRENDA POTTS

For Kansan Jamie Remmers, life went from peaceful to chaotic with the firing of a single shot on Dec. 7, 1997. That day, she killed one of the biggest whitetails ever shot in Kansas, and hands-down the world's highest-scoring buck ever taken by a woman. And as if all that weren't enough, the hunter was four months pregnant at the time!

Jamie got started hunting in 1982 because she "liked the outdoors and wanted to spend time with the rest of the family who hunted." The land her family hunts is primarily in alfalfa production, with some stands of timber and creek bottoms, along the Cottonwood River north of Wichita.

Folks in the area knew a giant deer was calling this part of Kansas home. In fact, locals had begun referring to him as "The Moose of Cottonwood River."

"My husband, Kent, saw it a few times during the morning on his way to work," Jamie says of the weeks leading up to her historic kill. The massive non-typical also was spotted by locals as he fed during the mornings or evenings. Most of the sightings occurred within a half-mile of where the deer and Jamie eventually would meet.

Main Characteristics: Huge main frame featuring super mass and extra-long beams.

JAMIE REMMERS, KANSAS, 1997

	Right Antler	Left Antler	Difference
Main Beam Length	29 4/8	27 4/8	2 0/8
1st Point Length	7 4/8	7 1/8	3/8
2nd Point Length	9 0/8	11 6/8	2 6/8
3rd Point Length	9 7/8	12 4/8	2 5/8
4th Point Length	7 2/8	8 2/8	1 0/8
5th Point Length	4 5/8	—	4 5/8
1st Circumference	6 2/8	5 6/8	4/8
2nd Circumference	6 1/8	5 6/8	3/8
3rd Circumference	7 5/8	6 5/8	1 0/8
4th Circumference	6 6/8	6 4/8	2/8
Total	**94 4/8**	**91 6/8**	**15 4/8**

MISCELLANEOUS STATS	
No. Of Points–Right	20
No. Of Points–Left	18
Total No. Of Points	38
Length Of Abnormals	63 1/8
Greatest Spread	28 3/8
Tip To Tip Spread	18 0/8
Inside Spread	23 2/8

FINAL TALLY	
Inside Spread	23 2/8
Right Antler	94 4/8
Left Antler	91 6/8
Gross Score	**209 4/8**
Difference (–)	15 4/8
Subtotal	**194 0/8**
Abnormals (+)	63 1/8
NET NON-TYPICAL SCORE	**257 1/8**

On the fifth day of rifle season that year, Jamie, Kent and longtime friend and hunting partner Jeff Riffel decided to conduct a deer drive. The plan was for Kent and Jeff to make a controlled push through some timber near the Remmers home. Jamie would set up near a creek behind the house as the two men set out to move some deer her way.

"Since I was four months pregnant, I didn't want to do much walking," Jamie says. "So after lunch, I walked over to the creek behind my house. A storm was coming, and it seemed to have the deer bunched up. We were hoping the drive would get something moving."

It wasn't long before a few does emerged from the timber. "I was watching the deer through the scope, checking them out for any sign of antlers," Jamie says. "I spotted the big buck about 400 yards out, but I didn't get a shot at him until he got to within 50 yards! When I shot, I saw him drop. There were a couple other bucks with him, and a 10-pointer and a 6-pointer trotted through the draw. The does were still mingling within 100 yards around me."

Jamie didn't wait for the drivers to emerge from the timber; she headed for her trophy. Kent and Jeff soon found her and inquired about her shot. They were shocked to see the 34-point monster lying

Jamie Remmers was four months pregnant when she got her trophy. Photo courtesy of Jamie Remmers.

before them. "We couldn't touch the antlers enough!" Jamie says of the celebration that followed.

They loaded up the deer and headed to the nearest town to show the rest of the family what Jamie had done. "We went through town with the buck in the back of the pickup truck. And we live in a small town. By the time we got home, the answering machine was full of calls and the garage was full of people," Jamie remembers. "My cousin's wife had gotten a deer that scored 200, and that was the biggest deer I had ever seen. But this buck was even bigger. We rough-scored it, and someone said it had to be in the top five in our state and probably the largest ever killed by a woman."

Whoever made those claims was right. The massive buck's net score proved to be 257 1/8 Boone and Crockett points, making him the world's highest-scoring whitetail ever shot by a woman!

The buck was taken in the prime of life, but not surprisingly, he had his share

of battle scars. "When they were cleaning it, they found a .22 bullet in the shoulder," Jamie points out.

Eventually, Jamie sold the rack to Bass Pro Shops. "I decided it would be a great way to share the deer and let other people see him," she explains. "They rotate him to other stores so more folks can get to see him. I have the original cape and a replica of the antlers.

"The best things about getting this buck are the memories and accomplishments and getting to meet a lot of really nice people," she claims. "I still keep in touch with some of the people I met because of the buck."

Actually, one of the funnier moments involving this deer resulted from the misinterpretation of a joke. "My husband was joking that, 'Two of them got the deer, but only one of them had a tag,'" Jamie says. What was meant as humor regarding Jamie's pregnancy led a hunting magazine to check with state wildlife officials to make sure the deer had indeed been shot legally!

And just how did things go in the maternity department? Well, a few months after Jamie bagged her monster buck, she gave birth to healthy daughter McKenzie Lee.

"She likes to call it *her* deer now," the proud mother says.

Chapter Thirty One

THE KELLY RIGGS BUCK

214 4/8 NON-TYPICAL, ILLINOIS, 1996

The *"Monster"* from the Nuclear Plant

BY RON WILLMORE

Throughout much of the 1990s, an amazing non-typical buck in central Illinois continually outsmarted many hunters — myself included. He was seen on many occasions, and several of his shed antlers were recovered, but in every instance he managed to stay one step ahead of his pursuers. I finally concluded that he led a charmed life and that he probably never would be taken by a hunter. He was indeed one of those rare "living legends" of the whitetail world.

Then, just when it seemed the buck would slip through the cracks and live out his natural lifespan, a local hunter beat the odds in a most unlikely fashion.

This tremendous animal made his home on and around a public bowhunting area adjacent to Clinton Lake, a power-plant reservoir in DeWitt County. The fact that he lived long enough to show his incredible genetic potential is directly related to where he lived, for Clinton Lake's unique management plan played a major role in the buck's development.

This program began in 1991 and was perhaps the nation's first to use bowhunting as a means of reducing a deer population while simultaneously improving trophy

Photo by Ron Willmore.

Main Characteristics: Sensational width and mass. Unique look with distinctive drop tines.

KELLY RIGGS, ILLINOIS, 1996

	Right Antler	Left Antler	Difference
Main Beam Length	23 4/8	20 7/8	2 5/8
1st Point Length	3 7/8	4 2/8	3/8
2nd Point Length	8 1/8	8 1/8	0/8
3rd Point Length	9 0/8	6 3/8	2 5/8
4th Point Length	7 6/8	4 0/8	3 6/8
5th Point Length	—	—	—
1st Circumference	5 7/8	5 5/8	2/8
2nd Circumference	5 3/8	5 6/8	3/8
3rd Circumference	5 5/8	5 6/8	1/8
4th Circumference	6 1/8	5 3/8	6/8
Total	75 2/8	66 1/8	10 7/8

MISCELLANEOUS STATS

No. Of Points–Right	15
No. Of Points–Left	12
Total No. Of Points	27
Length Of Abnormals	60 4/8
Greatest Spread	33 0/8
Tip To Tip Spread	28 6/8
Inside Spread*	28 6/8

* Spread credit cannot exceed length of longer main beam.

FINAL TALLY

Spread Credit*	23 4/8
Right Antler	75 2/8
Left Antler	66 1/8
Gross Score	164 7/8
Difference (-)	10 7/8
Subtotal	154 0/8
Abnormals (+)	60 4/8
NET NON-TYPICAL SCORE	214 4/8

hunting. Conducted jointly by the Illinois Power Co. and Illinois Dept. of Natural Resources, the special hunts gave lottery-selected archers a chance to hunt approximately 1,000 acres of prime mixed hardwood and cropland habitat bordering the reservoir.

Year after year during the life of the program, the property hosted hundreds of bowhunters. You might assume that such heavy pressure would wipe out the buck population, but special hunting regulations prevented that. A bowhunter on one of these hunts had to check in a doe from the property before he or she was allowed to shoot a buck. As a result, the harvest included far more of the former than of the latter.

Because the property had been unhunted for many years prior to 1991, and because the area had a well-deserved reputation for growing huge deer, most bowhunters willing to deal with this program's restrictive rules tended to be highly selective. As a result, around two-thirds of the mature bucks taken were large enough to make the Pope and Young record book. The program was successful not only in reducing crop damage and deer-automobile accidents, but also in allowing many bucks to reach prime age.

Over the years three full sets of the buck's sheds were found, along with three singles. The actual rack (worn at age 7 1/2) is on the mount with the wooden plaque. Photo courtesy of Ron Willmore.

an endless procession of busy fox squirrels. The hunter quickly turned his head — and was staring face to face with the largest buck he'd ever seen!

OK, now what do I do? Kelly thought. He and the buck decided to move

While there were many big deer on the property, throughout the years of these special bowhunts, hunters and motorists occasionally caught glimpses of one buck that stood out from the rest. During the first year of the program he was just 2 1/2 years old, but already he showed potential. By the time the 1994 hunt rolled around, he was 5 1/2 years old and had developed a rack with a wide spread, several drop tines and heavy palmation.

It was in November of that year, during shotgun season, that the great deer and Kelly Riggs first bumped into each other. On that cold day, Kelly had been sitting for more than five hours in his tree stand, which was on private land adjacent to the public bowhunting area. At around 3:30 p.m., he heard what he assumed was most likely just another in

at the same moment. When the dust had settled after the third shot from Kelly's slug gun, both hunter and hunted were a bit wiser. The buck was untouched.

Imagine how often that scenario must have been replayed in Kelly's mind afterwards. The real replay, however, was destined to take place almost exactly two years later, in November 1996, by which time the buck's rack and reputation had grown even more.

By then, the antlers' outside spread had pushed well beyond the 30-inch mark, and taking this trophy had become the dream of even more area hunters. Because the buck's core area was on the Mascoutin (Muh-SCOOT-in) Recreation Area, on the lake's northeastern side, he by now had become known locally as simply "the Mascoutin non-typical."

The special bowhunt in 1996 produced no shots at the buck by any of the participants, but he was seen on several occasions. Most of the sightings were at night as the buck crossed a highway separating the public hunting area from another tract. The non-typical had even been videotaped in late October in one of his sanctuaries adjacent to the public area, and on Nov. 13 he was once again caught on tape, this time near one of Kelly's stands on private land. He was favoring his left hind leg, but if he was badly injured, it didn't appear to be curtailing his interest in the ladies. In fact, he was with several does when seen on Nov. 13.

Kelly already had arrowed a P&Y buck on the private tract earlier in the fall, and his thoughts were on the upcoming shotgun season, which would open Nov. 22. In the meantime, he decided, he'd go coyote hunting instead.

So, on the morning of Nov. 19, the hunter was in a ground blind, watching for coyotes, when off in the distance he spotted deer. It was the huge non-typical, chasing does! Even at long range, Kelly could see that the buck was limping. The giant eventually re-entered the woods at a point near where one of Kelly's tree stands still hung.

So much for coyotes! Kelly returned home to replace his rifle with his bow, then went back to the woods. He eased into the tree stand near where he'd seen the buck that morning and settled in.

At around 4:15 p.m., the bowhunter spotted the buck approaching his stand through the timber. You're lucky to get even one chance at a super buck, and now it seemed Kelly was about to get his second! But the deer was approaching the stand head on, with no opportunity for a good shot.

The next couple of minutes dragged on for what seemed like hours. Finally, the non-typical stepped out into the edge of a shooting lane, broadside at 30 yards. The time had come for Kelly to act — if he could.

> *"The next couple of minutes dragged on for what seemed like hours. Finally, the non-typical stepped out into the edge of a shooting lane, broadside at 30 yards. The time had come for Kelly to act — if he could."*

"I could hardly get my bow drawn," he remembers. "I was shaking so bad that I pulled my shot off, and the arrow appeared to hit just in front of the deer's neck. The buck backed up a couple of steps and walked off."

For the second time in as many opportunities, Kelly knew he'd blown it! He was so distraught that he simply sat in the tree stand the remaining 30 minutes until the end of legal shooting time, all the while having a quiet but intense discussion with himself; then, he left the woods.

After a long night filled with doubt and disbelief — the kind bowhunters always put themselves through in such situations — Kelly decided he should return to the woods the next morning. Just after daylight, he began to search for his arrow. And he soon found it — covered with blood!

It would be difficult to describe the emotions the hunter felt when he learned he'd indeed connected. He still couldn't imagine how the arrow had passed through the animal when it appeared to have gone right in front of his neck. Kelly began to follow the blood trail.

It was a short one, leading just 80 yards to where the monster lay dead in the brush. The buck almost certainly had died before Kelly had even left his stand the previous evening. The shot had penetrated the neck and cut the jugular vein; because the arrow hadn't encountered any bone, it had passed right on through, as though having missed entirely.

Kelly Riggs strains to hold up the head of his massive Illinois non-typical. The buck, which has a 33-inch outside spread, was the state's highest-scoring trophy taken by a bowhunter in 1996. Photo by Tom Evans, courtesy of North American Whitetail.

was held in his honor right after the season ended. With a net score of 214 4/8 points, the deer turned out to be the highest-scoring non-typical by bow at the Illinois Deer & Turkey Classic in Peoria the following February, and he's among the state's most impressive bow kills ever. While his 1996 rack was actually smaller than the one he'd worn the year

To say Kelly was excited at this point would be to make a major understatement. After tagging and field dressing the deer — no easy task for an adrenaline-charged hunter to accomplish without slicing a finger — he discovered why the old buck had been limping. His left hind leg apparently had been clipped by a vehicle, breaking a bone. The fact that the injury had only slightly slowed the buck in his pursuit of does is testimony to the resiliency of whitetails.

Thus ended the long reign of the Mascoutin non-typical, a buck so well known in the area that a "wake" actually

before (at age 6 1/2), it still grossed 230 5/8 points and had 27 scorable points, with a 28 6/8-inch inside spread.

"The bottom line is that the Mascoutin non-typical is the star in this whole scenario," Kelly says. "God created the buck, and the buck is what should be honored, not the hunter who was lucky enough to get him.

"The intelligence of that buck, combined with the constraints of a quality deer management program, allowed him to grow up and fully mature before being killed. I just got lucky — twice!"

Chapter Thirty Two

THE PETER RUTKOWSKI BUCK

245 5/8 NON-TYPICAL, MINNESOTA, 1942

An Unlikely Trophy…
and an Even
More Unlikely Story

BY DICK IDOL

We all fantasize about sitting in that special place and having that "once-in-a-lifetime" buck walk into view. Of course, the location and the magnitude of the buck might vary greatly, depending on our experiences.

As for my own fantasies, I'm content to envision a "modest" 230- or 240-class non-typical with drop tines and massive antlers. (I don't get carried away with world records and such, just little fantasies that really could happen.) And my favorite setting would be in the wilds of the great North Woods, where few white men have ever trodden. The country is wild with wolves, moose, bears and old, gray-faced monarch bucks, most of which only seldom have crossed the paths of hunters. Small swamps teem with ducks, geese, mink and other wildlife, while lakes echo the mystical call of the loon. The pungent aroma of freshly fallen leaves and the bold, fermented aroma of acres of decaying berries and fruit add to the wild feeling.

Northern lights shimmer and dance across black, cold skies. And here, in a small, grassy swamp ringed by red willows, would be found the signature of my buck: giant

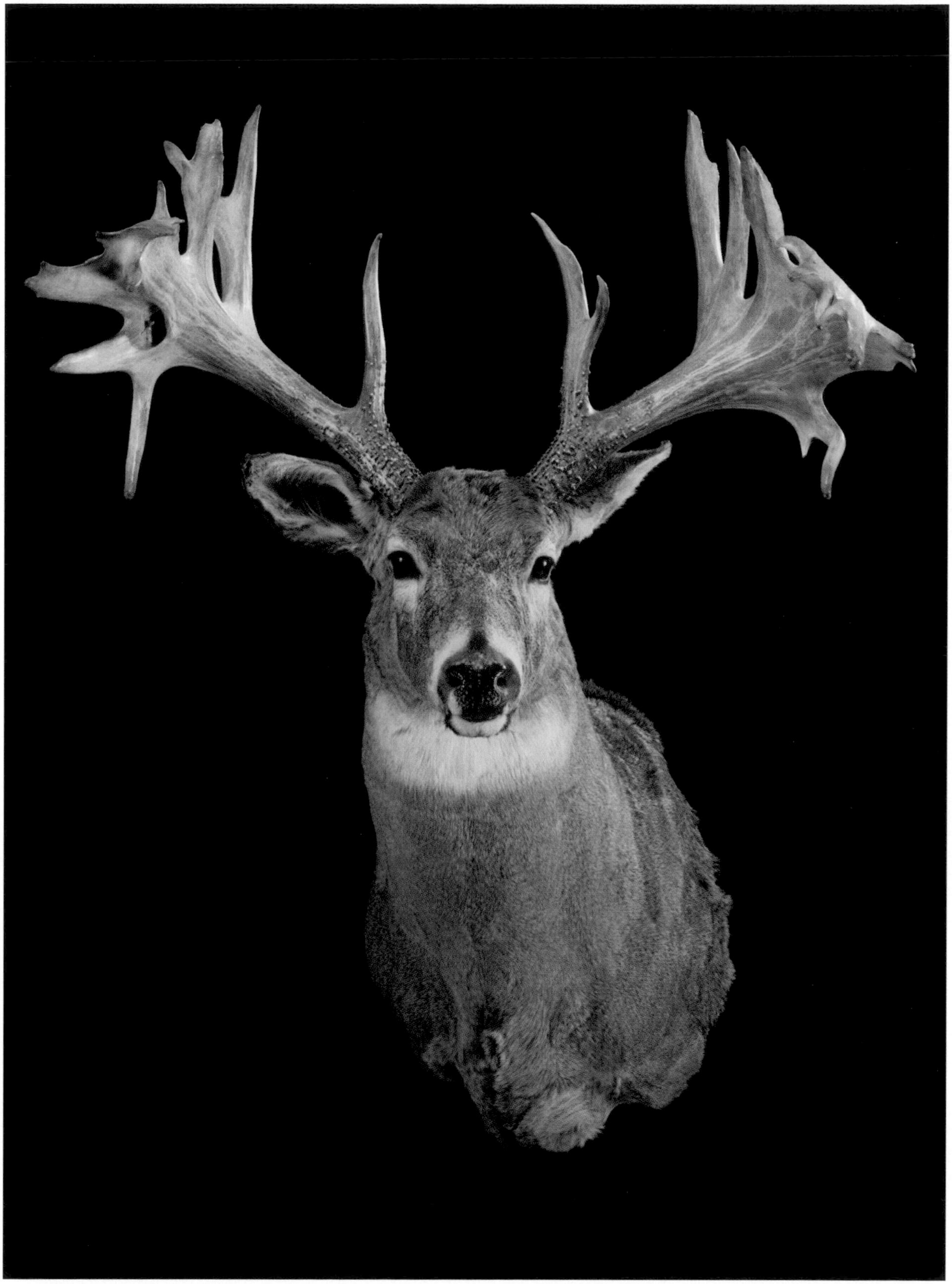

Photo courtesy of Bass Pro Shops.

*Main Characteristics:
Outstanding width
and 53 3/8" of mass
measurements.*

PETER RUTKOWSKI, MINNESOTA, 1942

	Right Antler	Left Antler	Difference
Main Beam Length	25 5/8	25 2/8	3/8
1st Point Length	8 3/8	9 4/8	1 1/8
2nd Point Length	10 4/8	10 7/8	3/8
3rd Point Length	7 7/8	7 5/8	2/8
4th Point Length	2 3/8	2 5/8	2/8
5th Point Length	—	—	—
1st Circumference	5 2/8	5 3/8	1/8
2nd Circumference	5 2/8	5 2/8	0/8
3rd Circumference	6 5/8	9 1/8	2 4/8
4th Circumference	7 0/8	9 4/8	2 4/8
Total	**78 7/8**	**85 1/8**	**7 4/8**

MISCELLANEOUS STATS	
No. Of Points–Right	12
No. Of Points–Left	12
Total No. Of Points	24
Length Of Abnormals	64 7/8
Greatest Spread	30 5/8
Tip To Tip Spread	20 6/8
Inside Spread	24 2/8

FINAL TALLY	
Inside Spread	24 2/8
Right Antler	78 7/8
Left Antler	85 1/8
Gross Score	**188 2/8**
Difference (–)	7 4/8
Subtotal	180 6/8
Abnormals (+)	64 7/8
NET NON-TYPICAL SCORE	**245 5/8**

scrapes dug deep into the moist, black soil and a line of ripped-up 10-inch birch trees dotting the area. For me, this would be that special place.

A similar setting was "that special place" for the late Peter W. Rutkowski when he bagged a tremendous northern Minnesota non-typical in 1942. Peter's now gone, but fortunately the story of his great buck has been preserved by his son, Wallace, who was 12 years old and present on that hunt.

The Rutkowskis lived on a farm in north-central Minnesota, but they generally drove roughly 100 miles to hunt deer near Big Fork and Scenic State Park, where their wilderness camp was located. Being located only about 60 miles south of the Canadian border, this was indeed wild country in those days. Almost the entire route to the camp was gravel roads used primarily for logging.

Most of the area was solid bush, with the exception of the odd hardy homestead. Such a harsh region was only marginally suited for farming, so most homesteaders who primarily depended on agriculture "starved out." But, there were many hardy souls who simply lived off the land. Logging was the primary source of income and a way of life for most, but many trapped during the winter, raised their own vegetables in summer gardens and grew chickens, hogs, milk cows and other livestock to supplement the larder. With homesteaded land under their feet, they needed no income except for the barest of essentials.

Deer and moose hunting in those days was an institution in itself. During the fall, towns came alive at night, as the day's hunts were relived over drinks. The frenzy of the crowd easily could have been mistaken for those boom towns during the gold-rush era. Autumn served as a vacation and festive occasion for farmers, city folks and others who annually looked forward to seeing old friends again, enjoying the good times and doing some serious hunting. A large percentage of these hunters were farmers from farther south who had harvested their crops and finished their farm chores for the year. The hustle and bustle of the nights was part of the trip, but the experience of the wilderness setting and the hunting itself were the featured attractions.

For many years, Peter and 10 to 15 other farmers and friends made their annual trek to the same location in the "big woods." Several days before each season, an advance party of three or four men would head to the site to prepare camp and do a bit of scouting. The camp consisted of a huge World War I army tent that would sleep 10-plus on one side and serve as a kitchen on the other.

Novembers in northern Minnesota generally are colder than an iron toilet seat at the North Pole, so camps had to be designed to provide warmth under adverse conditions. On the sleeping side, bales of hay were broken and fluffed out to a two-foot depth, then covered with horse blankets. The men slept parallel to each other in one long row, covering themselves with blankets.

A modified barrel stove sat squarely in the center and was the only source of heat; at the same time, it served as the kitchen stove, with its flat, homemade "griddle" on top. A large eating table sat in the kitchen, as did makeshift cupboards and other kitchen necessities. It was a cozy camp in a rugged harsh environment where men could listen to the howling of wolves as they dozed off.

On this particular hunt in November 1942, the advance crew had towed the trailer loaded with gear up as usual and had put the camp in order. Saturday would be opening day, so Peter took Wallace and another farming neighbor up on Friday. After getting settled in, Peter hunted both Saturday and Sunday without taking a deer. Because Wallace was only 12 at the time, he didn't actually carry a gun and hunt, but he did go out with his dad or another hunter each day.

On Monday, Wallace went out with one of the neighbors, and Peter went to watch a large slash about three miles from camp. Tree stands seldom were used in that region in those days, but many hunters would post overlooking prime areas, sitting or standing atop brushpiles, stumps or any other natural feature that provided some elevation. Or, they simply would stand at ground level and watch for game.

At about 8:30 or 9 on Monday morning, as Peter overlooked this logged-over area, he caught a glimpse of a huge buck making his way through the short, thick second-growth cover. Although Peter was a good shot, his short-barreled Winchester wasn't that accurate, and the caliber was too small for highly effective deer hunting in the brush. As the buck passed through a semi-opening Peter fired, and the deer was gone in a flash. From the buck's reaction, Peter was sure he'd been hit, and that suspicion was confirmed when he found a few hairs and sparse drops of blood.

"As Wallace penetrated the dense outer wall of the thicket, it opened into a room-like interior that was fairly dark. And before he even realized what was happening, he practically stepped on a huge outstretched buck!"

Small patches of snow were present in shaded areas, but not enough to help a great deal in tracking. After two hours of fruitless searching, Peter rather dejectedly headed back to camp for lunch. Later that afternoon, he spent another couple of hours combing the thick area, but to no avail. Finally, he concluded that the buck had traveled a very long distance before succumbing, or possibly wasn't fatally wounded.

At the time, Peter was a buttermaker by profession, and some business at home required him to return on Tuesday. In those days, farmers separated the cream off the milk and took it to buttermakers to be processed into cheese, butter and other dairy products.

On Wednesday evening, Peter returned to camp to resume his hunting, again taking Wallace with him. By now, 2 1/2 days after shooting the buck, Peter assumed the buck was gone forever.

However, that slash was one of his favorite honeyholes, so he decided to hunt it again Thursday morning. And this time, he took along Wallace.

Peter posted alone for the first couple of hours, as Wallace was preoccupied nearby with the many things a 12-year-old boy can find of interest in the woods. Around 10 a.m., having had no luck, Peter found his son and took him back to the area he'd been posting. Apparently, Peter had heard something moving in the brush, but he never could see its source. He'd now post again and send Wallace in a wide circle around him, hoping a deer might run his way.

The boy was feeling rather important as he began his wide circle. After he'd made his way through the thickets and tangles for a couple hundred yards, he came to a thick clump of spruce. As Wallace pushed through the dense outer wall of the thicket, it opened into a room-like interior that was rather dark. And before he even realized what was happening, he practically stepped on a huge outstretched buck!

The boy relaxed when he realized the animal was dead. After gathering himself, he began to yell for his dad to come over and see what he'd found. When Peter got there, he instantly recognized the wide, flattened antlers, and he knew his lost buck had been found. Apparently, the wounded animal had crawled into the spruce thicket, where he'd died and had remained undiscovered until being almost literally stumbled upon.

To this day, Wallace remembers the ancient swamp monster vividly. "His frame was huge, yet he was very poor," he says. "The rut was in full swing, so I suppose he was run down, because he really looked gaunt and lean. To me he looked like a gray ghost. Much of his head and neck was almost white. I've never seen one that color since. With his huge, palmated rack, long, gaunt body and unusual gray color, he seemed like a phantom of the spruce thicket, and I'll remember that sight forever."

The temperature was falling below 0° at night, so the dead buck was largely frozen; however, the meat already had spoiled from the lingering body heat. Peter chopped off the antlers, as it made little sense to attempt to haul a spoiled buck three miles back to camp. At least the antlers would serve as a great memento of the hunt and of Wallace's miraculous find. In such dense cover, they were indeed lucky to have found a wounded buck that had traveled several hundred yards after the shot.

The huge swamp buck caused quite a stir at camp and in the surrounding area. The fact that he was big wasn't news, for big bucks were common in those parts. The rack's webbing, however, was indeed rare. Even today, this impressive trophy remains one of the largest palmated whitetail racks in existence.

Extreme palmation, particularly on the left antler, marks this Minnesota giant. Photo by Dick Idol, courtesy of North American Whitetail.

Peter's 24-pointer certainly is spectacular in many respects. To begin with, he has tremendous spread, a characteristic that's rarely seen in areas of such dense cover. And the beam palmation is so great that although the base circumferences each measure an impressive 5 4/8 inches, they appear small relative to the rest of the rack. From there the beams just get larger, with the left side having circumference measurements of better than 9 inches! And as if all of that weren't enough, there are five drop tines!

It's sad that Peter didn't live to see the story of his hunt published, as I'm sure it would have meant a great deal to him. In some foolish way, it seems that giving exposure to a great buck and the hunter who got him makes them both "immortal."

This buck is certainly a legend and will remain so as long as there are fans of giant whitetails.

Chapter Thirty Three

THE SHAWN SEARS BUCK

248 4/8 Non-Typical, Indiana, 1990

A November Morning To Remember

By Larry Lawson

Hearing that a hunter's first antlered deer was a record-book buck inevitably brings to mind thoughts of "beginner's luck." But when young Shawn Sears pulled the trigger on the world's most impressive whitetail of the 1990 season, it wasn't simply a case of stumbling into a gold mine.

Shawn, then 26, already had been bowhunting in northern Indiana for a decade. He'd been well trained by his father, Bob, a veteran hunter with numerous big-game kills (including 25 deer with a bow) to his credit. And finally, Shawn had another big advantage that year: For the first time ever, he'd be using a gun.

We're not talking about just any gun, either, but one with a proven track record. Bob had decided to try a .357 Mag. handgun, meaning Shawn could borrow his trusty Montgomery Ward 12-gauge pump with rifle sights. Using this gun, Bob had downed every one of the many bucks at which he'd ever shot, in each case with only one round.

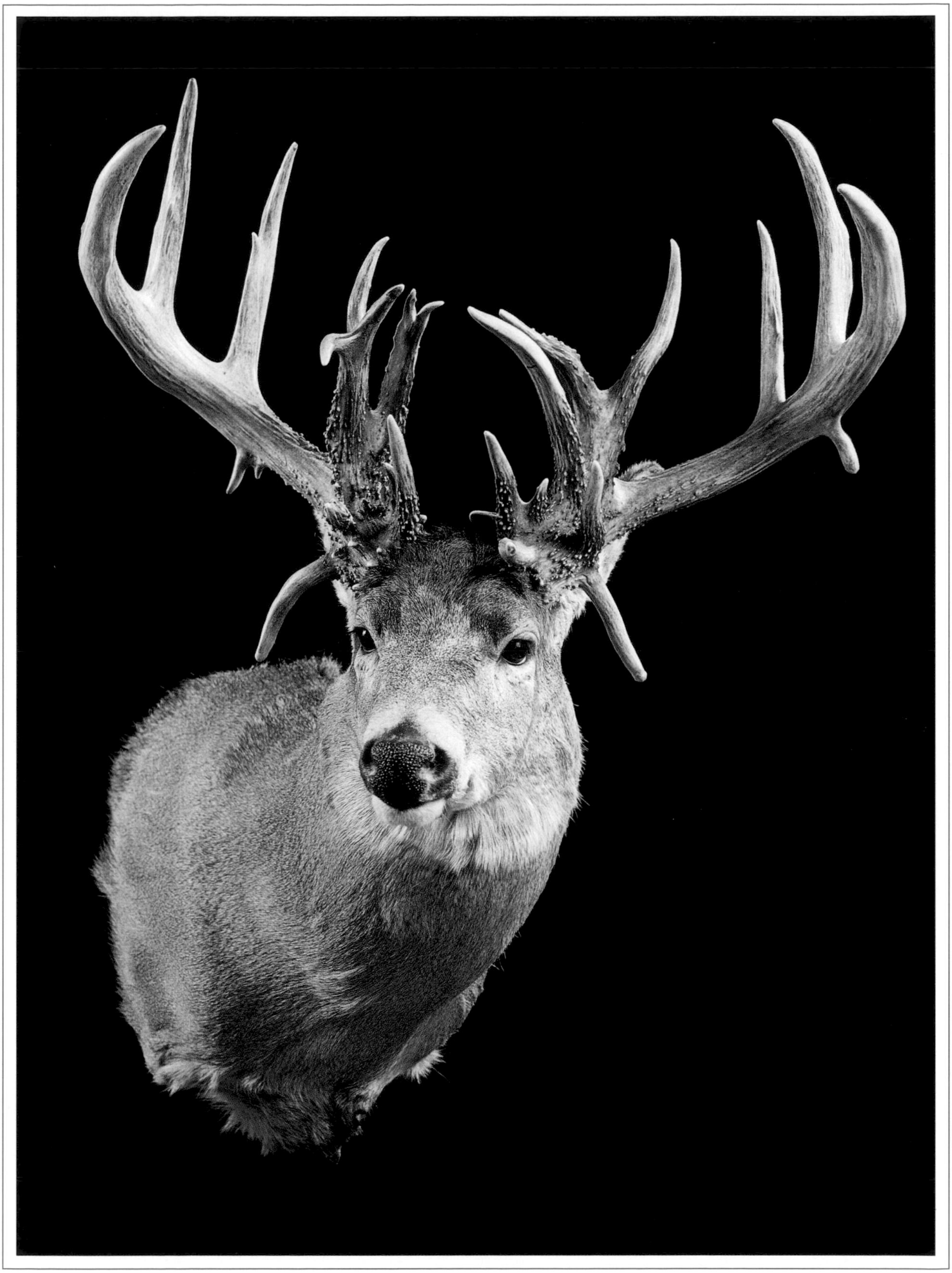

Photo courtesy of Bass Pro Shops.

SHAWN SEARS, INDIANA, 1990

	Right Antler	Left Antler	Difference
Main Beam Length	28 0/8	27 4/8	4/8
1st Point Length	8 7/8	8 5/8	2/8
2nd Point Length	9 4/8	7 7/8	1 5/8
3rd Point Length	8 7/8	9 2/8	3/8
4th Point Length	—	—	—
5th Point Length	—	—	—
1st Circumference	7 7/8	7 4/8	3/8
2nd Circumference	4 7/8	4 5/8	2/8
3rd Circumference	4 7/8	5 0/8	1/8
4th Circumference	4 5/8	4 2/8	3/8
Total	**77 4/8**	**74 5/8**	**3 7/8**

Main Characteristics: Basic 4x4 typical frame would make B&C with no abnormal points. Nearly all abnormals on brow tines or bases.

MISCELLANEOUS STATS

No. Of Points–Right	15
No. Of Points–Left	13
Total No. Of Points	28
Length Of Abnormals	76 5/8
Greatest Spread	26 2/8
Tip To Tip Spread	20 1/8
Inside Spread	23 5/8

FINAL TALLY

Inside Spread	23 5/8
Right Antler	77 4/8
Left Antler	74 5/8
Gross Score	175 6/8
Difference (–)	3 7/8
Subtotal	171 7/8
Abnormals (+)	76 5/8
NET NON-TYPICAL SCORE	**248 4/8**

The weather was cold and foggy as Shawn drove northward from his home in Kokomo to meet Bob and friend Clayton Ailor before dawn on Nov. 10. The men had hunted this area for eight years running, and sightings of several good bucks during early bow season had them back again.

En route, Shawn's mind drifted back to one huge buck he'd seen. The hunter had had only a glimpse of him, but that was enough to identify the deer as a giant.

While bowhunting the area, Bob and Clayton had found 5-inch-diameter rubs, as well as some active scrapes, in brushy thickets along this river bottom. There was serious big-buck activity in the area, including impressive rubs and scrapes not far from where Shawn had sat in bow season. His only change in tactics for the gun opener would be to sit even closer to the sign.

Despite heavy fog limiting visibility to only about 40 yards, dawn was breaking as

Shawn put down a trail of doe urine near his stand. Before the young hunter climbed into his stand he also placed a few earth-scent wafers around the area, hoping to cover any human odor left on the ground.

At 7:45 a.m., Shawn heard the report of Bob's .357 Mag. The shot must have been a good one, the young hunter finally decided, because there hadn't been a second one. But just in case, Shawn tightened his grip on the trusty shotgun.

Then, a faint noise caught his attention. Wiping the heavy fog from his glasses, Shawn turned slowly. A doe was coming directly on line with the scent trail, ambling toward him. And behind her was a buck — a big buck! He was 70 yards from the stand and closing fast!

Shawn had to make some quick decisions about which way to turn. Painful visions raced through his mind: *What if he shoots off to the left, into the brush... or to the right?* But fortunately, the two deer kept coming.

With sweating hands Shawn moved the 12 gauge into position. The buck was now less than 15 yards away, with his nose still on the scent trail — but then, he stopped and looked directly at the tree stand!

Years of waiting for just such a moment had culminated in the chance of a lifetime, and fear of missing gripped at Shawn's throat. With his heart pounding and his nerves just about gone, he could feel the tree shaking.

Don't get excited, he told himself as he slowly lowered the sights to just below the buck's chin.

Booooom! the shotgun roared.

The doe bolted at the sound of the shot, but the buck crashed to the ground.

Then, there was silence, except for the ringing in Shawn's ears. He tried to calm himself as he made his way out of the tree stand, but his adrenaline was still pumping wildly.

"Holy cow!" Shawn exclaimed as he walked up to the 28-point buck. He hadn't seen anything like this rack except in magazines!

Shawn field-dressed the trophy buck, then dragged him more than 200 yards before sitting down to rest. He just kept staring at the buck, still not believing his good luck.

Bob soon drove up in his truck. "Don't you know it's illegal to shoot elk in Indiana?" he asked his son when he saw the deer.

Shawn learned that Bob had shot a small buck with his handgun. They loaded up the big buck and headed off to get Clayton and the other deer. To Shawn's surprise, his dad's "small" buck turned out to have 10 points and a 19-inch inside spread!

Bob's deer dressed 175 pounds, Shawn's 195. Of course, Bob was quick to point out that the difference was because of the weight of the rack on Shawn's buck, and that's partly true. It actually did add several pounds to his dressed weight!

Because of the way in which many of the non-typical points spread out from the lower portion of the rack, the deer should be named "Medusa," after the mythological woman whose hair was a mass of wriggling snakes.

This is certainly a dream deer for any hunter. But the fact that father and son were able to share such a unique hunting experience might be an even greater trophy to cherish.

Chapter Thirty Four

THE KEN SHANE BUCK

---

186 5/8 TYPICAL, WISCONSIN, 2000

A Very Lucky Friday the 13th

BY KEN SHANE

When I met up with Randy Matthiessen in Minneapolis on Friday, Oct. 13, 2000, we thought it would be a good weekend to fill some doe tags in Wisconsin's Buffalo County. Instead, it turned out to be a good weekend for taking a state-record buck.

Randy and I do our best to manage the deer on the farm we hunt. To us, that involves taking as many does as legally possible and not shooting any buck that won't make Pope and Young's minimum score of 125 net typical points. Of course, judging a buck on the hoof can be a challenge, so to make it easy, we simply say, "If you have to think about whether or not it's a shooter, it's not a shooter!"

At around 5 p.m. that Friday we arrived at the farm we hunt, then changed clothes and headed to the woods. Randy chose a stand across the road, and I headed up a small valley behind the farm. The weather was unseasonably warm, so I knew the deer would be close to water. I chose a stand about 70 yards above a small dam, along the transition between a small grove of pines and hardwoods.

*Main Characteristics:
Beautiful 7x6 typical
frame with 4 tines of
10 4/8" or more.*

KEN SHANE, WISCONSIN, 2000

	Right Antler	Left Antler	Difference
Main Beam Length	27 1/8	26 4/8	5/8
1st Point Length	5 1/8	7 6/8	2 5/8
2nd Point Length	8 5/8	8 6/8	1/8
3rd Point Length	10 4/8	11 6/8	1 2/8
4th Point Length	10 7/8	11 1/8	2/8
5th Point Length	5 5/8	7 7/8	2 2/8
6th Point Length	2 4/8	—	2 4/8
1st Circumference	4 4/8	4 3/8	1/8
2nd Circumference	4 1/8	4 0/8	1/8
3rd Circumference	5 6/8	5 3/8	3/8
4th Circumference	4 4/8	4 2/8	2/8
Total	**89 2/8**	**91 6/8**	**10 4/8**

MISCELLANEOUS STATS	
No. Of Points–Right	7
No. Of Points–Left	8
Total No. Of Points	15
Length Of Abnormals	5 3/8
Greatest Spread	23 6/8
Tip To Tip Spread	13 6/8
Inside Spread	21 4/8

FINAL TALLY	
Inside Spread	21 4/8
Right Antler	89 2/8
Left Antler	91 6/8
Gross Score	**202 4/8**
Difference (–)	10 4/8
Subtotal	192 0/8
Abnormals (–)	5 3/8
NET TYPICAL SCORE	**186 5/8**

As I approached the spot, several does flushed from around the pond, and I silently cursed myself for arriving so late. I climbed into my stand at 5:15, and with the temperature around 70 degrees, opted not to wear my Scent-Lok hood. That decision later proved to be a risky one.

As I waited, I heard the farmer's tractor heading into the valley. I turned to watch behind me, in case the does would come up into the pines. Fortunately, the farmer made only one pass with his tractor and then headed back to the barn.

Once that noise was gone, I turned to face the ridge in front of me — and saw a buck scent-marking the overhanging branches. All I could see was antlers and leaves, but when he lowered his head, I knew he was the "Boonie" that had been seen in the area.

The buck was about 40 yards out and was heading straight toward me at a pace that ultimately would test my composure.

For 20 minutes he browsed on leaves and acorns, in no hurry to reach the freshly picked corn field 60 yards below me. He seemed so nonchalant in his approach that he even walked with a quartering wind.

Not wanting him to get too close, I drew when he was about 30 yards out. He looked directly at me but presented no shot. I felt naked as he stared my way —

Ken Shane's "doe hunt" turned into something much bigger. Photo by Pat Reeve.

it as if he were untouched. Then he disappeared.

Turning back to where the buck had been standing, I saw my arrow imbedded in a log. When I saw no blood on it, I started to play mind games with myself.

At 6:25 p.m. I decided to retrieve my arrow for a better look. Upon examination, I found it covered with tallow. Did I hit him low?

and then, as if nothing were wrong, he resumed feeding. I let down the bow.

It took the buck another 10 minutes to move only a few yards closer. Suddenly, as I felt the wind swirl and hit me on the back of my neck, he snapped his head up and looked directly at me. I thought, *This is it! Get ready!* But again, he lowered his head and kept feeding.

When the buck got to within 28 yards, I drew again and locked on, praying he would turn off the trail.

I'd been holding for well over a minute when the deer finally presented a quartering shot. His front leg was back, and I knew he had to step forward to make the shot work. As if on command he did so, and my instincts took over. I released my arrow, and in an instant he bolted back up the ridge.

I followed the deer for about 20 yards and then lost him in the brush. Through my binoculars I saw him about 30 yards out, standing with his tail up and flicking

I followed in the direction he'd run for about 10 yards but found no blood.

I backed out of the woods quietly and waited for Randy to return to camp. We headed back into the woods at 9 p.m. It didn't take long to find first blood, and with each step, the trail became more obvious. We'd covered only about 30 yards before Randy broke our code of silence. "I've got your deer," he said.

When I followed the beam of his flashlight, I saw the tall, massive rack protruding out of the leaves. I was overcome with emotion and thanked the Lord for helping me find my trophy.

My arrow had hit exactly where I'd aimed, taking the deer through both lungs at a quartering angle. He'd traveled only about 50 yards before going down.

In the spring of 2001, a Pope and Young panel awarded my trophy a final score of 186 5/8 net typical points, tying for the state archery record. Now, who says Friday the 13th is unlucky?

Chapter Thirty Five

THE LYLE SPITZNOGLE BUCK

258 2/8 NON-TYPICAL, IOWA, 1982

An Iowa Buck Worth Fighting For

BY ORLAN LOVE

The timber-laced grain fields of Iowa grow many world-class whitetails, and the party hunting allowed during shotgun season throws together competing groups whose passions and proprietary instincts can be inflamed by the sight of a monster buck.

So it was that in December 1982, in the wooded bottoms of the Iowa River, two parties of adrenaline-juiced Louisa County hunters would lock horns over a buck whose rack would prove to be the state's second largest of all time. When the cussing and shoving finally had ended, one hunter's scalp had been cracked open with the butt of another's shotgun, and the prize had been awarded to the man who initially had shot it: Lyle Spitznogle of Wapello.

Lyle, 28 years old at the time, had been hunting during the second of the state's two shotgun seasons with several companions when the world-class buck tried to race past him. "It was during the week, so we were down to a smaller party, maybe six or seven of us," Lyle recalls. "It was a normal mid-December day with temperatures in the mid-30s."

LYLE SPITZNOGLE, IOWA, 1982

	Right Antler	Left Antler	Difference
Main Beam Length	28 5/8	28 1/8	4/8
1st Point Length	11 0/8	10 1/8	7/8
2nd Point Length	12 4/8	10 1/8	2 3/8
3rd Point Length	11 4/8	11 5/8	1/8
4th Point Length	7 4/8	8 3/8	7/8
5th Point Length	—	—	—
1st Circumference	7 0/8	6 7/8	1/8
2nd Circumference	5 2/8	5 2/8	0/8
3rd Circumference	5 0/8	5 7/8	7/8
4th Circumference	4 5/8	5 1/8	4/8
Total	**93 0/8**	**91 4/8**	**6 2/8**

Main Characteristics: World-class 5x5 main frame plus 14 abnormal points. Brow tines of 10 1/8" and 11".

MISCELLANEOUS STATS

No. Of Points–Right	10
No. Of Points–Left	14
Total No. Of Points	24
Length Of Abnormals	55 7/8
Greatest Spread	26 2/8
Tip To Tip Spread	14 7/8
Inside Spread	24 1/8

FINAL TALLY

Inside Spread	24 1/8
Right Antler	93 0/8
Left Antler	91 4/8
Gross Score	**208 5/8**
Difference (–)	6 2/8
Subtotal	202 3/8
Abnormals (+)	55 7/8
NET NON-TYPICAL SCORE	**258 2/8**

Even though first-season hunters have first crack at the big bucks, Lyle's party always hunted second season, he says, because it was several days longer than the first season, had fewer hunters and typically was colder than the first season. Many of their favorite hunting spots included marshy areas that would freeze enough to permit foot travel during the second season.

The ugly confrontation occurred southeast of Wapello, in a low-lying area of grain fields, timber and swampland near where the Iowa River empties into the Mississippi.

Glen Brown, the first hunter in the party to see the trophy buck, was posted on a levee along the Iowa River, where Lyle and two other hunters were to conclude their drive.

Three bucks came out of the timber: a 3-pointer in front, then an 8-pointer and the big one, as big ones usually are, in the rear. "I could see a lot of antler on the big one," Glen says. "It got my adrenaline going."

Glen estimates the three bucks were between 90 and 100 yards from him. He froze, waiting patiently for a good shot until "they suddenly started scampering around, getting excited."

In an attempt to shoot the big deer, Glen aimed his pump shotgun over the back of the 3-pointer, but the 8-pointer got in the way. The slug dropped him.

Although the 8-pointer proved to have an excellent rack, Glen's attention immediately shifted to the two remaining bucks. (Iowa hunting regulations allow a shotgun hunter to continue to shoot as long as anyone in his immediate hunting party has an available tag.)

Glen knew he'd have to eject the spent shell and pump a live round into the chamber before firing again, and he was worried that this movement would frighten the two deer left. His fear was well founded. When he slid the pump, the 3-pointer bolted across an open field to the north, where another member of the party, Gene Lihf, shot him.

The big buck slipped into the timber, into the path of Lyle and the Schneider brothers, Duane and Howard, who were approaching from the opposite direction.

Lyle says the big buck, running at full speed, passed within 20 yards of him. He and Duane each fired several shots at the fleeing animal. "Duane did not get anything," Lyle claims. "I hit the big buck at least twice."

Glen says he heard the shots and heard Lyle holler twice that he'd hit the deer. He also heard the sounds of ice breaking in the swamp as the buck tried to escape.

Lyle had shot the buck in the lower jaw and in the abdominal cavity. The heavy lead slugs rolled the deer, but the buck regained its footing and disappeared, in a struggling gait, over a levee.

In Lyle's mind, there seems to be no doubt that his shots mortally wounded the buck. "We knew where it went," he says. "It was leaving a big trail of blood on the ground. We were going to give it a few minutes to bleed to death and trail it. We were confident we would find it." When Glen caught up with them, they told him that the wounded deer had run across the levee and out of sight.

"I found where it went through a barbed-wire fence," he says. "I found drops of blood on the ground, and from his hoof prints I could tell that his stride had changed, that he was slowing down."

Lyle says he was sure the buck wouldn't run far before it died. But as he and his hunting companions waited, giving the buck time to bleed to death, they heard shots on the other side of the levee.

As it turned out, a party of hunters who didn't have permission to be on that land had seen the mortally wounded buck and had started shooting at him.

While Lyle and friends advanced on the deer, Glen left the party to call the local Department of Natural Resources conservation officer, who turned out to be 22-year-old rookie Scott Kinseth.

When Lyle's party reached the buck, they found him dead, his throat slit by a member of the other party, one of their tags attached to a massive antler.

With the passage of nearly two decades, memories fade and witnesses die. Neither Lyle nor the conservation officer can now recall all of the details, but they agree that the situation — two groups of angry, shotgun-wielding men arguing over a big deer — could have turned out worse than it did.

"It was ugly," the officer says. "One guy was down on the ground, bleeding. He'd been hit with the butt of a shotgun, and someone had pulled a knife."

Lyle says he recalls the standoff as more verbal than physical. "Words were said and threats were made," he claims. "There was a little scuffling going on. A guy pulled a knife, but no guns were pointed. It was a little scary, but no one was really hurt."

A key eyewitness to the event helped to resolve the matter in Lyle's favor. Custer Walker, on whose land the incident had taken place, was running his traps and saw everything, Lyle says.

"When we heard the shooting on the other side of the levee, we could see old Custer up on top of the levee," Lyle remembers. "We went over to talk to him, and he told us what happened."

When Lyle's crew approached the dead deer, members of the competing party asserted their claim to it.

"They said they shot it," Lyle recalls. "We told them Custer saw the whole thing, and that's not how he saw it."

When the officer arrived, Custer told him the big deer had run across the levee and lay down in an open field, where it would have died if left alone. Sam Walker recalls that his late father, who died in 1992 at the age of 76, talked about the incident at the time.

"Dad saw the whole thing happen," Sam says. "What I got, this buck came running through nearly dead. It had been shot by Lyle and those guys, but then these other guys who had no business in there shot at it, too. I don't think they hit it. It was on Dad's property, and they didn't belong there, and that helped swing things in Lyle's favor, as I recall."

After hearing Custer's testimony, the officer awarded the deer to the hunter who'd shot it first, and that was Lyle.

Scott says he vaguely recalls the involvement of a Louisa County sheriff's deputy, Ron Gardner, who worked out an agreement to the effect that assault charges would be dropped in exchange for relinquishing any claim to the deer.

"That could be," Lyle says, "but I don't remember it that way. It's been a long time."

Ron has since passed away. No current employees of the sheriff's department worked there in 1982, and the department has no record of the incident.

Iowa law provides little specific guidance for settling cases in which one hunter shoots a deer first and another later tags it. In some cases the doctrine of "first blood" prevails, while in others the deer belongs to the hunter administering the final shot.

"You have to take a case-by-case approach to each incident and try to keep hunter ethics and principles of fair chase uppermost in mind," Scott notes.

His boss, DNR Law Enforcement Bureau Chief Lowell Joslin, agrees. "We've had it go both ways," he says. "When tussles come up, especially when the person who shot the deer doesn't find it right away, it gets nasty. It can get really nasty when big antlers are involved."

This buck certainly had big antlers; indeed, his wide, tall rack scores 258 2/8 net Boone and Crockett points. Among Iowa whitetails, only Larry Raveling's 282-incher from 1973 (featured in *Legendary Whitetails*) tops this one.

Lyle had the rack mounted by a local taxidermist. Naturally, that mount suffered from the fact that "the other guys

It's not hard to imagine that grown men might squabble over the Spitznogle buck.
Photo courtesy of Orlan Love and Lyle Spitznogle.

had slit the throat and ruined the cape." The rack has now been remounted and is on display at the headquarters of Bass Pro Shops in Springfield, Missouri.

The buck and the hunter dispute he engendered symbolize the basic fault of party hunting as practiced in Iowa and a few other states, according to Lyle. "I (couldn't) care less to go group hunting after that," he says. "It is too dangerous, too scary. It has been at least 10 years since I have gone deer hunting."

Despite occasional squabbles such as the one Lyle and his friends unfortunately found themselves in back in 1982, the Iowa shotgun season still has so very much to offer. The success rate is high,

and a hunter has more than a theoretical chance to shoot a whitetail buck of legendary proportions.

In a typical shotgun season around 70 percent of the participants harvest deer, according to Willie Suchy, the Department of Natural Resources biologist in charge of managing Iowa's herd.

Nutrition and age are key factors in growing large antlers. Iowa's abundant fields of high-protein soybeans provide optimum nutrition, and the later-than-average slug season gives bucks a better-than-average chance to reach maturity.

Put it all together, and you realize why Iowa frequently produces bucks worth fighting for.

Chapter Thirty Six

THE RICHARD STAHL BUCK

246 3/8 NON-TYPICAL, KANSAS, 1992

More Like a Bull Elk than a Deer

BY RICHARD STAHL

G oing into the 1992 Kansas bow season, I feared it could be the worst of my life. Although I'd been a bowhunter for years, in November 1991 I'd fallen while painting, fracturing my neck and losing much of the strength in my right hand and arm. Eventually I overcame this injury and learned to shoot a left-handed bow.

I broke more arrows than I saved over the first four months, but with many hours of practice shooting at a 3-D deer target, I began to regain some of my confidence. As an instinctive shooter, I could regularly hit the target in the kill zone out to 15 yards.

I failed to tag a buck during the early part of bow season, and eventually the early-December rifle season rolled around. I don't hunt with a gun, but many of my friends do. All through the short gun season I joked with the guys hunting the area, reminding them to "leave the big one for me." Well, they saw a big buck on several occasions, but no shots were fired. Only one small buck, an 8-pointer, was taken from my hunting area during gun season, and that deer was shot by the landowner.

*Main Characteristics:
Extreme width.
Unique non-typical
points off inside of
left beam.*

RICHARD STAHL, KANSAS, 1992

	Right Antler	Left Antler	Difference
Main Beam Length	27 7/8	26 1/8	1 6/8
1st Point Length	6 4/8	7 0/8	4/8
2nd Point Length	12 2/8	9 5/8	2 5/8
3rd Point Length	9 6/8	9 7/8	1/8
4th Point Length	9 4/8	6 4/8	3 0/8
5th Point Length	2 5/8	—	2 5/8
1st Circumference	5 1/8	6 6/8	1 5/8
2nd Circumference	4 6/8	5 0/8	2/8
3rd Circumference	5 1/8	5 4/8	3/8
4th Circumference	5 0/8	4 3/8	5/8
Total	**88 4/8**	**80 6/8**	**13 4/8**

MISCELLANEOUS STATS	
No. Of Points–Right	9
No. Of Points–Left	14
Total No. Of Points	23
Length Of Abnormals	62 6/8
Greatest Spread	30 6/8
Tip To Tip Spread	27 0/8
Inside Spread	27 7/8

FINAL TALLY	
Inside Spread	27 7/8
Right Antler	88 4/8
Left Antler	80 6/8
Gross Score	197 1/8
Difference (–)	13 4/8
Subtotal	183 5/8
Abnormals (+)	62 6/8
NET NON-TYPICAL SCORE	**246 3/8**

At last, Dec. 14 — opening day of the late bow season! I was out early, but the day turned out to be uneventful, with only one doe being seen. All day long I kept hearing warning cries of squirrels and birds.

The next day found me out even earlier, as I wanted to be deep in the woods by daylight. I often still-hunted a particular draw, and that's where I wanted to try my luck.

When I got there, I noticed some huge rubs. Big bucks in my area will take on hefty trees, but these rubs were unlike any I'd

seen. They were on hedge (Osage orange) trees 14 to 16 inches in diameter, and the trunks had been polished to a bright orange by the buck's antlers. This got my attention!

Not far away I found a saddle, a low spot where the heads of two drainages meet. After finding a tree to lean against, helping to hide my outline and make it easier to sit still, I waited for an hour to see if any bucks would come through. Finally, an 8-pointer trotted into view. I didn't want to shoot him, so I sat silently, letting him walk past at 10 yards.

No more than 10 minutes later, a small 9-pointer appeared. He seemed nervous and kept looking at those big orange rubs as though they were going to jump out at him. He didn't stay around long. Nothing more showed that day.

The next morning, the weather was overcast and damp, with the temperature in the 30s. Because the wind had shifted, I sneaked back into the area at daylight via a different route, one that forced me to go through the thickest part of the timber.

I was standing on the east side of the cedar-choked draw when I noticed a faint trail angling right toward those impressive rubs. I decided to stay there, rather than continue on. I located a large cedar and crawled beneath it to wait.

Right away, I was surprised by a red fox. He never knew I was there and simply strolled on past. I recall thinking that seeing a predator unalarmed at close range must mean I had a good setup.

It wasn't long afterwards that all my dreams turned to reality. One moment there was nothing around… the next, not 20 yards away stood a monstrous buck! He calmly put his nose to the ground and silently walked along the trail. I could tell he would pass within 12 yards of me and would be completely broadside when he did.

I don't remember actually shooting, only drawing my bow and then seeing the arrow hit behind the buck's right shoulder. He threw his head up and lunged forward, snapping the arrow in two as he crashed off into the thicket.

There I was, shaking and grinning all at once; I didn't know exactly how big the buck was, only that he was huge! After waiting for a solid hour, I finally started to follow his blood trail. It was an awesome sight, because there was blood everywhere.

I easily followed the sign for 60 yards or so, and there lay a 23-point non-typical!

With a 30 6/8-inch outside spread and tines sweeping forward and upward from the lower part of his left beam, he looked more like a bull elk than a deer. I couldn't believe my eyes.

To my knowledge, no one else ever had seen this buck, yet there he was lying right in front of me, bigger and more beautiful than anything else on earth. My best friend Jerry helped me with the happy chore of getting him home.

The rack green-scored around 246 Pope and Young points; after the mandatory 60-day drying period it shrank to an even 244. However, upon panel scoring, the final score was raised to 246 3/8, making the deer No. 4 by bow at that time. He also was the world's top bow-taken non-typical of 1992.

You know, after all was said and done, it turned out to be a pretty good bow season after all!

> *"With a 30 6/8-inch outside spread and tines sweeping forward and upward from the lower part of his left beam, he looked more like a bull elk than a deer."*

✦

Chapter Thirty Seven

THE TROY STEPHENS BUCK

198 0/8 TYPICAL, MICHIGAN, 1996

An Invitation to a State Record

BY RICHARD P. SMITH

Unlike many other big-game species, the whitetail doesn't discriminate on the basis of a hunter's bank account. And for that, Troy Stephens is thankful. This young resident of Jackson, Michigan, enjoys deer hunting, and since age 14 he's hunted as often as he can. However, the fact that he wasn't employed when the 1996 gun season rolled around limited his opportunity to hunt that year. So strapped was Troy for money that at the time, he didn't even own a gun or any hunting clothes. If he were to get a buck that fall, it would have to be as a direct result of some fellow hunter's generosity.

On the evening of Nov. 24, a friend invited him to hunt the following morning, and he gratefully accepted. Although Troy had been hunting elsewhere to that point of the gun season, using a Remington 12-gauge shotgun borrowed from friend William Gregory, he still had an unfilled either-sex tag in his pocket.

Roughly two inches of fresh snow covered the ground as Troy and his host crossed the property in the pre-dawn darkness. The host wanted to hunt a spot

Troy Stephens, Michigan, 1996

	Right Antler	Left Antler	Difference
Main Beam Length	29 2/8	29 4/8	2/8
1st Point Length	10 0/8	11 3/8	1 3/8
2nd Point Length	13 2/8	13 4/8	2/8
3rd Point Length	9 7/8	11 2/8	1 3/8
4th Point Length	9 3/8	9 0/8	3/8
5th Point Length	5 6/8	1 6/8	4 0/8
1st Circumference	5 2/8	5 1/8	1/8
2nd Circumference	4 6/8	5 1/8	3/8
3rd Circumference	4 7/8	5 2/8	3/8
4th Circumference	5 4/8	4 3/8	1 1/8
Total	**97 7/8**	**96 2/8**	**9 5/8**

Main Characteristics: Super brow tines of 10" and 11 3/8" as well as G-2 tines of 13 2/8" and 13 4/8" contribute to 214 3/8" gross typical score.

Miscellaneous Stats

No. Of Points–Right	9
No. Of Points–Left	7
Total No. Of Points	16
Length Of Abnormals	6 6/8
Greatest Spread	23 0/8
Tip To Tip Spread	6 6/8
Inside Spread	20 2/8

Final Tally

Inside Spread	20 2/8
Right Antler	97 7/8
Left Antler	96 2/8
Gross Score	214 3/8
Difference (–)	9 5/8
Subtotal	204 6/8
Abnormals (–)	6 6/8
Net Typical Score	**198 0/8**

toward the back of the property, so as they drove toward that location, they looked for a potential stand site for Troy.

At one point, they saw a major deer trail marked by numerous fresh tracks coming out of a corn field. A wedge of woods extended into the field where the trail was. It seemed a logical place for whitetails to move from the field into the woods without exposing themselves any more than necessary, so Troy decided to watch the well-used runway.

He set up a folding chair about 10 feet into the cover and was in position before dawn.

"Just as it started to get light, I saw two deer come out of the corn field," Troy says. "I could see shadows over the one deer's head, so I knew it was a buck.

"I was wearing real thick gloves, and had to take the glove off my shooting hand, so I could slip my finger into the trigger guard. I wasn't sure how good the buck was, but I was going to make him look at me. I dropped the glove hard on the snow. It was a still morning, so the sound of the glove hitting the snow was easy to hear.

"The buck looked my way and then put his head down and kept walking," Troy continues. "He was following a doe. I put the gun up and took my time, carefully putting the sights on him. The gun was loaded with buckshot and slugs, with buckshot in the chamber.

"My first shot hit him in the front leg, and he started limping," the hunter says. "After I shot, he started heading for the woods. I jumped up and ran after him. Then I took another shot, but I couldn't tell if that one hit him. Right before he got in the woods, I took one more shot, and he dropped right there."

A copper-plated 00 buckshot pellet to the brain is what stopped the trophy buck so quickly. Taxidermist Jim "Bass" Squires of Jackson, Michigan, found the pellet when he was removing the buck's skull plate prior to mounting.

After waiting a bit to ensure that the buck wasn't going anywhere, Troy walked up to him. It wasn't until the hunter lifted the rack that he realized the magnitude of what he'd done.

The rack has 16 points, 12 of which make up the typical frame. The gross typical score is a whopping 214 3/8, but 16 3/8 inches of deductions drop the net

After Troy Stephens (front) took his trophy, local deer hunter Jim Sezykutowicz came forth with the deer's previous sheds. Photo courtesy of Richard P. Smith.

to 198 0/8. Even so, the Stephens buck became the state-record typical with inches to spare.

The deer was estimated to be 4 1/2 or 5 1/2 years old. Troy says he found a chunk of lead in the meat when butchering the animal, evidence of an earlier encounter with another hunter.

After the season, Troy's taxidermist learned that the buck's shed antlers from the previous year had been found. In April 1996, Jim Sezykutowicz had picked them up just a half-mile from where Troy eventually shot the deer. The first shed was found near a cedar tree in a fence line, and a search of the vicinity turned up the second antler 70 feet away. The buck's 1995 rack would have scored in the 180s.

Jim and his son, Phil, each had seen the buck during the fall of 1995. Phil had spotted him on Oct. 1, the bow opener, while Jim had jumped him later in the month, on a pheasant hunt. But no one ever had been able to get a shot at this behemoth until Troy came along just over a year later.

The Troy Stephens buck is now on permanent display at Craig Calderone's Michigan Whitetail Hall of Fame Museum in the town of Grass Lake. Fittingly, that's just down the road from where this giant was shot.

❦

Chapter Thirty Eight

THE
SAM TOWNSEND BUCK

231 4/8 NON-TYPICAL, ILLINOIS, 1986

A Game Plan that Came Together

BY SAM TOWNSEND

As my eye caught movement on the ridge about 100 yards opposite me, I paused before installing the last screw-in step 18 feet above the Illinois fencerow. It was around 3 p.m. on a bright, sunny Nov. 6, 1986. Clinging to one tree while I rested one foot on a step in a second one, I focused my binoculars on the movement.

Exultation coursed through my veins; I was looking once again at the largest buck I'd ever seen. There was no mistaking his huge body or rack, which had bases as thick as my forearms. Even in photos, I'd never seen a deer of his size.

I'd first seen him momentarily during the 1984 bow season, in this same area. Then, in the fall of 1985 I'd spotted him twice, in each case well out of bow range. Now here he was again, and unaware of my presence. However, my joy was dampened by the fact that both my bow and camera were still on the ground as I was attaching the last step to a new stand setup. I couldn't move to retrieve them without being spotted. Every muscle in my legs quivered as I clung to the tree, trying to keep absolutely still.

SAM TOWNSEND, ILLINOIS, 1986

	Right Antler	Left Antler	Difference
Main Beam Length	26 0/8	25 6/8	2/8
1st Point Length	8 0/8	8 0/8	0/8
2nd Point Length	10 1/8	10 4/8	3/8
3rd Point Length	9 1/8	10 0/8	7/8
4th Point Length	8 5/8	10 5/8	2 0/8
5th Point Length	2 4/8	3 4/8	1 0/8
1st Circumference	7 5/8	8 3/8	6/8
2nd Circumference	5 7/8	6 0/8	1/8
3rd Circumference	6 0/8	7 0/8	1 0/8
4th Circumference	5 1/8	6 6/8	1 5/8
Total	**89 0/8**	**96 4/8**	**8 0/8**

Main Characteristics: One of the most massive bow bucks ever, with 52 6/8" of circumference measurements. Great typical frame grossing 203 7/8".

MISCELLANEOUS STATS	
No. Of Points–Right	11
No. Of Points–Left	10
Total No. Of Points	21
Length Of Abnormals	35 5/8
Greatest Spread	23 4/8
Tip To Tip Spread	11 1/8
Inside Spread	18 3/8

FINAL TALLY	
Inside Spread	18 3/8
Right Antler	89 0/8
Left Antler	96 4/8
Gross Score	**203 7/8**
Difference (–)	8 0/8
Subtotal	195 7/8
Abnormals (+)	35 5/8
NET NON-TYPICAL SCORE	**231 4/8**

Suddenly, I noticed an 8-point buck about 20 yards closer to me. As I watched him, he glanced over his shoulder, and a second 8-pointer moved into view. They circled each other warily, like two unfamiliar dogs, but my attention was drawn back to the king on the ridge. He started pawing a scrape and raking the ground with his rack, totally ignoring the two lesser bucks.

As I watched this monster, I was jarred out of my fascination by a noise behind me. I turned my head, and a third 8-pointer was standing 10 yards away, sighting up his nose right at me. What a helpless feeling! Never had I been surrounded by so many good bucks... and yet, for the moment, I could do nothing but hang on.

When I looked at this latest arrival, he turned and bounded off. I figured then that the show was over. But no! The two circling 8-pointers were watching him, heads up and ears forward, but they weren't alarmed. In fact, quite unexpectedly, they started walking my way!

At a range of 20 yards they passed me, then walked out into the open and stood there. I returned my attention to the big buck, which had calmly lay down, facing away from me. I studied him for a few minutes, then looked back at the two 8-pointers in the pasture. Incredibly, there were now three bucks there. Two of them had started an earnest shoving match, which turned into a push-and-crash battle with the clashing of antlers.

I feared the king on the ridge would come down to establish his dominance while my bow was still on the ground. But he'd merely stood up and had begun to rub a sapling, totally ignoring the fight scarcely 100 yards away. After thrashing the tree, he walked a few feet into the brush, still facing away from the fight. At about this time, the third 8-pointer started meandering back toward the big buck.

My legs had now been braced for nearly a half-hour, and they simply couldn't hold me any longer. I began slipping down the tree, one step at a time. Immediately, the two fighting bucks noticed me and were gone. When I then looked to the ridge, the big buck and his companion also had disappeared. I didn't see any of them again that day.

From that afternoon on, I started hunting the big buck with a dedication that wouldn't have been possible even the previous season, though I'd been bowhunting whitetails for 13 years with a high success rate. The new intensity with which I approached hunting came after the Illinois-Iowa Whitetail Classic at Davenport, Iowa, in April 1986. I'd ended the previous bow season on a note of frustration, because I hadn't been able

to locate the trophy buck, in spite of all of my efforts. As I listened to the speakers of the seminars at the show and talked to other trophy hunters, all of the trophy-hunting "rules" I'd ever read or heard finally began to sink in. Big whitetails are a different breed, and they must be hunted differently from other deer. I knew I had to change my hunting style.

The 150-acre pasture in which I was hunting had a wide creek running through it, with scattered stands of hardwoods and brushy areas lying among ridges and ravines. Corn and soybean fields bordered the pasture, and the terrain created a natural funnel which many bucks traveled through. Over the years my studies of the area helped me locate the best sites for my portable tree stands, which allowed me to respond to changing travel patterns of deer in the area.

To get within shooting range of this particular buck, I felt I'd have to get into and out of my stand undetected, time after time. After the 1985 season, I realized that if I made one mistake, he may disappear again. I didn't want him detecting my trail, and although I used attractant and cover scents, I didn't think there was any way to completely disguise human scent. Therefore, I needed stands placed to let me hunt with the wind from any direction.

I set up three stands, each around 25 yards (my ideal shooting range) into the edge of the brush. When using buck lure, I'd squirt it on the ground a bit downwind from my stand, where it hopefully would attract the buck's attention and give me a better opportunity for a shot.

That fall, I set three firm rules to keep from spooking the buck. Prior to the season, I soaked my rubber-bottomed pac boots all night in a baking soda-and-water solution, then scrubbed them clean. From then on, I only wore them to and from the stand and kept them in a plastic bag the rest of the time. Also, each time I walked across the pasture toward my stands, I stepped in every fresh "cow pie" I could find. After the ground froze, I began using scent pads with red fox urine. I also made sure I never smoked while hunting or left any litter in the area, and I carried a urine bottle for myself.

Finally, once I started hunting the buck, except to walk to and from my stands, I refrained from scouting the area for fresh rubs and scrapes. I always walked in from the direction that took the wind into consideration, even when this necessitated a roundabout route.

During the 11 days that followed my Nov. 6 sighting of the monster, I hunted that area exclusively, as the wind was favorable for doing so. I also was fortunate in that no one else was hunting the area at the time.

Nearly every day I sighted does and smaller bucks moving through the funnel my stands overlooked. One day I was tempted when a beautiful 10-pointer followed the buck-lure scent right into my shooting lane. But the memory of the massive buck kept my arrow on its rest.

On Nov. 18, for only the third time that season, wind conditions were perfect for a stand I'd placed near the ridge on which I'd first seen the giant buck 12

"Because I had to float the buck across the creek to get him to my vehicle, I didn't field dress him immediately. Thus, I had the opportunity to weigh him at the local locker plant. Although he was run down a bit from the rut, his live weight was an astounding 278 pounds, and he dressed out at 237."

days before. There was only a mild breeze, and the temperature was in the 30s. The sky was overcast and cloudy with an approaching storm: just the kind of day on which deer seem to move.

At around 7 a.m. I saw a spike buck, which slowly wandered past upwind of me. About a half-hour later a doe and a yearling walked past as well. Then, at around 8 a.m., movement to my right caught my eye.

Turning slowly in that direction, I saw the huge buck roughly 80 yards out and coming straight toward me. The first thing I noticed was his distinctive rack. He was walking purposefully and clearly was on a route that would take him right through one of my prepared shooting lanes.

I turned my body to the right and got into shooting position. He'd have to pass either on my right or left, and as I had a tree limb beside me, I had to try to figure which way he would go before choosing my final position. If he turned to his right, he'd be downwind of me, where I hoped my buck lure on the ground would distract his attention before he caught my scent. If he instead turned to his left, he'd be in a clear shooting lane.

When the deer was about 30 yards from me he turned to his right, passing through brush, which effectively screened him. I knew I'd have just one chance as he passed downwind, when he'd walk through a small opening. I went through my mental checklist as I started my draw: *arrow on rest... full draw… finger in corner of mouth… track him with the sight pin on his chest, right behind his front leg.*

As the buck stepped warily into the opening, I held up on releasing the arrow, because a small limb was silhouetted on his body. I made myself wait as he took two more steps. When he did I released, and the arrow sped to its target only 20 yards away.

Sam Townsend's years of planning and hard hunting for this massive brute paid off when he arrowed the giant on Nov. 18, 1986. Photo courtesy of Alan Foster.

I felt the shot was perfect in the millisecond the arrow took to get there. Sure enough, it buried itself to the fletching in his side. The buck exploded, running headlong, but I knew he wouldn't go far.

I did it! my mind yelled. I watched him crashing through the brush for about 50 yards, then he stopped abruptly, hesitated and folded onto the ground. While I hadn't been nervous until that moment, now I could hardly lower my bow, unsnap my safety belt and climb down. It seemed as if I were in slow motion.

I couldn't believe the size of the antlers; they were so big the deer's head was being held off the ground! The 21-point rack was as massive as I'd remembered, and I couldn't span either base with my fingers!

The cloudy sky fulfilled its promise, and sleet began to fall. By the time I'd finished tagging the buck and taking photos, it had turned to rain.

Because I had to float the buck across the creek to get him to my vehicle, I didn't field dress him immediately. Thus, I had the opportunity to weigh him at the local locker plant. Although he was run down a bit from the rut, his live weight was 278 pounds, and he dressed out at 237.

After the 60-day drying period for Pope and Young I had the rack officially scored by Mel Johnson, who came up with an entry score of 226 5/8 net non-typical. That was good enough to make my buck No. 2 in the state. A P&Y panel later elevated the final score to 231 4/8.

As I look back at the three seasons of single-minded determination required to take this buck, I realize that countless hours of scouting, planning, waiting and driving 60 miles round trip each time I hunted all were invested in making my dream come true.

But in the end, getting to wrap my hands around those massive antlers more than paid me back for my effort.

Chapter Thirty Nine

THE
JOE WATERS BUCK

280 4/8 NON-TYPICAL, KANSAS, 1987

What Happens When you Listen to Dad's Advice

BY DUNCAN DOBIE

Going into the 1987 Kansas firearms season, 26-year-old Joe Waters of Topeka was bent on making a comeback. He'd hunted whitetails off and on since age 16 but never had shot one. What's more, due to work, he hadn't been able to do any hunting at all for the past three or four years. It was high time to change his luck.

"My dad and I got permission to hunt on a friend's farm," Joe says. "It was located in the southwestern portion of Shawnee County, and it was only a few minutes' drive from both of our houses. The first day we scouted we saw five deer at a distance, but we couldn't tell what they were. We also found plenty of good deer sign, along with a huge set of tracks."

Typical of eastern Kansas, the land consisted of a number of long fields separated by narrow fingers of standing timber. To one side of this farm stood a 200- to 300-acre block of timber. "We chose several different stand locations where we could hunt from trees in the fingers of timber next to some of the open pastures," Joe says.

Photo by Jamie Boardman.

JOE WATERS, KANSAS, 1987

	Right Antler	Left Antler	Difference
Main Beam Length	25 3/8	25 2/8	1/8
1st Point Length	8 6/8	8 4/8	2/8
2nd Point Length	12 0/8	12 1/8	1/8
3rd Point Length	9 7/8	11 1/8	1 2/8
4th Point Length	5 5/8	5 7/8	2/8
5th Point Length	—	—	—
1st Circumference	6 1/8	6 4/8	3/8
2nd Circumference	4 5/8	4 7/8	2/8
3rd Circumference	4 3/8	4 4/8	1/8
4th Circumference	4 0/8	3 7/8	1/8
Total	**80 6/8**	**82 5/8**	**2 7/8**

Main Characteristics: 100 2/8" of abnormal points, including distinctive forked points on right antler.

MISCELLANEOUS STATS

No. Of Points–Right	16
No. Of Points–Left	13
Total No. Of Points	29
Length Of Abnormals	100 2/8
Greatest Spread	26 6/8
Tip To Tip Spread	18 2/8
Inside Spread	19 6/8

FINAL TALLY

Inside Spread	19 6/8
Right Antler	80 6/8
Left Antler	82 5/8
Gross Score	183 1/8
Difference (–)	2 7/8
Subtotal	180 2/8
Abnormals (+)	100 2/8
NET NON-TYPICAL SCORE	280 4/8

"A lot of these wooded areas served as natural funnels for the deer to move through, and many of them had hardwood trees that were easy to climb."

Joe's dad made another scouting trip several days before the season opener, and that day he glimpsed a huge buck. According to the eyewitness, the deer "looked like he had a brushpile growing on his head."

"Dad only had a doe tag, and he shot his doe on the first morning out," Joe remem-bers of the Dec. 5 rifle opener. "After that first morning, I hunted every day by myself. Dad dropped by the property once or twice to cut some firewood, and he always gave me a lot of moral support. He also gave me some good advice. He really wanted to see me shoot a nice buck."

Joe hunted every day that week. During that span he saw several does, but never a buck. He was off work on Thursday and Friday, and with the season ending at dark on Sunday, he planned to spend each morning and afternoon in the woods.

Zero deer were seen on Thursday, and Friday morning was a repeat. After lunch that day, Joe returned to his stand much earlier than usual.

"Dad kept telling me, 'The best time to be in your stand is when everyone else has left the woods,' and I was determined to get there good and early that afternoon," Joe says.

"It was about 1 p.m. when I climbed back up into the same tree that I had been in earlier that morning. By 3 p.m. my legs were cramping up, and I was really starting to get bored. Furthermore, I was really beginning to get frustrated, because I hadn't seen a single deer in almost two full days of hunting.

"Then, about an hour before dark, three does came up behind me," the hunter recalls. "I put the scope on that lead doe's shoulder and considered pulling the trigger. She was standing less than 30 yards away, and it would have been a fairly easy shot. But something made me hesitate. I kept thinking about all of the things my dad had said about being patient and sticking it out. I decided to hold out for a buck."

Moments later, the seemingly impossible happened. "I looked down, and I saw the body of a huge deer," Joe says. "I caught a glimpse of a massive rack. I couldn't believe it. It looked as though this deer was walking around with a brushpile on top of his head, just like my dad had said. The buck stepped out of some heavy brush about 30 yards away.

"He started moving through the trees toward the does, but it seemed like he

" It looked as though this deer was walking around with a brushpile on top of his head."

was always behind something," the hunter continues. "Finally, he stuck his head out from behind a tree. I decided to try for a neck shot. For a brief second after the shot he seemed to just stand there; then his legs seemed to fold up under him, and he dropped in his tracks."

Joe soon had driven to his dad's house to give him the news. "When I tried to describe the buck to him, I'm sure he thought I was exaggerating. Later, when we reached the deer, he was absolutely astounded," Joe recalls.

"You've got to get this rack scored," local game warden Jim Hale told Joe the next day. "It'll go high in the record book. And after somebody writes a story about you in one of the national outdoor magazines, I want your autograph!"

Jim was right about the buck's size and attention he'd receive from the national media. The non-typical tallied an entry score of 269 3/8 Boone and Crockett points, enough to surpass the state record by more than 10 inches! But amazingly, the best was yet to come. A panel of B&C measurers later raised the final score to 280 4/8 points! And naturally, as the world's highest-scoring deer of 1987, he ended up being featured in *North American Whitetail* magazine.

"Without my dad's help and persistence, I don't think I ever would have killed that buck," Joe admits. "I'll never forget those words he kept telling me over and over again: 'When everyone else is getting out of their tree and going back to camp, that's the time to stay there and stick it out.' That's exactly what I tried to do, and it sure did pay off!"

Chapter Forty

THE BOBBY WILLIS BUCK

252 0/8 NON-TYPICAL, OHIO, 1999

Everything that Could Go Wrong Did... and Didn't

BY BOBBY WILLIS

S ome days in the deer woods start out poorly and only get worse. But on rare occasion there are also days like Nov. 1, 1999 — which for me went from disaster to triumph. On Oct. 31, my buddy Marvin Pennix and I left our Kentucky homes and drove up to Jackson County, Ohio, to bowhunt. Although Marvin never had been to this farm, I'd hunted it enough over the years to know it held some big bucks. With the rut just starting, we planned to hunt up to two weeks if necessary.

Having already secured written permission to hunt the land, upon our arrival we set up camp, checked our gear and picked out a couple of trees to hunt from the next morning. We then turned in early, as we'd be getting up at 4 a.m.

The next morning we walked to our stands, going uphill for roughly a quarter-mile before separating. Perhaps 200 yards farther uphill, my penlight batteries started getting weaker, and as I started over a hill, the light went out entirely. Naturally, I realized I'd left my spare light at home. For several minutes, I tried in vain to get out

BOBBY WILLIS, OHIO, 1999

	Right Antler	Left Antler	Difference
Main Beam Length	29 2/8	29 2/8	0/8
1st Point Length	6 4/8	7 2/8	6/8
2nd Point Length	12 0/8	9 1/8	2 7/8
3rd Point Length	11 0/8	11 5/8	5/8
4th Point Length	8 2/8	10 3/8	2 1/8
5th Point Length	—	—	—
1st Circumference	5 6/8	5 6/8	0/8
2nd Circumference	5 3/8	5 5/8	2/8
3rd Circumference	5 0/8	5 7/8	7/8
4th Circumference	5 4/8	5 2/8	2/8
Total	**88 5/8**	**90 1/8**	**7 6/8**

Main Characteristics: Incredible score for a buck with no drop tines or big forks. World-class beams and mass.

MISCELLANEOUS STATS	
No. Of Points–Right	12
No. Of Points–Left	13
Total No. Of Points	25
Length Of Abnormals	59 7/8
Greatest Spread	23 0/8
Tip To Tip Spread	11 1/8
Inside Spread	21 1/8

FINAL TALLY	
Inside Spread	21 1/8
Right Antler	88 5/8
Left Antler	90 1/8
Gross Score	**199 7/8**
Difference (–)	7 6/8
Subtotal	**192 1/8**
Abnormals (+)	59 7/8
NET NON-TYPICAL SCORE	**252 0/8**

of a thorny greenbriar thicket in the dark. Finally, I opted to wait for more light. My hands already were scratched and bleeding, and I was perspiring heavily in the 48° air.

After I finally got to my tree, I leaned my portable stand and bow against it and put out some scent. As I started up the tree, I kept running into limbs. I had to cut off several to reach the right height, and in the still morning air it must have sounded as if the place was being timbered.

Once I had the stand up and my safety snap swung around to my back, I pulled up my bow and saw that the serving was unraveling, apparently having snagged on a briar. I rewound it, then used my lighter to melt the end and hold it in place.

As it began to get light, I began to realize that in my haste to get set up, I'd climbed the wrong tree. On top of that, my stand was pitching forward at a disconcerting angle, and a knot was poking me in the back. Yes, if anything could go wrong on a hunt, it had that day — and my hunt hadn't started yet!

While trying to get comfortable, I saw movement some 60 yards off in the brush. As I watched, a high-racked buck walked straight toward me over a bank, coming to within 40 yards of me on a woods road. He seemed to be looking right at me, and I figured he was investigating the noise I'd made earlier. After several minutes, he dropped his head and turned to go down the hollow.

The Willis buck was already in rut on Nov. 1. Photo courtesy of Jamie Willis.

Between then and 8:30, I saw only birds and squirrels. But when the deer activity finally got going, I was treated to an amazing display of rut behavior. On several occasions, single does ran past my stand from one direction or another, and bucks — some of them Pope and Young caliber — cruised through the area, either alone or in tandem with other bucks. One of the bucks that showed up was the giant I'd seen earlier, but he didn't come within range before walking out of my life once again.

Finally, I heard a heavy grunt and twigs breaking. The big boy was back! He came out of the brush and stopped about 70 yards away. With honeysuckle vines streaming from his antlers, he just stood there for three or four minutes, moving only his nose. Then, he started in my direction again.

As he got to within 20 yards, I drew and waited for a shot. Due to the brush, I was having trouble keeping my pin on him. But then he came out from beneath a leafy bush and stopped 17 yards in front of me.

When the arrow hit I saw blood, and with each leap I saw blood spray. The buck paused at 40 yards and then took off on a blind run, breaking brush as he went over a high point on the ridge behind me. The time was now 9:50.

Just over 30 minutes later, as I was sitting in my stand, I heard a truck start up beyond the ridge where the buck had disappeared. Not knowing who might be over there, I decided to start following the blood trail.

It went some 300 yards to the other side of the ridge before the blood trail ended. As I scanned the woods, trying to decide what to do next, I took a few steps and saw tall tines sticking up. My trophy was lying dead near another woods road.

"Marvin!" I shouted to my friend, whose stand was across the hollow. "Come over here! I think I just got a world-class buck!"

When Marvin reached me, he took one look and exclaimed, "Bob, you've killed an elk!" As it turned out, he'd heard the deer fall, but at the time he hadn't known what the sound was.

Official measurer Mike Dickess later confirmed the 25-pointer as an Ohio bow record at 252 0/8 net points, a score that also ranked him comfortably in bowhunting's all-time Top 10. And so, what started out as a bad day in the woods proved to be a great one instead.

And to top it off, the week after I got my deer, my buddy Marvin shot a nice 8-pointer on the same farm. Yes, that was one hunt we'll never forget!

CONCLUSION

BY LARRY L. HUFFMAN

Antlers: how intriguing a subject. As we have just seen, each set is like a fingerprint, in that no two are alike. Perhaps Dick Idol said it best in the first *Legendary Whitetails,* in which he stated that each set of antlers is as unique as an original work of art.

Man has always been intrigued by antlers, and they rank among the most popular collectibles with today's hunting fraternity. A high percentage of whitetail fanatics can easily recognize the antlers of the world's greatest bucks at a glance.

In fact, so great is the recognition of these special trophies that at a deer show a few years ago, an attendee's two-year-old son was able to name each of the 11 trophy bucks from the Legendary Collection that were on display. The boy impressed us to no end.

Many whitetail disciples prefer typical antlers. In fact, they would drive hundreds of miles to see the world-class typicals shot by James Jordan, John Breen or Milo Hanson. They admire the classic shape of a large typical rack, whether it features tall tines, a wide spread, extreme mass or some combination of those attributes.

These fans prefer typicals over non-typicals because they like the simple, clean form of a large 5x5 or 6x6 frame. As of this writing, only 14 typicals have registered net scores over the magic mark of 200 Boone and Crockett points, and of these, only five are basic 10-pointers.

As popular as huge typicals are, non-typicals probably are favored by even more members of the hunting community. For these antler enthusiasts, the more bizarre a rack is, the better. Many hunters would drive great distances just to view the "Hole In The Horn" buck or the giant harvested by Mike Beatty in 2000. Both of these bucks are from Ohio, but even though they have a similar appearance, their lives were separated by 60 years and 200 miles. The Beatty buck, which looks to be the world's highest-scoring hunter-taken buck of all time, is just one of the 27 non-typicals featured in *Legendary Whitetails II*.

So what draws so many hunters to non-typical antlers? Perhaps it is the great number of forms they take. The list of unusual features includes drop tines, split tines, multiple brow tines, palmation, double beams and extreme mass. The exact reasons for non-typical antler growth remain largely unknown, but certainly genetics plays a major role in their formation.

In the dedication of this book, I note that the hunters featured here are an elite group. They, their trophy bucks and their stories are a part of whitetail history. Very few hunters ever experience the thrill of taking such deer. I have personally been in the trophy rooms of many of the world's greatest hunters, and the one trophy missing from every one of these collections is a world-class whitetail

This is the highest-scoring whitetail buck of Larry Huffman's hunting career… so far. Like every other hunter, he dreams of even bigger ones. Photo courtesy of Larry L. Huffman.

buck. This goes to prove that taking a top whitetail buck is one of the biggest challenges in hunting.

Many people have asked me if I've ever harvested a B&C buck. My answer is, "Only in my dreams." Indeed, it has been a lifelong goal to down a buck that would meet or beat the minimum scores of 170 typical or 195 non-typical. My best buck to date had a score of 165 typical — close, but no cigar. Back several years ago I had an opportunity to take a non-typical that I estimate could have scored as high as 240, but some equipment failure foiled that opportunity. I have replayed that episode in my mind every day since then.

Between *Legendary Whitetails* and *Legendary Whitetails II*, we now have told the stories of 80 of the greatest bucks known to man. Their stories and photos give us substance to dream about, for they prove that every so often, hunters' dreams do come true.

Perhaps someday the world will get to read the story of how you took a legendary whitetail as well.